Understanding Shiite Leadership

In this book, Shaul Mishal and Ori Goldberg explore the ways in which Shiite leaderships in Iran and Lebanon approach themselves and their world. Contrary to the violent and radical image of religious leaderships in the Islamic Republic of Iran and Lebanese Hizballah, the political vision and practice of these leaderships view the world as a "middle ground," shying away from absolutist and extremist tendencies. The political leadership assumed by Shiite religious scholars in Iran and Lebanon has transformed Shiite Islam from a marginalized minority to a highly politicized avant garde of Muslim presence, revitalized the practice and causes of political Islam in its struggle for legitimacy and authority, and reshaped the politics of both the Middle East and the globe in its image. Utilizing approaches from social theory, history, theology, and literary criticism, the book presents these leaderships as pragmatic, interpretative entities with the potential to form fruitful relationships between Shiite leadership and the non-Shiite world.

Shaul Mishal is Professor of Political Science at Tel Aviv University and at the School of Government, IDC Herzlia. He is a Visiting Professor at Yale University, Visiting Scholar at the Center for International Affairs at Harvard, and Senior Fellow at the Harvard School of Public Health. He has authored and coauthored several books on Palestinian issues, including *West Bank/East Bank*, *The PLO under Arafat*, *Speaking Stones with R. Aharoni*, *The Palestinian Hamas* with A. Sela, and *Investment in Peace* with R. Kuperman and D. Boas. Mishal has authored numerous articles, which have appeared in many leading journals. He received his PhD in Political Science from the Hebrew University of Jerusalem.

Ori Goldberg teaches in the Department of Middle Eastern and African History at Tel Aviv University. He is the author of *Shi'i Theology in Iran: The Challenge of Religious Experience* and *Thinking Shi'a*, a collection of lectures examining Shiite culture, politics, and consciousness from various perspectives. Dr. Goldberg's research focuses on the comparative study of Muslim, Christian, and Jewish theological thought; Middle East politics and culture; and the critical role of religious thought in social theory and practice. He received his PhD in Middle Eastern History from Tel Aviv University.

PROBLEMS OF INTERNATIONAL POLITICS

Series Editors:
Keith Darden, *Yale University*
Ian Shapiro, *Yale University*

The series seeks manuscripts central to the understanding of international politics that will be empirically rich and conceptually innovative. It is interested in works that illuminate the evolving character of nation-states within the international system. It sets out three broad areas for investigation: (1) identity, security, and conflict; (2) democracy; and (3) justice and distribution.

For Arnon, Mira, Nazima, and Yehezkel,
Our roots.

Understanding Shiite Leadership

The Art of the Middle Ground in Iran and Lebanon

SHAUL MISHAL
Tel Aviv University

ORI GOLDBERG
Tel Aviv University

CAMBRIDGE
UNIVERSITY PRESS

CAMBRIDGE
UNIVERSITY PRESS

32 Avenue of the Americas, New York NY 10013-2473, USA

Cambridge University Press is part of the University of Cambridge.

It furthers the University's mission by disseminating knowledge in the pursuit of education, learning and research at the highest international levels of excellence.

www.cambridge.org
Information on this title: www.cambridge.org/9781107632677

First published 2014
First paperback edition 2015

A catalogue record for this publication is available from the British Library

Library of Congress Cataloguing in Publication data
Mishal, Shaul, 1945–
Understanding Shiite leadership : the art of the middle ground in Iran and Lebanon / Shaul
Mishal, Tel Aviv University; Ori Goldberg, Tel Aviv University.
    pages   cm – (Problems of international politics)
Includes bibliographical references and index.
ISBN 978-1-107-04638-2 (hardback)
1. Shiites – Political activity – Iran.   2. Shi'ah – Political aspects – Iran.   3. Political
leadership – Iran.   4. Islam and politics – Iran.   5. Iran – Politics and government – 1997–
6. Shiites – Political activity – Lebanon.   7. Shi'ah – Political aspects – Lebanon.   8. Political
leadership – Lebanon.   9. Islam and politics – Lebanon.   10. Political culture –
Lebanon.   11. Lebanon – Politics and government – 1990–   I. Goldberg, Ori.   II. Title.
JQ1789.A15M57   2014
320.955–dc23   2014002046

ISBN 978-1-107-04638-2 Hardback
ISBN 978-1-107-63267-7 Paperback

Contents

Acknowledgments

Our joint endeavor, which has been a while in the making, has benefited from the help of several devoted friends and colleagues. We are indebted to Jim Leitner for his generosity and interest. Ian Shapiro, of Yale University, shepherded this project from its inception. We received invaluable assistance from Raz Zimmt, Yair Samban, and Sofia Weibull. Eliran Bar-El saw us through the final stages of the process, offering both sage advice and tireless dedication.

Without Lewis Bateman, our editor at Cambridge University Press, his assistant, Shaun Vigil, and the three anonymous readers, this book would be completely different: less coherent, more complicated. Each in his or her own way reminded us that dreams require persistence and responsibility.

Introduction

When the political Shiite leaderships of Iran and Lebanese Hizballah emerged into the global light, the world could not be sure of what it was seeing. Were these new leaderships fundamentalist, conformist, or perhaps covertly realist? What knowledge was needed for better understanding of their worldview, strategic preferences, and conduct? There was no telling if Shiite leaders in Iran and Lebanon were stumbling blindly or walking proud.

Observers emphasize a rapid process of politicization, seemingly in direct contrast to the quietist, apolitical traditions of the new Shiite religious leadership. The assertion of overt political authority was an innovation bordering on the heretical for Shiite religious scholars. This embrace of conventions removed any notions of Shiite leadership as obsolete relics.

Article 2 of the constitution of the Islamic Republic of Iran (1980) declares the dominant role of religiosity in shaping the thoughts and actions of Shiite leadership.[1] The article states the following:

The Islamic Republic is a system based on belief in:

1. The One God (as stated in the phrase "There is no god except Allah"), His exclusive sovereignty and the right to legislate, and the necessity of submission to His commands;
2. Divine revelation and its fundamental role in setting forth the laws;
3. The return to God in the Hereafter, and the constructive role of this belief in the course of man's ascent towards God;
4. The justice of God in creation and legislation;
5. Continuous [religious] leadership (imamah) and perpetual guidance, and its fundamental role in ensuring the uninterrupted process of the revolution of Islam;

---

[1] For an astute analysis of Iran's constitution, see Asghar Schirazi, *The Constitution of Iran, Politics and State in the Islamic Republic* (IB Tauris, 1998).

6. The exalted dignity and value of man, and his freedom coupled with responsibility before God; in which equity, justice, political, economic, social, and cultural independence, and national solidarity are secured by recourse to:
   a. continuous *ijtihad* [religious decision making] of the *fuqaha'* [Shiite legal scholars] possessing necessary qualifications, exercised on the basis off the Qur'an and the *Sunnah* of the *Ma'sumun* [the twelve infallible Shiite Imams], upon all of whom be peace;
   b. sciences and arts and the most advanced results of human experience, together with the effort to advance them further;
   c. negation of all forms of oppression, both the infliction of and the submission to it, and of dominance, both its imposition and its acceptance.[2]

It is in fact religiosity, the practice and reality of religion, which serves as the core of the Islamic Republic, particularly its notions of leadership, virtue, and success. All these are defined in religious terms, accessed through a firm belief in God's sovereignty and fulfilled within a worldly social order.

Shiite Religiosity: A Comparative Perspective

The role of religiosity in political affairs is difficult to parse. For many scholars, the precepts of religious faith are incapable of supporting a full-fledged political system of beliefs and institutions. How is the very apparent religiosity of the Shiite leadership, particularly in the Islamic Republic of Iran, understood in the scholarly literature?

Hamid Dabashi, a leading scholar of modern Iran, begins his *Shi'ism – A Religion of Protest*[3] in the following manner: "Shi'ism is a festive gathering, a festival, a feast, a constellation of moral manners, a commitment, a conviction, a mobile memory – the centerpiece of it the iconic unsheathing of a dagger."[4] He goes on to say that "Shi'ism is the shimmering memory of an event, a dream, a single traumatic incident, condemned forever to try and remember itself: in vain ... Shi'ism is a blind faith, a reasoned reassurance, a moral mandate, an intellectual tapestry."[5]

Dabashi understands Shi'ism as a predominantly cultural entity. Shi'ism shapes the intangible aspects of being – morality, intellect, faith, reason, memory. Shi'ism runs deep, says Dabashi, and its main trait seems to be an ability to encapsulate profound contradictions.

Given this view of Shi'ism, Dabashi's thesis about the nature of political Shi'ism, and Shiite leadership, is not surprising: "My principal contention is that Shi'ism is predicated on a rather perplexing paradox – that it is morally triumphant when it is politically defiant, and that it morally fails when it

---

[2] Available online at http://www.iranchamber.com/government/laws/constitution_cho1.php
[3] Hamid Dabashi, *Shi'ism – A Religion of Protest* (Belknap Press, Harvard University Press, 2011).
[4] See Dabashi, *Shi'ism*, p. xi.
[5] *Ibid.*

politically succeeds."[6] Shi'ism "works" at the profound level of culture, says Dabashi. In fact, he claims even greater depth for Shi'ism as a motivating force. Dabashi links the Shi'i tendency toward social resistance to a Freudian guilty conscience caused by the martyrdom of the third Shi'i Imam, Hossein, at the battle of Karbala in 680 AD.[7]

Others cast Shiite religiosity within the framework of a struggle over naked power rather than over ideas. Ervand Abrahamian, in his *Khomeinism: Essays on the Islamic Republic*,[8] criticizes the commonly held opinion that Khomeini's Islamic regime was a fundamentalist one. Abrahamian demonstrates the inapplicability of fundamentalism to the realities of the Muslim world and the Islamic Republic. He explains that Khomeini did not offer blind adherence to a single sacred text, did not reject Western modernity, and did not accept other conventions of fundamentalism as it is known in the Christian West.

One of Abrahamian's reasons for rejecting the notion of Khomeini as a fundamentalist seems relevant for our discussion:

[T]he term "fundamentalist" conjures up the image of inflexible orthodoxy, strict adherence to tradition, and rejection of intellectual novelty, especially from outside. In the political arena, however, Khomeini, despite his own denials, was highly flexible, remarkably innovative, and cavalier toward hallowed traditions. He is important precisely because he discarded many Shiite concepts and borrowed ideas, words, and slogans from the non-Muslim world. In doing so, he formulated a brand-new Shi'i interpretation of state and society. The final product has less in common with conventional fundamentalism than with Third World populism, especially in Latin America.

The term "populism" needs some added elaboration. By it I mean a movement of the propertied middle class that mobilizes the lower classes, especially the urban poor, with radical rhetoric directed against imperialism, foreign capitalism, and the political establishment. In mobilizing the "common people," populist movements use charismatic figures and symbols, imagery, and language that have potent value in the mass culture. Populist movements promise to drastically raise the standard of living and make the country fully independent of outside powers. Even more important, in attacking the status quo with radical rhetoric, they intentionally stop short of threatening the petty bourgeoisie and the whole principle of private property. Populist movements, thus, inevitably emphasize the importance, not of economic-social revolution, but of cultural, national, and political reconstruction.[9]

Abrahamian subverts both Dabashi's explanation of political Shi'ism and the conventional understandings of religious rule. Khomeini's regime was, according

---

[6] See Dabashi, *Shi'ism*, p. xvi.

[7] See Dabashi, *Shi'ism*, pp. 9–13. Hossein, the third Imam (religious ruler) of the Shiite community following its secession from the majority of the Islamic world, was slaughtered on the plains of Karbala by a vastly superior Sunni force, which had ambushed him at the spot. Hossein's death is reenacted each year as a passion play, on *Ashura'*, the most solemn of Shiite holidays.

[8] Ervand Abrahamian, *Khomeinism: Essays on the Islamic Republic* (University of California Press, 1993).

[9] See Abrahamian, *Khomeinism*, p. 17.

to Abrahamian, quite comfortable with foregoing much of its religious heritage and commitments. Moreover, while the powers that be in the Islamic Republic appear to be motivated by cultural and religious norms, in reality they are mobilized by a class struggle over the allocation of political means and social prestige. According to Abrahamian, Shiite religiosity in the Islamic Republic is a ploy on the part of the bourgeoisie, meant to mobilize the lower classes to preserve the class interests of the former. Religiosity is, then, a derivative element within the Iranian social sphere. It motivates genuine social processes, but mostly under use or manipulation by ulterior forces and motives.

Said Amir Arjomand, a prominent scholar of the Islamic revolution and its aftermath, represents an additional version of the materialist view. In his *The Turban for the Crown: The Islamic Revolution in Iran*, Arjomand explains the revolution by doing two main things: "putting it in the context of the relationship between Shi'ism and political order in the history of Iran, and ... comparing it to other revolutions."[10]

The role of religiosity in the unfolding of the revolution is, according to Arjomand, a historical one. Since 1501, Shi'ism has been the state religion in Iran. Shiite religious leaders have been part of a dual power structure, combining their spiritual authority with the stately, temporal authority of the king in power. As the Iranian state grew in strength and complexity, the religious establishment enjoyed a unique position.[11] Its leaders were fully integrated into the state elite while maintaining continuous, intimate contact with the Iranian masses through their networks of students and through their religious rulings.

The religious leaders could thus hardly shy away from offering stringent criticism of the state. The 1979 revolution was carried out by a broad coalition effort uniting socialists, wealthy merchants, landowners, and Western-educated liberals. Still, it was seen as Islamic because the unique position of the religious establishment allowed it to form a nexus for the various elements desiring change.

According to Arjomand, Shiite religious leaders skillfully took advantage of this state of affairs. They did all they could to expand their power at the expense of other forces. Arjomand explains their motivation:

What alerted the mind of Khomeini and a number of other Shiite jurists to the immense possibilities for the expansion of Shiite hierocratic power was: (1) the opportunity to lead a crusade against foreign, imperialist domination that had presented itself recurrently since the nineteenth century; and (2) a desperate struggle for the very survival of the Shiite religious institutions against the onslaught of the modernizing Pahlavi state, beginning in the 1960s and becoming more intense in the mid-1970s.[12]

---

[10] Said Amir Arjomand, *The Turban for the Crown: The Islamic Revolution in Iran* (Oxford University Press, 1988), p. 15. Arjomand has also written the influential *After Khomeini: Iran Under his Successors* (Oxford University Press, 2009).

[11] For a thorough historical review, see Arjomand, *The Turban for the Crown*, pp. 11–75.

[12] See Arjomand, *The Turban for the Crown*, p. 76.

Arjomand's explanation highlights two motivating forces for religious leadership. First, he describes a nationalist, class-based struggle against foreign domination; second, a struggle for materialist survival against the state, a struggle over resources and institutional power. Religiosity itself does not play an independent role as a motivator and mobilizer. It is a tool, a means, a bonding agent. Religiosity, thus, is evaluated within a historical context. Its relevance on its own terms is, at best, of secondary importance.

We began our discussion of current literature by asking how this body of knowledge considers religiosity and its role in the thought and actions of Shiite leadership. Despite their differences, the views described earlier share a similarity in this regard. They all consider religiosity as a reflection of ulterior forces and motivations. For Dabashi, religiosity reflects powerful psychological processes, the logic of which is shared by all human beings. Guilt, desire, longing – these all find expression in religious practices. For Abrahamian, religiosity reflects the dynamics of social history, as well as a human tendency for grand, ideological visions. He conducts effective comparisons across temporal and geographical boundaries.

Within such comparisons, religious practices express broader patterns of social and individual behavior. For Arjomand, religiosity is a reflection of power struggles between economic classes. The religious scholars represent a concrete set of financial and political interests, and they protect those interests against competition. Religious practices and ideologies are a reflection of the material powers that drive and regulate social orders.

High Ground and Middle Ground

Shiite heritage has always been grounded in texts.[13] Shiites have been, throughout their history, a persecuted minority. Shiite communities have hardly had the opportunity to entrust their collective memory to state institutions, despite the existence of several Shiite states throughout early Islamic history. The task of conducting a meaningful life has thus been entrusted to the scholars capable of studying and interpreting these texts. This scholarly religious leadership acknowledges the absolute extremities of values and interests, but consciously opts to forge its own path. We will refer to this in-between domain as the middle ground.

The leading scholars of the new brand of Shiite leadership – Dabashi, Abrahamian, and Arjomand – apply what may be called a high-ground approach to religion and religiosity. Both may be explained and justified by recourse to a higher, more basic organizing principle: psychological processes, economic forces, historical narratives. Often, religiosity is seen to be meaningful mainly

[13] In this respect, Shiite theology is very much akin to Jewish theology, which views the Torah as a "Tree of life to those who take hold of her" (Proverbs 3:18), online at http://www.biblegateway.com/passage/?search=Proverbs+3&version=NIV

as a reflection of these higher principles. It is rarely perceived as an independently influential component within Shiite reality.

In contrast, the religious middle ground as we understand it plays a significant part in shaping that reality. This understanding does not contradict a psychological description or an economic description, but seeks to complement them by highlighting the dynamic, negotiated nature of Shiite religious experience and its influence on Shiite political reality. The middle ground is not relativistic, flaccid, or benign. The boundaries of the middle ground are solidly defined by unimpeachable truths.

One such truth is the faith in God as sole sovereign, rather than the state or the people. Life in the middle ground acknowledges these truths as horizons, but it rejects them as destinations. An object of aspiration, these horizons may motivate, but in reality they are unreachable. The middle ground resists the ultimate satisfactions of absolute truths just as it acknowledges and is inspired by such truths.[14] Resistance toward unassailable answers and absolute stability is a hallmark of middle ground life and politics. The extraordinary nature of life in the middle ground requires different forms of reading and understanding, which stray from the beaten path.

The Religious Roots of the Middle Ground: Void, Interpretation, Friction

We present the Shiite middle ground through a three-dimensional grid. We refer to these dimensions as *Void*, *Interpretation*, and *Friction*. Shiite faith begins with a void. The Twelfth Imam, the Mahdi, the infallible Shiite leader descended from the holy seed of the prophet Muhammad, awaits Judgment Day when he will return as the Shiite messiah.[15] His absence, alive but not present, leaves a gaping hole at the heart of Shiite consciousness. No single leader can replace him. Yet, the community cannot remain without an authoritative guide. The void, never whole, stands in direct contrast to the subjective, rational wholeness of the modern individual from which Western politics and philosophy emerge. The inviolable individual, always maintaining singular integrity and coherence, could hardly survive in the shadow of the void.

In the absence of the Imam, interpretation is the main practice of the Shiite community. With infallible authority suspended, no truth or order claim to be more than an interpretation. Authority is based on a constant processing

---

[14] For a discussion of the relationship between absolute questions and intellectual practice, see John Caputo, *Philosophy and Theology* (Abingdon Press, 2006).

[15] For the definitive treatment of the Islamic Messianism in general and Shiite messianism in particular, see Abdulaziz Sachedina, *Islamic Messianism* (State University of New York Press, 1981). Sachedina is remarkable among scholars of Shi'ism for combining rigorous historical study, a keen theological sensitivity, and an understanding that this combination should continuously strive for relevance with regard to the current state of Shi'ism. His *The Just Ruler in Shiite Islam: The Comprehensive Authority of the Jurist in Imami Jurisprudence* (Oxford University Press, 1988) is another work synthesizing these seemingly competitive directions.

of the world, on adaptation and participation. A virtuous society is one that engaged more in interpretation than in attempting to live out static perfection. Interpretation is the core rationale of the Islamic Republic of Iran, just as it is the dominant dynamic allowing Lebanese Hizballah to remain unscathed despite the coalition of forces seeking the organization's weaknesses.

Friction is the practical axis of the Shiite middle ground. Different voices and interests coexist within this whole, without relinquishing their differences. The eternal and the mundane, the national and the communal confront each other and cooperate with each other within the friction of the middle ground. Often, friction challenges the procedural, bureaucratic rationale of Western societies. Such societies ground their integrity and morality in the smooth, neutral stability of the democratic process. Friction is negotiable, contextual, and dynamic.

The most publicized aspect of Iran's foreign policy, its nuclear prospects, can serve to illustrate these issues.[16] Pundits and politicians repeatedly state that a nuclear Iran is an unacceptable risk to the Middle East and beyond.[17] However, when seen in a middle ground context, Iran's nuclear policy is not determined by high-ground calculations. The focus does not seem to be on acquisition or detonation. Rather, Iranian policy seems to leverage the friction caused by nuclear negotiations into diverse global influence.

Iran uses the controversy around its nuclear prospects to further engage with different countries. It is the nuclear agenda, placing Iran at odds with the United States, that allowed it to develop close ties with Venezuela. Observed differently, it is the nuclear agenda that allows Iran to convey different messages to different international parties. Juggling the different Iranian statements addressed to the United States, the International Atomic Energy Agency (IAEA), the EU, Brazil, and others makes Iran a hub of regional and global policy. It is here that one encounters the logic of the middle ground in immediate fashion. The potential to change the world, to touch absolute boundaries, is a constant temptation.

The politics of Shiite leadership reflect an understanding of the world simultaneously innovative, pragmatic, and traditional. The middle ground takes on the politics of the extreme, whether that extreme is universal or highly particular. The middle ground reframes the debates between state and non-state actors, religious and secular forces, local communities and global societies.

The resurgence of the middle ground opens up real possibilities for transcending or dissolving impasses plaguing global politics. Middle ground leaderships are on the rise in diverse countries throughout the world. They may

---

[16] For a diverse analysis of Iranian foreign policy over the past two decades, see Anoushiravan Ehteshami and Mahjoob Zweiri (eds.), *Iran's Foreign Policy: From Khatami to Ahmadinejad* (Ithaca Press, 2011).

[17] For a broad historical survey of Iran's nuclear history, see David Patrikarakos, *Nuclear Iran: The Birth of an Atomic State* (IB Tauris, 2012).

be found in Latin America, Asia, on the Indian subcontinent, and in Africa. They have the existing order in their sights. The example of Turkey is a telling one. For nearly two decades, the EU has refused to accept Turkey as a member. Turkish leadership traditionally adopted a position of acquiescence. Since the rise of Turkey's Justice and Development party (2002), headed by Recep Tayyip Erdoğan, this position has changed dramatically. Turkey marches to its own drum. It seeks positive relations with Iran, a long-standing rival, turns to the United States for support, and significantly dampens relations with the EU.

Attempts to describe these changes in Turkish policy as "Radicalization" or "Islamicization" miss the far-reaching changes taking place in the country.[18] Erdoğan has embarked on a consistent reform of Turkish constitutional politics. He has successfully taken on the extra-democratic authorities enjoyed by the Turkish military and high courts. In the process, he has expanded the scope of public participation in Turkish electoral politics.

Erdoğan's policies cannot be merely addressed as fundamentalist on the one hand or cynical on the other. He has, like counterparts in India[19] and Brazil, rejected the notion that one must support or reject the current conventions of global politics. Erdoğan is a political reformist and a true believer, behaving like both an international statesman and a parochial village elder. We view Erdoğan, in similar fashion to Shiite leaderships in Iran and in Lebanon, as defining his leadership through friction rather than exclusion.

Where We Are Going and How We Get There

Understanding Shiite Leadership strives to understand Shiite leadership through the interaction between its worldview, its surroundings, and its conduct. We seek to present the conceptual tools required for approaching and engaging with Shiite leadership on its own terms. The first four chapters deal with the components of the Shiite worldview and environment. The following four chapters examine Shiite leaderships in action, exploring a variety of contexts and courses of action. The concluding chapter combines both aspects into a unified narrative, considering history, theology, and practice through the eyes of an imagined Iranian Shiite individual.

The first two chapters focus on the leadership's quality of interpretation. Its evolution, both historical and theological, is also the story of Shiite leadership itself. The initial void in Shiite public life, the one left by the Twelfth Imam

---

[18] For a nuanced, interdisciplinary anthology on religion in Turkish public life, see Ahmad T. Kuru and Alfred Stepan (eds.), *Democracy, Islam and Secularism in Turkey* (Columbia University Press, 2012).

[19] For a history of Indian democracy, see Ramachandra Guha, *India after Gandhi: The History of the World's Largest Democracy* (Harper Perennial, 2008). For a history of Brazil and its transformation under Luis Ignacio Da Silva (Lula), see Richard Bourne, *Lula of Brazil: The Story so Far* (University of California Press, 2009).

who resides with God as a Messiah-in-waiting, was filled by the interpretative leadership of the religious scholars. They were the ones qualified to mediate divine revelation into practical rules for human life. They were also those who provided human lives with a semblance of holiness, a link to a transcendent truth.

Still, interpretation was hardly ever politically construed in a formal sense. Khomeini's 1979 revolution rejuvenated traditional Shiite practices and principles, marginalized under the authority of Iranian Shahs over the past 500 years, shining a new light on them and casting them as inherently political. This political form of interpretation rejects absolutist ideologies, opting for ongoing friction within society.

Interpretation provides a key principle of the middle ground, its reality and its leadership. It allows for both an acknowledgment of the void and a commitment to creating a meaningful life from this void. It provides cohesion while leaving room for difference and adaptation, tension, and, most of all, the absence of a clear-cut resolution.

Chapters 3 and 4 examine the cultural and geopolitical environments in which Shiite leadership operates. Middle ground reality is diverse. It includes several spaces – communal, institutional (state), and the frontier – without any single space achieving prolonged dominance over others. Boundaries between these spaces are porous and flexible. This is so because middle ground reality is not a part of the perfect, single-spaced reality of divine creation. Middle ground reality is a human construct.

For nearly forty years (1941–1979), Mohammad Reza Pahlavi, the last Shah of Iran, attempted to create a state based on a single space. He sought to follow the notion of single civic space of Western states, one which provides a sense of community alongside institutional coherence and national identity. Khomeini's Islamic Republic, however, reveled in its multiplicity of spaces – community, state institutions, and frontier.

What are the unique features of each space? What role does each fulfill with regard to the other spaces of Shiite society? To what extent does the presence of Shiite leadership within these spaces affect its policy and practice? We highlight these issues in order to demonstrate how the power and effectiveness of Shiite leadership are related to its simultaneous presence in different spaces.

The following three chapters examine friction management by Shiite leaderships in Iran and Lebanon. Interpretation and space serve as two lenses, or a pair of spectacles, with which to observe the reality of friction. Friction drives the various modes of behavior exhibited by Shiite leadership. These chapters elaborate the ways in which Shiite leadership in Iran and Lebanon regulates friction.

The three dimensions of Shiite middle ground reality – void, interpretation, and friction – sustain each other. All three dimensions shape each other simultaneously. The initial void rejects absolute truths. The resulting necessity of interpretation denies a single space or person the possibility of dominating the middle ground. Friction provides both the basic principle of motion and the elaborate structure for Shiite leadership.

The notion of middle ground challenges the discourse of victory and defeat embraced by current global politics. The Arab Spring of 2011 provides another type of challenge. In both cases, revolutionary narratives defy the convention of a linear plot. While incumbent regimes are unseated by these middle ground forces, the process of nation building following such upheavals is as unpredictable as it is imminent.

Conservative and pragmatic, embracing and solitary, the politics of the middle ground as practiced by Shiite leadership are a worldview as well as a way of life, not just means to a high-ground end. How does Shiite leadership measure up to prevalent leadership types in other parts of the world? What can one learn from it about truths we hold to be self-evident? This course of inquiry will be taken up in the concluding chapter.

That chapter consists of an imagined encounter with Hossein B., an archetypical Iranian protagonist in the story we tell. His life reflects diverse issues: the advent of the Islamic Republic of Iran in 1979, the relationship between religion and politics, and the extent to which the practice of interpretation, as well as awareness of multiple spaces, have shaped individual and collective consciousness. Hossein B. will be a Tocquevillean figure, serving as a guide through various experiences of Shiite life. Looking at Shiite leadership through this lens will allow us to end our voyage on a note of promise.

As mentioned earlier, *Understanding Shiite Leadership* provides the conceptual contours of Shiite leaderships in Iran and Lebanon. We focus on their middle ground dynamics and logics, most emphatically on the role of friction as their organizing principle. These leaderships are constantly in motion; evaluating, adapting, aligning and realigning. Those engaging with Shiite leaderships – decision makers, scholars, and observers – should come to expect the recasting of insurmountable differences as platforms for dialogue, and of hardline rigidity as pragmatic realism.

I

Leadership as Interpretation

A profound conflict between divine perfection and earthly reality stands at the heart of religious faith. However devout one may be, the purity of the primary tenets of faith exists in tension with the pragmatic necessities. Early Islam resolved this conflict through state institutions. *Sharia* (Islamic law) served as the inspiration for the codification of these institutions during the three centuries following the death of the Prophet Muhammad in AD 632.

According to *Sharia*, the leader represents both divine will and human order; he is the center, the axis around which society spins; he is the beginning and the end for every social process in society. He oversees economic competition, the administration of justice, and the security of the state and its institutions. The leader's authority grants viability and motion to the flow of human relations and social interaction.

After Abu Bakr, the Prophet Muhammad's father-in-law was selected to replace him as ruler, or Capliph. Abu Bakr's supporters, who included the majority of the Islamic community, are known as Sunni Muslims, those who observe the prophet's tradition (*Sunnah*). A minority group refused to recognize the right of any but Muhammad's cousin and son-in-law, Ali, or his descendants to govern the Islamic faithful. These dissidents referred to themselves as the Shi'a (faction) of Ali. Individual adherents were called Shiites. From the time of Ali's death in AD 661, Shiite leadership grew in parallel fashion to Sunni leadership. A unique religious consciousness was formed, which shaped the nature of the leadership's involvement and participation in government.

The eleven successive heads of Ali's family received the title of Imam, meaning "infallible spiritual leader." The twelve Imams were the direct proof of God's existence, the unique link Shiites enjoyed to divine will and word. Their leadership was the doctrinal reason for the Shiite withdrawal from the Sunni majority. Their followers are still referred to as *Twelver*, or *Imami* Shiites.[1]

The absence of the Twelfth Imam negates any possibility for a leader in the Sunni vein. In doctrinal terms, Shiite leaders following the Imams cannot command a similar allegiance. The authority of Shiite leadership is drawn from its ability to recognize and value *difference* between doctrine and reality without trivializing either element. Shiite leadership operates under the premise that difference is here to stay. The interpretation of difference is the key to understanding the authority wielded by Shiite leadership.

In the Shiite view, the hallmark of a virtuous Shiite society is allowing different Shiite parties to engage each other rather than preferring one party over the other in definitive fashion. Non-religious political leaders are recognized and accepted. They administer the state and see to the streamlining of daily life. These leaders are judged on their performance, but they do not pretend to play a role in shaping the religious core of Shiite identity.

The vanishing of the Twelfth Imam exacerbates the struggle between heavenly ideals and practical reality. In the absence of the Twelfth Imam, Shiite society lacked leadership that was both divinely mandated and capable of managing a social order. Interpretation became the foundational skill of those who would be religious leaders. It was highly specialized and required rigorous training, thus forming a distinct community of scholarly leaders within Shiite society.

The history of the relationship between the two communities – the scholarly elite and the lay believers – encompasses the history of Shiite leadership and society. The critical expression of Shiite political culture was in Iran, the location of the Shiite Safavid Empire (est. 1501).[2] The Safavid Empire was the first to grant official power to Shiite scholars (*fuqaha*). Scholars were incorporated into the political establishment and were thus forced to adapt their traditional quietist position to the realities of political power.

The Shiites of Iran were not a part of the Sunni Ottoman Empire. The territories known today as Iraq and Lebanon, however, were Ottoman provinces until the Empire's demise following World War I (1923). Shiites in the Ottoman Empire, therefore, lived under Sunni rule. Still, the Shiites of Iraq and Lebanon did not challenge the Sunni Ottoman state. Shiites in Ottoman Iraq and Lebanon continued to live as minorities, outside the shadow of Sunni power and leadership.

Shaping Shiite Consciousness

The scholarly community was the pillar of Shiite leadership. The rise of this community began under the leadership of the Sixth Imam, Ja'afar Al-Sadiq

---

[1] For a concise introduction to Twelver Shi'ism see: Moojan Momen, *An Introduction to Shi'i Islam* (Yale University Press, 1985).

[2] See: Kathryn Babayan, *Mystics, Monarchs and Messiahs: Cultural Landscapes of Early Modern Iran* (Harvard Center for Middle Eastern Studies, 2003) particularly pp. 3–47.

(d. AD 765). According to Shiite lore, he decided that Shiite scholars should withdraw from political leadership. He did so as a result of the persecution to which Shiites and their leaders were subjected and his conviction that it would not end while the Shiites attempted to exercise political authority.

This trend became particularly noticeable after the vanishing of the Twelfth Imam (AD 874), when Shiite scholars began a long process of removing themselves from the public and institutional realm. Shiite scholars dealt with a restricted variety of theological pursuits. One aspect of scholarly activity was the study of grand philosophical questions, discussing divine attributes or debating the primary versus the created nature of the world. Another was the collection and transmission of *hadiths*, the sayings of the Shiite Imams and members of their households. This devotion to the Imams underscored the provisional nature of any leader claiming absolute authority in the absence of the Twelfth Imam.

Private law – torts, contracts, civil disputes – constituted a third area of activity for Shiite scholars. They made rulings regarding matters of private law and communal welfare. The scholars followed a strict interpretative framework that limited their ability to express personal opinions. Individual reflection was not encouraged. Religion became synonymous with law for the public – that is, the community of Shiite believers. This was not the law of the state, and was not enforced by state institutions.[3]

Shiite scholars saw their role as representatives of the law, achieved through training in textual interpretation. Muslims believe that God created the world with all its laws intact and whole, and that one of the religious duties of humans is to ascertain divine law and apply it. The scholars provisionally recognized the authority of state rulers in "secular" matters, but remained committed to their religious interpretative duties.

Alongside the scholarly elite, Shiite society consisted of a lay community of believers. One is born into the community by virtue of being born into the faith. Communal solidarity was founded on the shared beliefs of Shiism and on the day-to-day praxis of the community. The virtues of *taqiyah*, the Shiite doctrine allowing the faithful to keep a low public profile, constituted the principal tenet of this community. This doctrine manifested some of the most basic Shiite practices, including quietism, pietism, a strong, inward looking sense of community, and a pervading insularity. Significantly, it meant that Shiites did not have to profess their beliefs at the top of their lungs.

These features of communal Shiism originated in the tale of the Karbala Massacre (AD 680), which relates the tragic death of Imam Hussein, the Third Imam and younger son of Ali, the First Imam.[4] Hussein, who was denied the

---

[3] See: Nikkie R. Keddie, *Scholars, Saints and Sufis: Muslim Religious Institutions since 1500* (University of California Press, 1978), pp. 211–30.

[4] Names of Arab protagonists have been transcribed so as to preserve Arabic pronunciation. Names of Iranian protagonists (often spelled similarly in Persian and Arabic) have been transcribed so

right to inherit his father's position, was summoned to aid the Shiite residents
of Kufa in today's southern Iraq. When he arrived at the plains of Karbala, not
far from Kufa, he found that he had become the victim of a ploy. Ten thousand
Sunni soldiers awaited him, led by Yazid, the son of the Sunni ruler Muawyieh.
Hussein and seventy-three of his followers went into battle and, according to
Shiite tradition, were brutally massacred.[5]

The trials and tribulations of Imam Hussein before his death, and especially the massacre, are commemorated and reenacted each year with a passion
play on the main Shiite holiday, *Ashura*, the tenth day of the (Islamic) month
of Muharram. Hussein's story was traditionally seen as the epitome of Shiite
experience. It emphasized a life of suffering and bowing before the inevitable,
seemingly preferring the world to come over the temptations of the present,
and clearly distinguishing Shiites from Sunni Muslims.[6]

The stories of Imam Hussein and the Shiite history of persecution were both
significant in the development of appropriate codes of behavior within the
Shiite community. Still, religious convictions were a cornerstone of communal
life, not the platform for a political order. Faith was an intimate matter. Shiites
were taught that Islam was about what you felt in your heart more than how
you lived your life. This stands in contrast to the Sunni belief, which considers
living in an Islamic state and obeying an Islamic ruler as supreme embodiments
of faith. Whereas the Shiite community of believers accepted the authority of
the Shiite scholars (*fuqaha*) on matters of worship and spirituality, they did not
view them as a political authority.

There is no better way to follow the evolution of this narrative than by
identifying three historical phases that characterize the behavioral modes of
Shiite leadership toward the state's authority: withdrawal, presence, and participation. Withdrawal and increasing presence characterized Shiite leadership
until the nineteenth century. The last phase, participation, began during the
nineteenth century and is discussed in Chapter 3.

Withdrawal

The most prominent period of withdrawal for the Shiite leadership came under
Sunni rule. Most Shiites lived under Sunni rule from the eighth century until
the establishment of a Shiite state in Iran at the turn of the sixteenth century.
Shiites acknowledged the authority of the Sunni state but remained quietist and
indifferent toward it. Both Shiite communities – scholars and lay believers –
were connected at their core. Their membership was often overlapping; both
shared disdain for the power of the state, even when accepting it. The scholarly

as to preserve Persian pronunciation. Thus, the Third Imam is Hussein, but our imaginary inter-
locutor later in the book will be Hossein.
[5] For a contemporary analysis of the battle of Karbalah, as well as preceding events, see Ehsan
Yarshater, *The history of al-Tabari, Volume 19* (SUNY Press, 1991).
[6] For an analysis of Shi'a beliefs, sects and experiences, see al-Hasan ibn Musa al-Nawbakhti,
Shi'a Sects (Kitab Firaq al-Shi'a) (Islamic College for Advanced Studies Press, 2007).

leaders were not just religious authorities decreeing doctrine from ivory towers. They were active participants in the daily life of the lay Shiites.

Within the scholarly community, however, there was no clear hierarchical order. Scholars rose to prominence based on intellectual merit and the informal social network within the lay community. Networking at various levels was essential to the operation of the scholarly leadership and the community of believers. Both accepted the political authority of Sunni rulers, which filled the vacuum left by the scholarly withdrawal from political power. Neither community was constructed around centralized, regulatory authority. Both opted for a looser, network-based structure. The scholarly leadership attained compliance by exercising continuous, simultaneous presences at various levels of Shiite society.

Both communities – scholars and believers – recognized the authority of the Sunni state in Iran and throughout the Ottoman Empire. Shiites recognized the authority of rulers who were not the Imams, but only in a provisional fashion. Under these circumstances, the Shiite scholars served as spiritual leaders to the common believers, providing solace, advice, and religious rulings when necessary.

From the fifteenth century onward, this type of relationship thrived between the communities of Shiite society and the Sunni state. Iraq and Lebanon became provinces of the Sunni Ottoman Empire, the epitome of centralized authority.[7] The Ottoman Empire consisted of a multitude of peoples and religious communities that were ruled by the Sultan. The Sunni Ottoman Sultan allowed his subjects unprecedented degrees of religious autonomy. Yet this autonomy was dependent on the communities' recognition of the Sultan's absolute political authority. Shiites in Iraq and Lebanon were generally content to recognize Ottoman rule. In the absence of their Twelfth Imam, they treated the Sultan as a default authority.

The social ethic of withdrawal was challenged between the sixteenth and eighteenth centuries when the Safavids, Shiite rulers of Iran, installed Shiism as the state religion. Shiite scholars no longer wholly rejected political engagement. They gradually became more involved in political reality.[8]

Presence
The second phase in the evolution of Shiite leadership is marked by increased presence in the political realm. The rise of the Safavid state in Iran provided the Shiite scholars based in Jabal 'Amel (today in Southern Lebanon) and the holy cities of Iraq with an opportunity to gain political leverage. The Safavids, originally members of a militant, mystical order, rose from the planes of Anatolia

---

[7] For an insightful examination of Ottoman-Arab relations during this period, see Jane Hathaway and Karl Barbir: *The Arab Lands under Ottoman Rule: 1516–1800* (Longman, 2008).

[8] This historical account is based on Said Amir Arjomand, *The Shadow of God and the Hidden Imam* (Chicago University Press, 1987), pp. 32–65.

at the end of the fifteenth century to conquer and unify the Iranian provinces under their rule.[9]

Although the Safavids conquered and unified Iran, their authority lacked acceptance. Having converted to Shiism during the fifteenth century, Safavid leaders sought to install Shiism as the state religion so as to command the loyalty of the population. Their campaign to obtain this loyalty began when Isma'il Shah, the founder of the dynasty, declared himself to be descended from the Seventh Imam and continued when he adopted many of the traditional forms of Persian, pre-Islamic government, including the title of Shah.

The Safavids also offered benefits to those who recognized their rule. They were especially quick to reward the existing religious establishment in Iran, which was mostly Sunni and encouraged these scholars to convert to Shiism. They also invited Shiite scholars from abroad to Iran. Most of those who came were associated with the prestigious scholarly community in present-day Lebanon, further endowing their rule with religious legitimacy. Loyal scholars received state appointments and salaries as well as a chance to join the imperial elite.

Although the Shiite sages acknowledged the legitimacy of the Safavid kings, at no stage did they recognize Safavid authority as absolute. They perceived the Safavids as responsible for administration, economic order and security. The scholarly leadership, therefore, developed into religious traditional elite with the support and funding of the state, with no demand for direct participation or involvement in state affairs. Safavid rule allowed for the joint, yet separate development of the Iranian state and the scholarly community. Although they relied on the state for institutional backing, the scholars also created religious venues for the religious justification of Safavid rule.[10]

Personalizing Presence – Taqlid

It was under the Safavids that the concept of *taqlid* (emulation) became influential within the Shiite community.[11] The Shiite scholar, according to this notion, is a model to be emulated by the lay faithful in all areas of life pertaining to religion. This included matters regarding civil and family law, ritual observance, and social issues traditionally within the purview of the local religious establishment. The presence of religious scholars within Iranian politics and society thus grew significantly. The authority of the scholars became linked to their personal status while remaining outside the limiting protocols of state rule.

[9] For two enlightening analyses of the Safavid state, see Newman, *Safavid Iran*; Savory, *Iran under the Safavids*.

[10] This historical account is based on Moojan Momen, *An Introduction to Shi'i Islam: The History and Doctrines of Twelver Shi'ism* (Yale University Press, 1987), pp. 105–46; Said Amir Arjomand, *The Shadow of God and the Hidden Imam* (Chicago University Press, 1987), pp. 122–70.

[11] See: L. Clarke, "The Shi'i Construction of Taqlid", *Journal of Islamic Studies* 2001 12 (1): 40–64.

A *marja-ye taqlid* (source of emulation) was selected for his piety, his religious knowledge, and his ability to address the needs of the constituency that looked to him for inspiration. This last criterion was especially relevant as the *marja*'s authority was not legitimated by a clear, undisputed institution. Instead, his authority was dependent on his ability to continuously demonstrate the relevance of his knowledge and skills under changing circumstances. When a *marja* died, his rulings entered the canon of Shiite thought, but his followers were to cease emulating him.

The attainment of *marja* status was a dynamic, flexible process. The prestige and jurisdiction of a *marja* was determined by his ability to command a large following. A *marja*'s students acted as his representatives in villages, towns, and cities, spreading his rulings as definitive. He acquired such students by publicly demonstrating the financial ability to support them. This capacity, in turn, was very dependent on the willingness of the community of believers to pay the religious taxes levied by the scholars in their role as representatives of the Imams. A mutual dependence was formed. Scholars required support and constituents. Believers sought a bonding agent to ensure the coherence of communal bonds. Each community supported and was sustained by the other.

The Shiite scholars and the lay believers became intertwined, yet had no clear relations of authority. Neither could claim control over the other. Both seemed to contract and expand in uncoordinated fashion, and both overlapped each other significantly. Gradually, the authority of the Shiite Safavid state over both eroded. The state was in no way qualified to shape the "Shiiteness" of either community. As the senior scholars joined the state elite, they grew distant from the laity as well as from their juniors.

The *usuli-akhbari* Dispute

Tensions among the Shiite scholars came to a head in the seventeenth century when an internal struggle took place within the scholarly community, which resulted in the formation of two religious schools of thought: one calling itself *usuli* (authentic), and another, often called *akhbari* (text-based). The *akhbaris* rejected the *taqlid*-based, personal authority of the *maraji'* (the sources of emulation). They offered a model based on internal salvation obtained through the individual study of the sacred texts. Spiritual elevation was to occur through the study of texts and the recasting of daily life in the light of those texts.[12]

The *akhbaris* marginalized the role of personal scholarly mediation between the human and the divine. They believed in the individual application of the divine word, expressing disdain for the adaptive, communal character of the *usuli* normative structure. The *akhbari* school also argued that all believers

---

[12] On the *usuli-akhbari* debates, see Robert Gleave, *Scripturalist Islam: The History and Doctrines of the Akhbari Shi'i School* (Brill, 2007), pp. 1–30.

must literally follow the words of the prophet and the twelve Imams as they appear in Muslim Scripture.

The *akhbari* school placed great importance on linguistic and textual skills. They argued that the words of the scripture must be understood correctly. Knowledge of Arabic, the language of Scripture, was implied, as was a high literary proficiency. *Akhbaris* refuted the dogmatic expertise of the *usuli* sources of emulation. They insisted that the texts themselves held the answers to all questions that might arise in the life of a believer or in society as a whole.

At a first glance, the *akhbari* school seems to be extremely egalitarian. It presented anyone who wished to devote time to reading and interpretation with a single road map to individual salvation. In practice, however, this school imposed a blunt hierarchy separating the rich, literate minority from the impoverished majority that could not even read the sacred texts.

The *usuli* scholars, on the other hand, grounded their authority in the current realities of their constituents. Theirs was a societal vision. They had an astute understanding of politics. Through the principle of *taqlid*, the *usulis* began to accumulate informal influence both within the ruling circles and among the general public. Placing a focus on the concept of personal emulation, the *usulis* cast religious doctrine into the present, adapting and evolving their rulings in close correspondence with the diverse needs of the believers.

As the seventeenth century moved forward, the struggle between the two scholarly schools intensified, but the political context changed. The *usuli* scholars, originally from Lebanon, had a higher status and more political clout than their competitors. This was attributed to their close relationship with the monarchy which had brought them to Iran. They therefore began to identify themselves with the state's interests. *Usuli* scholars received powerful positions in the service of the Safavid monarchs; intermarried with court officials, rich landowners, and traders; and became full-fledged members of the imperial elite. The *akhbari* school was, under these circumstances, subversive as a result of its preference for individual salvation through textual study over the daily life of the community. Rejecting existing social reality in favor of a more inward mode of salvation presented a problem to those in power. The *usuli* scholars, who were closely allied with the monarchs and owed them some of their social status, had something to lose should the status-quo be disturbed.

The *usuli* school disdained mysticism and the desire for inner salvation. Contrary to the *akhbaris*, the *usulis* argued that God had created rules to guide individual and social life. This knowledge, they insisted, was highly applicable rather than philosophically abstract. According to the *usulis*, this knowledge should be sought and interpreted by the scholars, who were the most skilled interpreters in Shiite society.[13]

---

[13] For an illuminating discussion of the changing contexts within the *usuli-akhbari* debate, see Juan Cole, *Sacred Space and Holy War: The Politics, Culture and History of Shi'ite Islam* (IB Tauris, 2005), pp. 58–77.

Under the leadership of Ayatollah Mohammad Baqer Majlisi (1616–1698), the *usuli* scholars began to actively oppose what they perceived as *akhbari* social supremacy.[14] This opposition took the form of a campaign to separate piety and devotion from the study advocated by the *akhbaris*. Picking his weapon from the *akhbari* arsenal, Majlisi compiled huge collections of *hadiths*, or tales of the Imams and the prophet, on which *usuli* jurists came to base their rulings. Thus, he linked *usuli* rulings to a clear holy text. Majlisi and his comrades extolled the virtues of piety while linking it to a legalistic approach to holy texts. This stood in opposition to the inward study advocated by their rivals.

Majlisi soon acquired a solid popular base, in part because of the inherent elitism of the *akhbari* creed. Especially relevant to the *usuli* cause was the reluctance on the part of *akhbaris* to actively seek political power. Majlisi and his followers, therefore, continued to codify Shiite religious conduct. They wrote guides for the correct performance of prayer, speech and diction, the ritualistic repetitions of Quranic verses, and other practical aspects of religious life.

They standardized and transformed mystical rituals alongside quasi-religious rituals of divination, charm-writing, and so forth. These actions were unprecedented in the Shiite world. Daily Shiite practices had previously been diverse and highly local. These rituals served as the platform for Majlisi's transformation of Shiite popular religion. The *usuli* school emerged victorious and has remained the dominant Shiite school since the seventeenth century.

Usuli Shiism and the Safavid State: A Concluding Note

Usuli dominance paved the way for a new relationship between scholars, believers, and the Safavid state. Scholars moved to establish direct authority over the community of believers. They did this in two ways. The first was by equating religion with law and presenting themselves as the group most capable of understanding and applying divine law to daily life. The scholars perceived themselves as the final arbitrators of the law, as well as the ones divinely charged with discovering the law through interpretation. The *usulis* took the practices of traditional piety, and transformed them into a highly formalized religion.

Majlisi's streamlining of Shiite popular religion addressed the needs of the believers, which preferred a reconciliation of authority, hierarchy, and communal traditions. The community of believers was able to develop locally, based on the personal relationship of the religious leader to his community. The structure of power and authority within the local community was closely attuned to the needs of its localized public.

---

[14] For a thorough treatment of Majlisi's life and works, see Colin Turner, *Islam without Allah? The Rise of Religious Externalism in Safavid Iran* (Curzon Press, 2001).

This alliance between scholars and lay believers grew more open and stable toward the end of the Safavid era (circa 1700).[15] The Safavid state, which previously served as a center meant to alleviate the vacuum at the core of Shiite society, no longer commanded clear allegiance from either scholars or believers. Both became involved in a political process that was based on engagement and dialogue. Both maintained their own agendas and networking. Still, both recognized the importance of communication and consensus building between the two communities.

The line separating scholars and lay believers was blurred and ambiguous. The medium that the community of believers provided for the scholars' activities encouraged a mutual dependence between the two. Lay believers saw the legitimate authority of the scholars as an alternative to the waning authority of the state. The constant, continuous interpretation of scripture and sacred law in relation to current events was the key to the ongoing legitimacy of scholarly authority.

---

[15] See: Newman, *Safavid Iran*, pp. 81–116.

2

The Quest for Authority

The participation of the Shiite scholars in state politics grew significantly following the collapse of the Safavid dynasty in the early eighteenth century. Seeking to take an active role in shaping the public sphere, political engagement became the order of the day. Still, this engagement was not tantamount to a direct assumption of political power. The scholars swore allegiance to the Shahs during Friday prayers; they received state salaries and favors, acknowledging the sovereignty of the kings in return. This remained the state of affairs, *mutatis mutandis*, throughout the eighteenth and nineteenth centuries. It was under the Pahlavi Shahs that the division of powers began to change, until the violent paradigm shift of Khomeini's 1979 Islamic Revolution. To better understand this growing political participation, one should trace the contours of the conceptual array that shaped and directed the transformation of Shiite leadership between the rise of the Qajar dynasty (1795) and Khomeini's revolution (1979).

The Consolidation of the Scholarly Community

The nineteenth century saw a semi-institutional order begin to form among the Shiite scholars. This change was related to the rise of the Qajar dynasty (1795) and the reintroduction of centralized rule to Iran, following seventy years of political chaos. It is the internal upheavals of the religious establishment to which we now turn.[1]

Following the rise of the Qajari regime, the system of *taqlid* (emulation), reached a higher level of institutionalization that was conducive to the creation of a more hierarchical order within the scholarly community. The number

---

[1] For an innovative historical review of the period, see Robert Gleave, *Religion and Society in Qajar Iran* (Routledge, 2009).

of scholars and sources of emulation grew under the Qajars. The community of scholars began to recognize a hierarchy of *maraji*, or sources of emulation. At the top of this hierarchy sat the supreme source of emulation, known as the *marja-ye a'ala-ye taqlid*. In the early nineteenth century, Mortaza Ansari became the second *marja* accorded such an honor. He decreed that all believers must adhere to the leadership of a *marja*, and insisted that such *maraji* must be alive, not dead. This approach increased the relevance and presence of Shiite leadership in the lives of its constituents. This process, initiated by Ansari, grew to maturation with Khomeini's revolution in both Iran and Shiism.[2]

Ansari reorganized the financial network of the religious establishment based on the support provided by the lay believers. This support came partly in the form of a tax, originally payable to the Imam or to his representatives in his absence, and partly as voluntary contributions. Ansari decreed that the proceeds of this tax were to be spent addressing the needs of the believers, and he authorized local scholarly leaders to spend them in this fashion. Through these measures, Ansari validated the authority of the scholars.

Ansari focused his efforts predominantly on the internal structure of the scholarly community. These efforts immensely strengthened the authority of the scholars over the believers. The changes promoted by Ansari had less impact on the scholars' relations with the state. The Qajar state remained marginal in the shaping of Shiite leadership. When the authority of the Qajar state began to weaken during the nineteenth century, the scholars preferred not to fill the resulting political vacuum. They largely focused on expanding their presence among the believers.

Under the Qajar monarchs, the government awarded contracts to foreign firms and governments to perform a great variety of public services, from the collection of customs to the laying of railways. Westerners flooded into Iran during the nineteenth century. British and Russian representatives played increasingly significant roles at the Qajar court. Western entrepreneurs made their presence felt in all sectors of Iranian society. Increasingly, the traditional economy based on land and patronage gave way to foreign-dominated capitalism.

The scholars disapproved of the degree of Western economic and political interference in Iran. They did not do so on the basis of a clear ideological point of view or to simply protect personal interests. Instead, the senior religious scholars feared that the Qajar Shah was trying to cement his own power at their expense by allying himself, through the sale of concessions, with the Westerners. They feared that they would lose their influence on both rulers and followers. The scholars had long enjoyed influence over Shiite believers and social welfare without being blamed for political mistakes. The Qajar reforms were a threat to this fragile balance.[3]

---

[2] For a detailed account of Ansari's work, see Juan Cole's chapter in: Nikkie Keddie (Editor), *Shi'ism: From Quietism to Revolution* (Yale University Press, 1986), pp. 40–6.
[3] See Arjomand, *The Turban for the Crown: The Islamic Revolution in Iran*, pp. 20–34.

Nationwide Activism

The twentieth century witnessed the growth of unprecedented tension between state authorities and Shiite leadership. Although most scholars remained loyal to the Qajar Shahs, dissenting voices began to be heard and acquired a following. In 1892, the scholars took on the Qajar monarchy directly in a movement referred to as the "Tobacco Rebellion," after the Shah awarded a comprehensive tobacco concession to a British firm. This firm was to handle the growing and processing of tobacco from the plant stage to the finished cigarette. Although the Shah had granted numerous other concessions prior to 1892, those had not had much impact on Iranian society.

The tobacco concession, however, touched the lives of almost every Iranian. The terms of the agreement required landowners to allow British inspections of their fields, forcing merchants to submit to foreign supervision over one of their largest sources of income. This increased the sensation, common among Iranians at the time, of ongoing Western encroachment on the Iranian way of life.

Several groups approached the senior *marja* at the time, Mirza Hasan Shirazi, requesting that he take a public position on the concession. In response, he issued a *fatwa* (religious ruling) forbidding all Shiite believers to touch all tobacco products, whether to grow, process, transfer, sell, or consume them. As a result, the entire nation stopped smoking, including many members of the court, which forced the Shah to revoke the concession. For the first time, a scholar had actually challenged state authority, but neither the scholars nor the believers pushed on for scholarly political control of the nation.[4]

The Shiite scholars and the state clashed again in 1905–6, during Iran's so-called Constitutional Revolution. The revolutionary movement reflected general discomfort with the Shah's absolutist policies. Intellectuals with Western education, who opposed the Shah's absolutist politics, offered the constitution as a symbol of sovereignty and justice. These intellectuals attracted the merchants and landowners, who were once again displeased with the Shah's efforts to shatter the balance of power in Iran. They also attracted several top religious scholars who publicly opposed the Shah, granting legitimacy to the constitutionalist struggle. Most of the senior scholars, however, opposed a constitution, seeing it as a threat to the role of religion in shaping public policy.[5]

The political struggles of the Qajar era largely took place among elites, as the two groups contended for authority in the newly forming public sphere. The political upheaval hardly affected the lay believers. The Qajar state lacked common norms and shared beliefs required to mobilize solidarity, or to effectively shape the social and economic aspects of daily life.

---

[4] See Nikki Keddie, *Religion and Rebellion in Iran: The Iranian Tobacco Protest of 1891–1892* (Routledge, 1966), pp. 35–64.

[5] For a history of the constitutional revolution, see Vanessa Martin, *Islam and Modernism: The Iranian Revolution of 1906* (Syracuse University Press, 1989).

The state's weakness was exacerbated by the view shared by both Shiite communities regarding the triviality and negligibility of the state. The language of Shiite Islam appeared to possess some political potency, but it had yet to lead to the creation of a religiously inspired political movement. This changed in 1925 when a military officer named Reza Khan overthrew Ahmad Shah Qajar and crowned himself Reza Shah Pahlavi.

Collision

The ascendance of the Pahlavi regime brought about a profound shift in the relationship between the religious leadership and the Iranian state. The Pahlavis and the scholars' community tested each other's boundaries throughout the twentieth century, each attempting subtly to dominate the other. During the 1950s and 1960s, this balance was shaken by a far-reaching initiative on the part of Mohammad Reza Shah Pahlavi. He attempted to concentrate all political and cultural power in the monarchy. It was Ayatollah Khomeini who responded to this challenge by radically reinterpreting his religious standing to include direct political authority.

In 1925, Reza Khan, a military officer, established the Pahlavi dynasty, crowning himself Reza Shah Pahlavi. Pahlavi was one of the ancient languages of pre-Islamic Iran, and Reza Shah sought to establish a clear connection to this heritage. He wished to make Iran into a world power. When he looked to the West, he saw a higher quality of life, sophisticated educational systems, powerful militaries, and superior technology. Most of all, he was impressed by the notion behind the principle of the Western state. Its power, in his view, lay in its unity, which in turn resulted in a coherent institutional structure. He saw the Western state as playing two simultaneous roles. First, it was a core of political power, granting its citizens a stable existence and a prosperous life. Second, he saw the state as a symbolic entity, a community granting its members a social and visionary context larger than their individual lives.[6]

These two realms of leadership – the symbolic and the political – had been separated in Iran for centuries. Reza Shah assumed that this unity of functions exhibited by the Western state was responsible for the unimpeachable legitimacy it enjoyed. In turn, he believed this legitimacy allowed the state to assume a monopoly on both making laws and enforcing them. Reza Shah embarked on a process of reform, aimed at unifying the Iranian state under his monarchy. The community of believers was to be dismantled and turned into a community of citizen-subjects. Its complex networks and alliances were to be remade, with each individual professing fealty to the state.

Reza Shah set about achieving his desired goal in diverse forms. He concentrated on incorporating Iran's rural areas more fully into the nation by expanding the infrastructure, building roads, and laying railroads. He expanded the

---

[6] For an attempt to broadly consider Reza Shah's rise to power, see Cyrus Ghani, *Iran and the Rise of Reza Shah: From Qajar collapse to Pahlavi Power* (IB Tauris, 2001), pp. 376–412.

state's education system, initiated adult education programs, and opened Tehran University. The Ministry of Education initiated a state-sponsored curriculum for all schools. For the first time, Persian was systematically taught to Iran's ethnically diverse population. These changes improved the level of education in Iran, but they also enabled indoctrination in the new supremacy of the monarchy and, formed the basis of a civil, nationalist identity. Reza Shah identified himself as a faithful Shiite even though he stripped the scholars of the jurisdiction over law and education.[7]

Shiite Scholars could continue teaching or practicing law, but only if they became civil servants licensed to operate by the state. The scholars managed to pass the state licensing examinations in small numbers. Still, when they did, they rapidly saw their privileges, which were granted under the previous rulers, stripped away. Licensed scholars became mere bureaucrats, offering services required by the subjects of the Iranian monarch. The scholarly community was thus diminished to an executive arm of the state. The scholars were elegantly shoved aside and then co-opted, becoming civil servants. Their new dependence on the state for their livelihood diminished their ability to challenge the Pahlavi regime.

Reza Shah sought a new balance of power, with the country united under his monarchy. To achieve this goal, he focused on making the state felt in the lives of its citizens. He moved to affect quick and efficient economic change, strengthening Iranian industry and agriculture. He was reluctant to come out directly against the scholars and often professed his allegiance to Shiite Islam.

Following the demise of the Ottoman Empire in 1923, he considered forming a republic molded after Ataturk's new venture in Turkey. He consulted with the religious scholars, who opposed the idea. Publicly, he credited them with persuading him to change his mind. Thus, despite the threat to scholarly livelihoods, the fragile balance tipped but did not completely collapse. For the most part, scholarly leaders backed him, as they had backed previous leaders of the Iranian state over the course of centuries.[8]

This coexistence ended with the abdication of Reza Shah in favor of his son, Mohammad Reza. Reza Shah's rule came to an end in 1941 when the British and the Russians forced him to abdicate his throne because of his sympathies for the Nazi regime. Mohammad Reza succeeded him with Allied agreement, and – for the first twelve years of his reign – he ruled under U.S. influence. A U.S.-engineered coup d'etat prevented Mohammad Reza Shah's dismissal in 1953.

---

[7] For a detailed discussion of Reza Shah's reforms, see Donald Wilber, *Riza Shah Pahlavi: The Resurrection and Reconstruction of Iran* (Exposition Press, 1975); and Ervand Abrahamian, *Iran Between Two Revolutions* (Princeton University Press, 1982), pp. 102–48.

[8] See Shahrough Akhavi, *Religion and Politics in Contemporary Iran* (SUNY Press, 1980), pp. 23–59.

Mohammad Reza Shah reasserted his authority following the events of 1953, confident of U.S. support. He sought to exceed his father in transforming Iran. Mohammad Reza Shah wished to replace Islam as the principal component of Iranian identity with a new secular vocabulary, grounded in the monarchy and the pre-Islamic history of Iran.[9]

The Shah's Effect

During the reign of the Pahlavis, the state redefined its authority, nearly eliminating the Shiite scholars' interpretative authority. The Pahlavi state also sought to change the religious affiliation of Shiite believers, turning Shiite society into a national society of subject-citizens loyal to the state. During the rule of Mohammad Reza Shah, the scholarly community was dependent on the state both for its livelihood as well as for its legitimacy. The link between Shiite scholars and lay believers was significantly marginalized.

Mohammad Reza Shah actively sought to shift the focal point of Iranian identity from the Shiite community of believers to a nationalist Iranian monarchy[10] Mohammad Reza Shah presented a centralized, unified, and westernized model of authority, placing the state above the alliance of Shiite communities. Mohammad Reza Shah sought to impose a single, monolithic identity, that of a citizen-subject. The difference-based model of traditional Shiite identity, capable of including within itself diverse affiliations, was seen by Mohammad Reza Shah as a threat to his monarchy and as the force keeping Iran from attaining its rightful place in the world.[11]

The Pahlavi monarchy called for containing all other forms of authority. The state tried to cast itself as the sole interpreter of Iran's past by applying absolutist structured authority. By doing so, Mohammad Reza Shah provoked the quietist scholarly leadership into response. His attempt proved alienating to many Iranians and was ultimately vanquished by the revolution of 1979.

As long as the Shah did not directly combat the scholars, the religious leaders did not oppose him publicly. The community of scholars split into three camps. The largest one wished to continue with quietist policies, seeing no need to directly embrace or reject the Shah. A second group cooperated publicly with the regime and enjoyed religious appointments throughout the country. The third group, which directly opposed to Pahlavi policies, included many future leaders of the Islamic Republic.

This group consisted mostly of mid-level religious scholars whose local constituencies lay in large villages or provincial towns where the faithful did not

---

[9] For an example of the Shah's self-perception, see Mohammad Reza Shah Pahalvi, *Answer to History* (Stein & Day, 1982).

[10] See Arjomand, *The Turban for the Crown*, pp. 75–102.

[11] For the most extensive review of the Pahlavi educational system, the lynchpin of the Pahlavi attempt to restructure Iranian identity, see David Menashri, *Education and the Making of Modern Iran* (Cornell University Press, 1992). Menashri provides an analysis of the social perception and mechanisms guiding the battle of identities in Iran.

identify with Mohammad Reza Shahs' policies of rapid Westernization and indoctrination. They were provincial, imbued with the spirit of the lay believers. They resisted attempts by the elitist leadership of the scholarly community to interfere in their lives. On the other hand, as faithful members of the scholarly community, these mid-level scholars were reluctant to disobey their leaders. It is this group, led by Ayatollah Khomeini, that served as the platform for the emergence of revolutionary Shiite leadership.[12]

Khomeini: Becoming a Leader

Since assuming the role of *rahbar*, Supreme Leader of the Islamic Republic of Iran, Khomeini has become less a man, more an avatar.[13] Web sites galore celebrate Khomeini as a true Imam, offering hagiographical accounts of every aspect of his life, from birth to the memorable funeral at which his body was almost torn to pieces by a crowd numbering in the millions, ecstatically bereft at the passing of their leader.[14] His life and thought is referred to incessantly by the leadership of the Islamic republic, his legacy is seen as the most comprehensive yardstick for measuring practical achievement and doctrinal purity. Attempting to reduce this bounty of cultural forces into the chronology of a single life must be simplistic at best. Still, a biography is necessary for providing an initial historical background to Khomeini's work, as well as for orientating us within the general Iranian historical context.[15]

Khomeini was born as Ruhollah Musavi in the town of Khomein, about 300 kilometers southwest of Tehran. He was born on September 24, 1902 to Mostafah, the son of a land-owning family in the region and to his wife, Hajieh Khanum. His was a family of Musavi Seyyeds, meaning that they claim descent from the prophet through the Seventh Shiite Imam, Musa al-Kazim. Religion was always a family profession. Originally, the family came from northeastern Iran, but immigrated to India in the eighteenth century. Khomeini's grandfather moved to the holy city of Najaf. He never returned to India. He struck up a friendship with a landowner from the Khomein area, returned there with him, and settled in the town.

Khomeini's father, Mostafa, trained for the clergy as well. He married the daughter of a high-ranking cleric and went with her to Najaf in 1892. This was

[12] See Akhavi, *Religion and Politics in Contemporary Iran*, pp. 91–116, 159–80.

[13] For an innovative account of Khomeini's transformation during his reign as Supreme Leader and following his death, see Daniel Brumberg, *Reinventing Khomeini: The Struggle for Reform in Iran* (University of Chicago Press, 2001).

[14] For example, see: http://www.inminds.co.uk/khomeini.html

[15] The biography presented is a synthesis of several biographies, including Hamid Dabashi's biographical sketch (see Hamid Dabashi, *Theology of Discontent* (NYU Press, 1993), pp. 409–84), as well as Amir Taheri's highly controversial yet informative biography (see Amir Taheri: *The Spirit of Allah: Khomeini and the Islamic Revolution* (Hutchinson, 1987)). For the fullest, book-length biography available, see Baqer Moin, *Khomeini: Life of the Ayatollah* (Thomas Dunne Books, 1999).

a heady time for a young cleric in training. In December of that year, the chief Shiite cleric, Mirza Hassan Shirazi, directly challenged the Qajar Shah. The Qajars had engaged in selling off state services as concessions to foreign firms or governments.

As part of that policy, they sold the concession for tobacco-related services, from growing the leaf to its processing into cigarettes. This was perceived as an imposition on the most private of Iranian private spheres. Shirazi ordered a boycott of all tobacco products on religious grounds of impurity, and an entire nation stopped smoking. The Shah was forced to cancel the concession.[16] This challenge by the clerics served to increase their reputation, and marked the beginning of their direct involvement in politics.

However, Mostafa returned to his family's estate and settled down to live the quiet life of a local nobleman. He enjoyed the prestige his religious schooling gave him, but did not fulfill the duties of a country cleric. He was a recognized social presence in the area. When three local warlords began to extort money and produce from the people of the region (the central government was, at the time, not strong enough to collect its own taxes and farmed these services out to powerful local figures), Mostafa decided to ride and ask for help from the provincial governor. The two warlords ambushed him and shot him on the road to Arak, the provincial capital. Ruhollah was six months old.

Khomeini was raised by his mother and aunt. He received his early education at home and at the local religious school, studying with local teachers and with his older brother, Mortaza, later Ayatollah Pasandideh. In 1919, he began to study at the seminary in Arak, led by the noted Shiite cleric Ayatollah Abdolkarim Ha'ei Yazdi. One year later, in 1920, Ha'eri was asked to move his seminary to the city of Qom and to transform that city's seminary into a leading one. Ha'eri agreed, and Khomeini followed his teacher to Qom.[17]

Khomeini embarked on a traditional course of Shiite higher education, immersing himself in the canons of Shiite law and ethics. However, his initial interests were rather unorthodox for seminary students – philosophy and mysticism. Many seminary students studied privately with teachers of mysticism, as the subject was not usually a part of the official curriculum. Khomeini studied with some of the philosophical mystics and luminaries of the age, including Ayatollah Muhammad Ali Shahabadi.[18] Khomeini began teaching mysticism and philosophy in 1928, long before he took up teaching advance Shiite law. Although he was certainly known and revered as a legal expert, his philosophical and mystical interests remained with him and were dealt with in several of his works.

Khomeini rose rapidly through the ranks of the Shiite scholars. Before his turn to revolutionary rhetoric, he served as personal secretary to Ayatollah

---

[16] For a detailed survey of the Tobacco Rebellion, see Keddie, *Religion and Rebellion in Iran*.
[17] See Moin, *Khomeini*, pp. 1–20.
[18] See Dabashi, 1993, p.410–11.

Hossein Borujirdi, the most venerated Shiite scholar in Iran, the supreme source of emulation. He expressed reserved criticism of Mohammad Reza Shah's reforms, but never explicitly came out against the monarchy. Khomeini was a popular teacher at the high Shiite seminaries in Iraq as well as in Iran, specializing (as mentioned earlier) in civil law and philosophical mysticism.[19]

Khomeini's embrace of radical activism in 1963 grew out of his assessment that the Shah's reforms represented a real threat to both Shiite communities, lay and scholarly. He was most concerned with the Shah's desire to destroy the unique pattern of communication and engagement that had developed between the two communities in the seventeenth century and had been maintained since. He recognized the Shah's plan to portray scholarly authority as obsolete and the threat in the Shah's attempts to provide an alternative social, cultural, and historical vision.

Khomeini did not initiate actions to pursue the removal of the Shah until Mohammad Reza enfranchised women in 1962. In 1964, the Shah exiled Khomeini, who found refuge first in Turkey and then in Iraq in 1965. He lived in the Shiite holy city of Najaf in Iraq until 1978 when Saddam Hussein expelled him. During his time there, he taught classes on various subjects, including mysticism and contract law.

Khomeini's most famous class dealt with the question of the Shiite scholarly community – political leadership. Departing from centuries of Shiite scholarship, he argued that Shiite scholars must insist on taking active political roles. The notes from this class, transcribed and published illicitly, became the seminal text of the Islamic revolution – *velayat e-faqih* (the governance of the jurist).

Khomeini's Argument

Khomeini's vision was framed within the context of a scholarly discussion, testing the limits established by his elders in Najaf. When the Grand Ayatollah Kho'i was asked by his students in the late 1960s if Shiite scholars were permitted to openly assume the mantle of political governance, he answered in the negative. Khomeini did not shy away from the fact that he was engaging in creative interpretation, stating: "If the only proof I had were one of the traditions I have been citing, I would be unable to substantiate my claim."[20]

Khomeini's interpretation sought to actively alter political reality, doing away with quietist arguments. Particularly, he opposed the notion that Shiite Islam should no longer seek institutionalization, owing to the occultation of the Twelfth Imam. He claimed that Shiite Islam was capable of such institutionalization and that those who administered it should be well-taught in Islam. He also argued that the authority of the scholars was sufficient to

---

[19] For a thorough biography of Khomeini, see Moin, *Khomeini.*

[20] See Hamid Algar (Translator), *Islam and Revolution: Writings and Declarations of Imam Khomeini* (Mizan Press, 1981), p. 99.

continue collecting the religious tax (*khums*) on behalf of the Imam in the Imam's absence.[21]

Khomeini's argument was based on his understanding of interpretation as the root of political practice.[22] He demanded political leadership for the scholars. According to his belief, they were the most qualified interpreters, as well as the ones with the strongest work ethic and commitment to the public good. Khomeini saw the world as a text to be constantly read, interpreted, and mediated. Khomeini was an innovator when he argued for conferring leadership on the scholarly community. Still, the notion was not unprecedented in Shiite circles. Khomeini's disciples, however, made the conceptual leap to the actual, overt demand for authority.

Khomeini's conception of a virtuous Islamic society emphasized negotiated, interpretative authority. Khomeini surmised that he could not present a convincing challenge to the Shah's sweeping reforms without providing a semblance of authority for Iranian Shiites already grown accustomed to the role of a functioning state. He demanded authority for the scholars, yet one that was far removed from the absolutist model propounded by the Shah. Khomeini saw the authority of the scholarly community as grounded in the scholars' ability to serve as interpreters and mediators.[23]

In Khomeini's vision, the scholarly community was uniquely capable of discharging two tasks simultaneously. He saw the role of the scholars as fostering national identity among the community of Shiite believers while promoting religion among citizens of the Iranian state. This was to be carried out within a functioning, difference-based order. This type of authority was dependent on the never-ending process of interpretation and adjustment. It saw the process not just as a means to attaining an ideal, but as an end in and of itself.[24]

Khomeini saw the scholarly community as occupying the middle ground of Shiite society. He suggested that both sources of identity, state, and community of lay believers should acknowledge the scholarly community as a source

---

[21] For an illuminating, detailed analysis of Khomeini's creative engagements with various hadiths in *velayat-e faqih*, see Michael M.J. Fischer Mehdi Abdi, *Debating Muslims: Cultural Dialogues in Postmodernity and Tradition* (University of Wisconsin Press, 2002), pp. 122–46. Professor Fischer's work, including *Iran: From Religious Dispute to Revolution* (University of Wisconsin Press, 2003), is a model of clarity and compassion, a critical anthropological approach to the Islamic Republic and its formative revolution.

[22] For a seminal discussion of interpretation as a basis of cultural and normative authority in the Western canon, see Hans Georg Gadamer, *Truth and Method* (Continuum, 2004).

[23] For a thorough, innovative discussion of the tensions involved in the practice of interpretation, see Paul Ricoeur, *The Conflict of Interpretations: Essays in Hermeneutics* (Northwestern University Press, 2007). For an immersing treatment of the hermeneutic craft, see Paul Ricoeur, *From Text to Action: Essays in Hermeneutics II* (Northwestern University Press, 2007).

[24] For a different analysis of Khomeini's political project, see Dabashi, *Theology of Discontent*, pp. 409–84.

of authority. Yet, Khomeini's goal was not to condense both into a single, scholarly-dominated vision.[25]

The Shah politicized the traditional relationship between the political elites and Shiite scholars by appealing directly to the Iranian public for political support. He treated Iran's citizens as political capital to be disposed of at will. Khomeini did the opposite. He created a message and formed organizations that allowed for continuous engagement between scholars and laity without negating existing differences. Khomeini believed that maneuvering between the two groups was desirable and feasible.

According to Khomeini's argument, the scholars were the most capable of mediation as they closely affiliated both with community of believers and with the state. Khomeini's notion of interpretative authority sought to allow both community and state to exist separately, yet interact within a dynamic balance.[26]

Life as Interpretation

On January 3, 1988, Khomeini sent a letter to Mikhail Gorbachev, then still the General Secretary of the Communist Party of the USSR. The letter was seen as a curiosity at the time because it implored Gorbachev to embrace Shiite Islam as a cure-all remedy to his country's existential crisis.

However, the letter also contained several comparisons made by Khomeini between religious and irreligious societies. He refers to "Materialists" and "Theists," highlighting the contrast between Iran and the Soviet Union. For the purposes of our discussion, it is also possible to read the excerpt (in the following quotes) as a revealing discussion of the differences between high-ground and middle ground understandings of reality. Khomeini's text appears in italics, with our commentary in regular font:

I have found it necessary to remind you to reflect once again on the materialistic and theistic world views. Materialists consider sense to be the sole criterion of knowledge and are of the opinion that whatever cannot be known through the senses falls outside the realm of knowledge. They identify existence with matter and consider as nonexistent anything that has no material body.

Khomeini identifies the focal point of Shiite consciousness and awareness, the void. In this void are a God that cannot be seen or approached, but also the Twelfth Imam, the Messiah who will restore justice and fairness when the Day of Judgment comes.

---

[25] For a unique discussion of Khomeini's political theology, see Ibrahim Moussawi, *Shi'ism and the Democratisation Process in Iran: With an Emphasis on Wilayat al-Faqih* (Saqi Books, 2012). Moussawi is head of media relations for Lebanese Hizballah, and editor of the organization's newspaper.

[26] For an informative translation of Khomeini's *velayat-e faqih* (Islamic Government), see Algar, *Islam and Revolution*.

Inevitably, they regard the world of the unseen-God Almighty, Divine Revelation, Prophethood and the Resurrection-as mere fiction. On the other hand, theists consider both sense and reason to be the criteria of knowledge, and maintain that whatever can be known through reason lies within the realm of knowledge, although it is not perceptible. To theists therefore, existence is inclusive of both the unseen and the manifest. For a thing to exist it is not necessary to have a material body.

Human life stands between the seen and the unseen. It is never, clearly, one or the other. The basic method for leading a meaningful life consists of mediation and interpretation. How can one make sense of an unseen, unapproachable truth, if not through interpretation of signs and glimpses?

The Holy Qur'an reprobates the fundamentals of materialistic thought and, addressing those who say: "We shall never believe in thee until we see God manifestly"; the Qur'an proclaims: "Vision comprehends Him not, and He comprehends all vision; and He is the knower of subtleties, the Aware." I should not like to present here Qur'anic arguments concerning Divine Revelation, Prophethood and the Resurrection which from your point of view are debatable. In fact I do not wish to entangle you in the twists and turns of philosophical arguments, particularly those of Islamic philosophy. I will content myself by presenting one or two simple, intuitive examples of which even politicians can avail themselves.

Khomeini underscores the fact that, for him, the differentiation between the middle ground life and the high-ground life is not a matter for abstract, philosophical discussion. The tenets of religion are just as real as human life, and both should be addressed through a similar framework – that is, the middle ground.

It is self-evident that matter, whatever its nature, has no awareness of self. Consider a stone statue: each side is ignorant of the other side, whereas human beings and animals, we clearly observe, are aware of their Surroundings. They know where they are, and have some idea of what goes on around them. There must be, then, an element in men and animals that transcends matter and is separate from it, living beyond the life of matter. Intrinsically, man seeks to attain absolute perfection. He strives, as you well know, for absolute power over the world; he is not attached to any power that is defective.

If he has the entire world at his command, he naturally feels inclined to have command of another world once he is informed of its existence. No matter how learned a person may be, if he learns of some other branch of knowledge, he naturally feels inclined to attain mastery of that branch of knowledge also. Therefore, there must be some Absolute Power and Absolute Knowledge to which man is attached. It is God we all seek, although we may not be aware of it. Man strives to attain Absolute Truth, so that he may be annihilated in God. Basically, the desire for eternal life that is inherent in every individual is proof of the existence of an Eternal World to which destruction cannot find its way.[27]

---

[27] Available online at: http://www.ghadeer.org/english/imam/letter%20Imam/callto/callto2.html.

Man strives for perfection, yet it is clear that man cannot reach perfection. God, according to Khomeini, is the only one who is perfect. We always want more, but we are also always in the presence of what we do not know. Our life exists between what we know and what we do not know. Eternity, everlasting life; these are validated by our all too short lives, our interests and desires, our struggles. Perfection is what we want, but not what we have. The sole effective way to create order and solidarity is through interpretation, in the middle ground.

It is the interpretative dimension of Shiite leadership that maintains sizable distance from fundamentalist adherence to a fixed creed.[28] The new Shiite vision, as defined by Khomeini, is an attempt to produce a middle ground political reality. This middle ground vision acknowledges and sustains diverse voices and viewpoints. Each one maintains its autonomy, but none grows strong enough to maintain dominance over others for a prolonged period of time.

In fact, the lack of fundamentalism is not exclusive to Khomeini's school within Iran, but characterizes Arab Shiite communities as well. Historically, the Lebanese confessional polity has remained multifocal, without clear preference toward a single religion. Lebanese Hizballah, despite advocating an Islamic Republic in the Iranian mode, has refrained from taking active control of the Lebanese State. In post-Saddam Iraq, Shiites hold many key positions at the national level, including the prime-ministership, but they also occupy a place of pride in opposition circles. This diversity is apparent in Iraqi religious circles as well.[29]

---

[28] For an intense, authority-centered, Christian understanding of the Liberal/Fundamentalist divide, see J.I. Packer, *Fundamentalism and the Word of God* (Eerdmans, 1958). Although this is a dated, Christian book, it presents the challenges offered by fundamentalism to liberal notions of authority in very effective form.

[29] For a definitive review of Iraqi Shi'a, see Yitzhak Nakash, *The Shi'is of Iraq* (Princeton University Press, 2003). For an innovative attempt to integrate the various levels of Iraqi Shi'ism, see Imranali Panjwani (editor), *The Shi'a of Samarra: The Heritage and Politics of a Community in Iraq* (IB Tauris, 2012).

3

Void and Spaces

Space is the domain of social interactions. It is not necessarily physical or terri-torial. Simply put, space is the dimension in which one no longer exists alone. In space, one understands oneself in relation to other people, things, groups, institutions.[1] Shiite society exists in three separate yet connected spaces[2]: com-munal, institutional, and frontier.

Communal space is organized around primordial loyalties, informal net-works, and shared core values.[3] Institutional space, primarily the realm of the state and public institutions, is the social dimension concerned with the distri-bution of official power. The frontier is the space of longing. It is inhabited by the Shiite myths. The frontier also marks a tangible territorial border, which separates the land one possesses from the land one desires.

The Communal space is local, either the space in which one lives or from which one originates. Communal space is grounded in the shared experience of its inhabitants. The affiliations between community members stem from "the subject's ... sense of the 'givens of social existence' – speaking a particular language, following a particular religion, being born into a particular family, emerging out of a particular history, living in a particular place; the basic facts, viewed again, from the actor's perspective, of blood, speech, custom, faith, res-idence, physical appearance, and so on."[4]

Communal space, thus, includes residential arrangements, kinship systems, circuits of praxis, and networks of economic affiliations. This dimension also

---

[1] For a foundational discussion on human geography, see Yi-Fu Tuan, *Space and Place: The Perspective of Experience* (University of Minnesota Press, 2001).

[2] For a broad analysis of space as a defining social concept, see Henri Lefebvre, *The Production of Space* (Wiley-Blackwell, 1992).

[3] In use of this term, we are following Clifford Geertz, *Interpretation of Cultures* (Basic Books, 1973), pp 255–310.

[4] Geertz, *The Interpretation of Cultures*(Basic Books, 1973), p. 6.

denotes social divisions between particularistic groups across residential, ethnic, class, occupational, and religious lines.[5]

Decisions within the community are rarely overt. Instead, direct participation and consensus building by members of the community mark both the evolution and execution of communal decisions. That is, communal space often shies away from formal institutions and procedures. Still, social and cultural aspects of communal space are elaborate, even though they often manifest themselves in the form of mundane reality. The frontier is a geopolitical as well as an imagined place, growing out of shared beliefs, common destiny, a mythical past, and a grand political design.

The frontier is not autonomous. It is profoundly connected to its communal counterpart. Communal space is organized around the notion of the local and the day-to-day. The frontier deals with utopia, with an ideal notion of the collective.[6] Each space complements the other. The frontier broadens the horizons of the occupants of communal space, providing them with a vision that links them to spaces beyond the local or the immediate. Communal space, on the other hand, grounds the collective identities and grand ideas of the frontier in the realities of individuals and social groups.

Institutional space is the realm of the state that provides the basic structure for institutional space. Its recognizable aspects are the executive organs of government.[7]

The national borders and the state institutions sustain each other. While the state recognizes its debt to communal space and to the frontier, it views itself as regulating the ambitions of both. Institutional space becomes increasingly occupied with obtaining and maintaining the power necessary to impose its rationality over the frontier and the community.

Institutional space regulates the volatile relationship between the accessible real and the lofty ideal. It functions as a buffer between communal space and the frontier. This border should be dynamic and flexible in order to manage the relations between the other two spaces. Communal space and the frontier have their own internal logics and justifications. Neither overtly requires the other to exist fully. Institutional space, however, exists through these two spaces.

---

[5] See James Scott, *Domination and the Art of Resistance: Hidden Transcripts*, (Yale University Press, 1990); Diane Singerman, *Avenues of Participation: Family, Politics, and Networks in Urban Quarters of Cairo* (Princeton University Press, 1993).

[6] Michel Foucault highlights the utopian nature of the frontier and the constant critique of other spaces that it represents. Michel Foucault, *Of Other Spaces*, accessible online at: http://foucault.info/documents/heteroTopia/foucault.heteroTopia.en.html.

Benedict Anderson views the frontier and its existence as crucial for the formation of a national, "imagined" community, see his, *Imagined Communities* (Verso, 1991);

Henri Lefebvre distinguishes between perceived, conceived and lived space, seeking to stress the importance of understanding modernity in spatial terms.

[7] For a definitive description of institutionalism as a mindset see: Walter Powell and Paul Dimaggio (editors), *The New Institutionalism in Organizational Analysis* (University of Chicago Press, 1991).

The three types of spaces are archetypes, simplified models of nuanced socio-political and religious phenomena. In reality, one can hardly find spaces as clearly demarcated as we have described. Instead, one finds groups and individuals whose consciousness and worldviews embody a fusion of different perceptions, contradicting and complementing each other simultaneously. In peaceful times, the inner tensions between communal, institutional, and frontier spaces rarely cause conflict. Groups and individuals are often able to prioritize the competing visions and demands. In times of crises, however, the tensions between the various spaces may be exacerbated. Groups and individuals may have to prioritize the needs or demands of one space over those of the other two.[8]

The Evolution of Shiite Spaces

Following the dynamic interaction of the three spaces reveals that in the Shiite case, the interaction led to the creation of two parallel axes. The first regards institutional space, which begins as a marginal phenomenon in terms of its ability to shape religious identity, and gradually grows stronger and more dominant. The second axis is that of the alliance between communal space and the frontier. Each axis challenges the other, and each seeks to dominate the other.

Until the twentieth century, both axes maintained a parallel, autonomous existence. Before the rise of the Safavids in the sixteenth century, the state played a marginal role in the formation of religious identity. During the Safavid and Qajar periods, institutional space grew more dominant, but still maintained a separation from the axis of communal space and the frontier.

It was only under the Pahlavi Shahs, especially under Mohammad Reza Shah (1953), that institutional space began to expand, threatening to swallow the two other spaces whole and subjecting them completely to the power of the state. Pahlavi leadership was a high-ground leadership. The Pahlavi Shahs sought a functioning order and committed to the creation of a new reality in Iran through the destabilization of existing structures. The Shah sought to transform both communal space and the frontier, unifying them within the spatial confines of the state.

Khomeini and his Islamic Republic represent a different perception of the state. Khomeini created a new institutional discourse, basing his vision of the state on the open-ended, flexible alliance between communal space and the frontier. Within the Islamic Republic, all three spaces continued to exist autonomously with Shiite leadership serving as the ultimate mediator. The Islamic Republic under Khomeini thus redefined leadership, injecting the Shiite traditions of the middle ground with new political vitality.

---

[8] For a creative examination of the relationship between space and the political, see Nigel Thrift, *Non-Representational Theory: Space, Politics, Affect* (Routledge, 2007).

The Absence of Institutional Space

Persecuted minority groups draw much of their strength and cohesion from their communal space. As the group is unable to dominate the halls of institutional power, its members focus on daily survival. Persecuted minorities often engage in drawing clear distinctions between members of their community and outsiders. Minority identity is constructed out of oppositional relationships alongside in-house communal affiliations and networks.

The Sixth Shiite Imam, Ja'afar al-Sadiq (d. 765 AD) rejected any claims on the part of the Shiite community to assume political authority. This rejection amounted to a suspicion and resulting distance from institutional space. He initiated two new directions for Shiite leadership. The first related to legal authority, and the second to metaphysics and religion.

Al-Sadiq charged Shiite leaders with deciding matters of civil law impacting the Shiite community. Whether Shiites lived in a Sunni or a Shiite state, the Shiite community of believers maintained its own norms and legal system through its scholars' community. In addition, Al-Sadiq made Shiite leaders responsible for interpreting questions of religion and disputing the attributes of God, as well as the nature of messianic deliverance.[9]

Shiite scholars considered it their duty to collect the tales and traditions of the Imams. They used them as the basis for learned treatises and judicial decisions on issues as diverse as civil and contract law and the occurrence of Judgment Day. In the early days of Shiism, the twelve Shiite Imams provided both legal and religious guidance, communicating directly with God and mediating between frontier and communal spaces.[10]

The twelve Shiite Imams were infallible, according to Shiite tradition, because they enjoyed direct contact with God. They were, therefore, able to translate and apply God's words to the daily experiences of the Shiite community. When the Twelfth Imam vanished, the Shiites lost their guide and mediator, as well as their immediate contact with the divine. The religious scholars were not able to communicate directly with God, as the Imams could. They assumed the role of interpreters. It was their responsibility to interpret current reality in light of the teachings of the Imams.[11]

The frontier became the space that demonstrated the bond between myth and reality in Shiite tradition. In many ways, the frontier was a defense against the misery and hardship that defined Shiite reality. Still, frontier space was never wholly composed of redemption visions.

From the eighth century until the rise of the Safavid Empire in 1501, most Shiites lived under Sunni rule. Still, Shiites did not consider Sunni leaders to be fully legitimate. In Iran, officially Shiite since 1501, a separation of powers

9 See Momen, *An Introduction to Shi'i Islam* pp. 72–6.
10 See Mohammad Ali Amir-Moezzi, *The Divine Guide in Early Shi'ism – The Sources of Esotericism in Islam* (State University of New York Press, 1994), especially pp. 61–98.
11 Ibid.

existed between Shiite rulers and Shiite scholars. The former were charged with defending the integrity of the state, whereas the latter oversaw religious and spiritual allegiance and welfare. Institutional space, even under Shiite rulers, did not play a major part in the shaping of religious identity.

Sunni rulers were able to impose material conditions on Shiite communities. Yet, they rarely succeeded in convincing their Shiite subjects to view themselves as part of a broader polity. The Shiite longing for the frontier remained, for the most part, outside the scope of the Sunni state. It was primarily an abstract, visionary space, criticizing through its very existence the indignities suffered by Shiites at Sunni hands.

The scholarly gatekeepers of the frontier devoted themselves to a religious and judicial discourse, aimed at converting divine command into realizable norms for Shiite communities. At best, they partially succeeded in implementing these norms, as they lacked institutional power. Still, the relations between the frontier and communal space remained intense and close-knit.

Adjusting to Institutional Space

The rise of the Shiite Safavids heralded the return of institutional space to dominance.[12] For the Safavids, the frontier was a powerful presence. The Safavid ruling elite based their political legitimacy on claims to direct descent from the Seventh Shiite Imam, Musa al-Kazim. Thus, the mythical figures of the Shiite frontier played very tangible roles in Safavid political culture. For the Safavids, the frontier was not just a space of longing. It was a very real territory to be dominated, a source of authority, and a space in which various social groups could unite behind a single political power.

The scholars, identified with both frontier and communal spaces, began to appreciate the power and stability offered by the Safavid state. In effect, institutional space and frontier space – that is, the Safavid state and the community of scholars – allied in an effort to dominate communal space; in other words, the space of the Shiite lay believers.

The interaction of the frontier and the state expanded when the Safavid Shahs invited high-ranking Arab Shiite scholars from the great schools of Jabal 'Amel in today's Lebanon to Iran to occupy the top positions of their new religious establishment.[13] The Safavid Shahs rewarded these scholars with state-backed jurisdiction over both the educational system and the legal system. In their educational and legal capacity, they began constructing the principle of *taqlid*. Under this doctrine, each member of the Shiite laity was required to seek a scholarly source of emulation to follow in all aspects of life related to

---

[12] See Newman, *Safavid Iran*, especially pp. 1–25.

[13] This was not entirely unusual: itinerant scholars and peripatetic intellectual and scholarly traditions were fairly common in the sixteenth-century Muslim world and would continue to be so until the fall of the Ottoman Empire. For further reading, see Babayan, *Mystics, Monarchs and Messiahs*.

worship and devotion. Within a century, the Arab community of scholars had become a part of the Persian Safavid elite.

Shiite society acknowledged Safavid authority and respected the territorial space of the state. Nonetheless, the state did not acquire the authority to define either the informal structure of communal space or the idea-based contents of the frontier. The state fulfilled the administrative functions of government, protecting the state's borders, collecting taxes, and performing other such duties. Still, the Safavid state did not play a significant role in the life of the Shiite community or in shaping the frontier.

Under the Safavids, the interdependence of the communities described earlier brought about the reconfiguration of Shiite society. The frontier, the space of longing and myth, was reintroduced into the mainstream of Shiite culture in the form of a new popular religion. The *usuli* scholars, dedicated to the notion of *taqlid* (emulation) and the advancement of scholarly personal authority, produced numerous treatises on rituals and popular religion. For example, they codified particular prayers to be offered up to specific Imams at given times.

The *usuli* scholars prescribed amulets and created intricate formulas for performing *istiftah*, the random perusal of works of scripture to answer questions related to daily life. This ritualized, mass-oriented public religion appealed to the needs of the lay believers. They embraced it eagerly, elevating the scholars to a status they had not previously enjoyed, expanding their financial and political support for the scholarly community.[14]

The merger of the frontier and communal space was achieved through the religious interpretative skills of the scholars. They were, in fact, charged with the task of regulating the frontier. Shiite scholars collected the tales and traditions of the Imams. They were responsible for adapting this raw material into a detailed and comprehensive code applicable to human, as opposed to divine, existence.

The need for such dynamic mediation between scholars and believers was directly linked to the collapse of the Safavid state in the eighteenth century.[15] Frequent attacks by local warlords, combined with the deterioration of Safavid infrastructure, were responsible for their fall. Communal space and the frontier were connected at their core. The tensions between the two spaces were complemented by their mutual dependence. What emerged was a new Shiite society imbued with the spirit of the frontier but speaking the language of communal space. This process of emergence continued throughout the rule of the Qajar dynasty, which began at the turn of the nineteenth century.

---

[14] For an integrative analysis of *usuli* practice and theory in the life of Ayatollah Majlisi, see Turner, *Islam without Allah*, pp. 148–78.

[15] For further reading on the institutional disorder in Iran during most of the 18th century, see Michael Axworthy, *The Sword of Persia: Nader Shah, From Tribal Warrior to Conquering Tyrant* (IB Tauris, 2009).

Although the community of scholars did not assume direct political power, the scholars reasserted their authority over the Shiite community by actively challenging the Qajar state on several occasions. Their role in challenging Qajar policies embellished their reputation as defenders of the people.

A prime example is the Tobacco Revolution of 1892, when, after a concession for the growing and processing of tobacco had been granted to a British firm, Iran's most senior scholars boycotted all tobacco products. The entire country stopped smoking and the Shah was forced to rescind the concession. Another example is Iran's 1905–1906 Constitutional Revolution.[16] Religious scholars were influential on both sides of the debate over the constitution's capability for limiting the Shah's authority. These two examples reflect the growth of Shiite society from the interaction between the frontier and communal space, bypassing the authority of the state.

The Institutional Challenge

Reza Shah

Reza Shah's rule led to the formation of Iran's first unified, monolithic state infrastructure. Reza Shah believed that, under its rightful monarch, the state should retain sole authority over all aspects of its citizen-subjects' lives. His state sought to take over communal space. The community of believers was to be replaced by a state of citizens. All aspects of the state created in his image were to resound with an Iranian identity. This was meant to diminish the spatial diversity of Shiite society.

While Reza Shah maintained a working relationship with Iran's land-owning and trade elites, he also took on the scholars in an efficient, indirect manner. Reza Shah stripped the scholars of their executive authorities in the fields of law and education. His state established ministries of education and law that were broadly modeled on European parallels. The scholars were relegated to civil servant status, service providers for the new citizens who could engage in religious activities in their spare time.

Reza Shah was careful not to relinquish his Shiite identity. Despite professing admiration for Ataturk's reforms, he refrained from creating a republic modeled on Ataturk's secular state-building in Turkey. He publicly announced that his decision was the result of consultation with top scholars. Reza Shah identified himself as a Shiite lay believer, although he made it clear that this had minor relevance to his new, single-space state.

Reza Shah emphasized the development of a modern economy in Iran. He industrialized the country and built extensive roads and railroads. He opened

---

[16] For additional material on the tobacco rebellion, see Keddie, *Religion and Rebellion in Iran*. For additional readings on the constitutional revolution, see Janet Afary, The Iranian Constitutional Revolution, 1906–1911: Grassroots Democracy, Social Democracy & the Origins of Feminism (Columbia University Press, 1996).

Iran's first institution of higher education, Tehran University, in 1936. He formed an adult education program, striving to bring all Iranian citizens to a minimum standard of skill and competence in reading, writing, and arithmetic. All these measures were aimed at creating a clearly defined Iranian civil space. This monolith stood in stark contrast to the blurred nature of Shiite communal space.[17]

Mohammad Reza Shah

Mohammad Reza Shah actively sought to identify and eradicate threats to the institutional coherence he wished to impose within all three spaces – the institutional, the communal, and the frontier. In 1963, he initiated what he called the "White Revolution," the purpose of which was to conclude the task begun by his father. Mohammad Reza Shah's ambitious plan called for the neutralization of all rival sources of power.

The Shah's revolution took on the structure of land ownership in Iran.[18] Mohammad Reza Shah feared the wealth of the big landowners. His father promoted the interests of the land-owning class, seeing them as potential allies in his attempt to revitalize Iran's economy. Mohammad Reza Shah, who wished to establish his authority on cultural as well as material grounds, could not tolerate any opposition from any sector within Iranian society.

More than the landowners' wealth, he feared their influence over the millions of peasants who tilled their lands as tenant farmers. The White Revolution nationalized great tracts of land, including the Shah's own personal holdings, and passed them over to the peasants. This measure had a far-reaching effect on the traditional structure of Shiite society, removing a powerful, age-old hierarchy and placing agricultural communities strictly under the authority of the new monolithic state.[19]

Mohammad Reza Shah did not stop there. He used the new educational platform to promote his visionary political agenda. The textbooks published under this program linked every aspect of collective life in Iran to the monarchy, ignoring religious communal affiliations.

Reza Shah justified his authority by pointing to his success in modernizing Iranian society. He created a unified Iranian state under his rule, imbuing it with technological and economic vitality. Mohammad Reza Shah went further. He claimed his monarchy was a direct link in the chain begun by the ancient Persian kings (to 600 BC). To highlight that connection, Mohammad Reza Shah changed the Iranian calendar. Rather than marking chronological time

---

[17] See Arjomand, *The Turban for the Crown*, pp. 59–70.

[18] For more on Mohammad Reza Shah's land and economic reforms, see Ervand Abrahamian, *Iran between Two Revolutions*, pp. 419–49. See also Abrahamian's *A History of Modern Iran* (Cambridge University Press, 2008), pp. 123–54.

[19] See Asghar Schirazi, *Islamic Development Policy: The Agrarian Question in Iran* (Lynne Rienner, 1993).

as before and after the birth of Mohammad or Christ, he set it to Cyrus the Great's ascent to the Persian throne. He then commemorated 2,500 years of Persian monarchy (1971) in an extremely ostentatious manner, inviting world leaders to the festivities but restricting public access to the celebrations.[20] In effect, he sought to replace the founding myths of Shiite religiosity with the myths of Iran's pre-Islamic past.

Mohammad Reza Shah's efforts to transform Shiite society into a secular, nationalist society, and increase the power of institutional space, were unprecedented. When his father, Reza Shah, took on the scholars, his reforms impacted institutional space. The scholars did not actively oppose Reza Shah's measures because he did not attempt to destroy their traditional stronghold, the frontier. He allowed the scholars to maintain their position as guardians of Shiite religious collective memory, even while he was formulating an alternative collective memory in his image.

Mohammad Reza Shah followed a much broader initiative. By providing for his monarchy an ancient, historical origin that kept its distance from Islam, he threatened the very reason for the existence of the frontier and thereby the Shiite community of scholars. He denied the Shiite scholars any significant role in the shaping of Iranian public consciousness. Institutional space, as he envisioned it, would completely subdue not only communal space, but also the Shiite mythical frontier.[21] The state he envisioned could exist only if it discharged the duties of both communal space and frontier.

Mohammad Reza Shah took on the relationships of difference which comprised the core of Shiite social order in Iran. His monolithic state could not survive if it were to acknowledge the intricate engagements between communal space, the frontier, and traditional Iranian institutional space. The distinctions between these spaces, essential for their interaction in the Shiite middle ground, posed a direct threat to the Shah's unitary vision.

The Shah saw the diversity and negotiated nature of the middle ground as a major source for Iran's weakness. His revolutionary intentions sought a pervasive overhaul of the Iranian public sphere. The threats that the Shah's vision posed to the status and authority of the religious leadership were the force behind Khomeini's counter-challenge, the transformation of the benign middle ground into a viable political ideology.

---

[20] See: Moshe Halberthal and Avishai Margalit, *Idolatry* (Harvard University Press, 1998) for a remarkable statement of monotheism's utter condemnation of replacing divine glory with human-like idols. The book profoundly illustrates the argument later made by Khomeini against the Mohammad Reza Shah with regard to the latter's abandonment of Islam for the glories of ancient Iran.

[21] For a concise review of Mohammad Reza Shah's policies, see Arjomand, *The Turban for the Crown*, pp. 71–87.

4

Khomeini's Middle Ground

Understanding Khomeini's vision of the Iranian state as an Islamic Republic requires exploration of his effort to reframe the interpretative traditions of Shiite leadership by creating a state based on the politics of the middle ground. The 1979 revolution placed overt political authority directly in the hands of the scholarly leadership. This was the first time in Iran's history that Shiite scholars assumed political authority. The relationship between state, community, and frontier thus shifted significantly.

Initially, the majority of Iran's Shiite leaders chose the traditional course of acquiescence and quietism. They were motivated by the tradition of eschewing political authority, as well as by recognition of Mohammad Reza Shah's superior resources and popular support. Active opposition centered on a small group of middle-rank scholars under the leadership of Ayatollah Khomeini. The future leader of the Islamic Republic saw the Shah's reforms as an existential threat. Khomeini led protests against the Shah in 1963 and found himself exiled from Iran for his efforts.[1] During sixteen years of exile, Khomeini transformed himself. The man who was a pillar of the scholarly community until the age of 61 became a political firebrand.

Political authority, Khomeini suggested, should belong to the scholars, they were to be made rulers because of their interpretative skills. They were the ones qualified to carry out the interpretation that constitutes the cornerstone of a virtuous society.[2] Why, according to Khomeini, should a virtuous society be based on interpretation? First, a virtuous society cannot be one that exists solely within a single, homogenous space. Khomeini claimed the pretense of

---

[1] See Moin, *Khomeini*, pp. 92–128.
[2] See Khomeini's most famous political treatise, *velayat e-faqih* (*Hokumat e-Eslami*) [Government of the Legal Scholar or Islamic Government] as translated by Hamid Algar. Accessible online at: http://www.al-islam.org/islamicgovernment/.

objectivity, which lies in such a perception of society, is heretical. God is the sole sovereign and legitimate legislator. Absolute truth, which is implied in a hegemonic order, exists only in perfect, divine space of eternity. Human truth is flawed and contextual, but it is also multifocal, holding within it differing worldviews and perceptions. Diversity is the primary trait of human society constructed on this truth.

Human society, which encompasses communal and institutional space as well as the frontier, is a work in progress in spatial terms. It is an interaction between different levels of religious existence: ritual, knowledge, and faith.[3] The Shah asked his subjects to give up their affiliations with the frontier and communal space. Khomeini suggested a model that allowed and encouraged Shiites to remain present in all three spaces that had been the core of Shiite society for centuries.

Khomeini reinterpreted the tradition distancing Shiite scholars from politics. In the first centuries of Shiite history following the disappearance of the Twelfth Imam, he argued, the frontier was perceived as a space of longing, loaded with myths. For the persecuted Shiite minority, the frontier became an unfulfilled alternative to the reality in which they lived. Under the Safavids (1501–1722), the frontier slowly began to have a bearing on the daily life of Shiite communal space. The interpretative labors of Shiite scholars in the frontier gradually became a platform for increasing political power.[4]

The frontier, with its growing proximity to the community, served as the basis of a popular religion enacted in Shiite society by *usuli* scholars in the seventeenth and eighteenth centuries. As the Qajar state deteriorated in the nineteenth century, the scholars identified themselves with popular protests and actively took on the Shahs of Iran. During Iran's constitutional revolution (1905–6), the scholarly camp was divided. Many prominent scholars vehemently opposed a constitution, claiming it was a heretical profession of human sovereignty. Others, however, supported it and produced scholarly studies explaining the ways in which scripture condoned and supported its tenets. Despite their differences, both parties made political use of interpretation, slowly moving from the periphery to the center of Shiite Iranian society.[5]

Khomeini perceived his revolution to be the conclusion of this historical process. Interpretation, he claimed, should no longer be simply the means by which ends are enforced. This approach to the role of interpretation, he argued, could easily lead to the Shah's experiment in absolute rule. To avoid this outcome, Khomeini claimed that interpretation itself is an end and not a means. Interpretation, therefore, should be the guiding principle of Shiite society. What

[3] See Mohammad Mojtahed Shabestari, *iman va-azadi (Faith and Freedom)* [Entesharat Tarh-e No, 1379], pp. 117–38.
[4] For a critical analysis of Khomeini's interpretative work in his *velayat-e faqih*, see Fischer and Abedi, *Debating Muslims*, pp. 122–46.
[5] See Arjomand, *The Turban for the Crown*, pp. 34–58.

began as a method of applying sacred texts to daily conduct would now become the key to Khomeini's Shiite state.

Khomeini's interpretative middle ground perception was the most effective way to repel Mohammad Reza Shah's high-ground vision for Iran – that is, the formation of a secular, homogenous, and sovereign society. A virtuous society, claimed Khomeini, was one that recognized and sustained the differences between its components. The way to do this was to place the frontier at the heart of Shiite society. The community of religious scholars thus emerges as the most qualified entity to assume the mantle of political leadership.

Khomeini's State in Action

The idea of the state as based on interpretation found its clearest expression in the constitution of the Islamic Republic of Iran, first ratified in 1980 and then amended in 1989.[6] Khomeini's vision of Shiite society inspires the founding of a functioning Shiite state, a merger of the Shiite community and state institutions with the religious frontier. Article 4 of the constitution reads:

All civil, penal, financial, economic, administrative, cultural, military, political, and other laws and regulations must be based on Islamic criteria. This principle applies absolutely and generally to all articles of the Constitution as well as to all other laws and regulations, and the wise persons of the Guardian Council are judges in this matter.[7]

Because this article of the constitution applies to all other articles, any act of the state must be evaluated in accordance with Islamic criteria. These criteria are not defined in the constitution itself. Instead, the most venerable scholars in the land are required to deduce them in each case. Interpretation is, therefore, the key to maintaining both the rule of law and a virtuous society. It is a sacred responsibility, entrusted to the most capable scholars. The frontier is the space of interpretation, lying at the heart of society envisioned in the constitution.

The notion of communal space is maintained in Article 8:

In the Islamic Republic of Iran, "enjoining good and forbidding evil" (al-'amr bilma'ruf wa al-nahy 'an al-munkar) is a universal and reciprocal duty that must be fulfilled by the people with respect to one another, by the government with respect to the people, and by the people with respect to the government. The conditions, limits, and nature of this duty will be specified by law. (This is in accordance with the Koranic verse "The believers, men and women, are guardians of one another; they enjoin the good and forbid the evil." [9:71])

---

[6] For an astute, comparative assessment of religion and constitutional orders, see Ran Hirschl, *Constitutional Theocracy* (Harvard University Press, 2010).

[7] All English translations of the constitution quoted from the following Web site: http://www.iranonline.com/iran/iran-info/Government/constitution.html.

This article, entitled "community principle," is directed at communal space. Still, one may notice that even in this case, communal space is set against the context of other spaces, most clearly institutional space inhabited by the state.

The citizens' loyalty to the state is preserved in Article 9:

In the Islamic Republic of Iran, the freedom, independence, unity, and territorial integrity of the country are inseparable from one another, and their preservation is the duty of the government and all individual citizens. No individual, group, or authority, has the right to infringe in the slightest way upon the political, cultural, economic, and military independence or the territorial integrity of Iran under the pretext of exercising freedom. Similarly, no authority has the right to abrogate legitimate freedoms, not even by enacting laws and regulations for that purpose, under the pretext of preserving the independence and territorial integrity of the country.

This loyalty is broadly framed. It includes the preservation of the freedom and unity of the Iranian nation. The framers of the constitution are quick to point out loopholes. Preserving sovereignty cannot serve as a pretext for abrogating legitimate freedoms. The whole system of checks and balances requires dynamic interpretation to be effectively upheld. Interpretation is most effectively performed in the frontier.

The constitution constructs the different branches of power in Iran, with no branch having absolute power over all others in any specific field. Even the supreme leader, the highest-ranking position in the Islamic Republic, can be replaced. This is an expression of middle ground reality in which no single actor can or should achieve prolonged dominance over all others.

The difference between the leadership of Khomeini and the Shah is demonstrated most clearly with regard to the division of power within the Iranian state. Like his visionary contemporaries in the region (David Ben Gurion in Israel, Ataturk in Turkey), the Shah attempted to do away with millennia of history and culture. He imposed a new Iranian identity, based on an incorporation of pre-Islamic history and secular westernization. His working formula for a new Iranian state was, therefore, based on two ideals that clashed with the Iranian realities.

In contrast, Khomeini's vision had flawed, mediated, and contextual middle ground reality. He built his strength on the creation of effective communication between the community of lay believers, the scholarly community, and the state. Whereas the Shah focused on superimposed extremes, Khomeini encouraged a return to the traditional mode of diverse and dynamic friction.[8]

Khomeini's Vision of Resistance

Khomeini's political vision includes a significant dimension of resistance. He rejected the Shah's attempts to create a non-mediating state, a source of power

---

[8] For a systematic treatment of Khomeini's vision of authority, emphasizing the tension between militant and scholarly trends within Shi'i tradition, see David Menashri's "Ayatollah Khomeini and the Velayat-e Faqih," in *Militancy and Political Violence in Shi'ism*, Assaf Moghadam (ed.) (Routledge, 2011), pp. 49–70.

beyond challenge or interpretation. This resistance to extremes was directed not only at the Shah, but at the world at large.

Khomeini's sentiments are clearly reflected in a letter he wrote on July 16, 1988 to the members of the Iranian parliament. The letter explained his decision to sign a ceasefire with Iraq, ending the brutal, eight-year war between the two countries. Khomeini begins the letter with a detailed description of Iran's dire military situation. He provides facts and figures, supplied by various politicians and military commanders, describing why Iran stands no chance of victory.

Having dispensed with the facts, Khomeini then devotes half of the letter to a statement of personal faith. He begins by identifying Iran's unique place in the world:

O God! You are aware that we do not collude even for a moment with America, the Soviet Union and other global powers, and that we consider collusion with superpowers and other powers as turning our back on Islamic principles.

O' God! We are alone in a world of polytheism, blasphemy, division, money, power, deceit and double-dealing, and we seek your help.[9]

Khomeini sees Iran as a "non-power." He understands that the labeling of one-self as a "power" indicates a desire for totality, a placing of the self at the extreme. His Iran cannot ally itself with any such power, regardless of ideology or agenda. The Iranian middle ground resists the world of powers and super-powers, with its extremist and corrupting values.

Khomeini identifies and commits to this resistance in his letter when he says:

O' God! In the entire history, whenever prophets, guardians and Ulama decided to be the peacemakers of societies and intertwine practice with knowledge, and organize societies devoid of corruption and decay, they faced resistance from the Abu Jahls and the Abu Sofyans [opponents of Prophet Muhammad] of their time.

From the middle ground, Khomeini is prepared to go to war, to sacrifice millions of Iranians and to forego personal and national honor. Still, this is done through engagement, rather than extremist fealty to a preconceived grand vision. Resistance does not deny or exclude. It is waged through continuous engagement and mediation.

Khomeini's understanding of resistance as essential to the politics and life of the middle ground leads us to Lebanese Hizballah. The organization, known for its worldview of *muqawama* (resistance), elaborates Khomeini's vision expressly along similar lines.

Lebanese Hizballah

The Shiite reality in Lebanon differs from the Iranian reality in a crucial way. Shiites in Iran have lived under lay Shiite leaders for more than 500 years.

[9] See http://www.cfr.org/publication/11745/letter_from_ayatollah_khomeini_regarding_weapons_during_the_iraniraq_war.html.

The motivation for the Shiite doctrine of withdrawal from the state, which began in times when state authorities were often persecuting Shiites, gradually grew obsolete in Iran. Shiite scholars did not accept Iran's Shahs as religious authorities. Still, the scholars interacted more and more with the Iranian state. They used the regime's stability and the effectiveness of the state to maintain their roles as mediators between the Shiite community and frontier vision.

The political history of Lebanese Shiites is one of marginalization.[10] Throughout four centuries of Ottoman rule in the region, Shiites remained a persecuted minority. Even when they were not actively persecuted, Lebanese Shiites were at the bottom rung of the social ladder. Most of them were subsistence farmers, tilling the relatively arid land of today's southern Lebanon.

After World War I, when the Allies created the Lebanese state under French Mandate, Christian Maronites and local Sunnis shared responsibility for home rule. The Druze, a fiercely independent sect that withdrew from Islam in the eleventh century, also received some consideration. The Shiites did not. They remained pawns in a game that took place among the elites of the Sunni and Christian factions.[11] Throughout the first half of the twentieth century, the Shiites accounted for 19 percent of Lebanon's population. Still, they were ignored by the Lebanese state. The National Pact of 1943 divided governmental power between the various Lebanese denominations. The president of the republic was to be a Maronite Christian, the prime minister was to be a Sunni, and the speaker of parliament – the least influential of the three top positions – was to be a Shiite.[12]

In the 1960s, Musa al-Sadr, a young member of Iraqi Shiism's most prestigious family, arrived in Lebanon to serve as the leading scholarly authority for the city of Tyre.[13] Sadr represented a new type of Shiite scholar, one who demanded a significant role for Shiites in national politics and who sought to politicize a stolid Shiite public.

Sadr was profoundly influenced by Khomeini's emerging vision of the Shiite scholars as political leaders, present in all three spaces of Shiite society. During the following decade, Lebanese politics began a process of transformation. Sadr's insistence on direct participation in Lebanese political discourse was also shaped by the escalation in interfaith and interethnic hostilities in

---

[10] See Augustus Richard Norton, *Hezbollah: A Short History* (Princeton University Press, 2007), pp. 1–46.

[11] For a critical history of Lebanese nationalism, see Kamal Salibi, *A House of Many Mansions: The History of Lebanon Reconsidered* (University of California Press, 1990).

[12] See http://countrystudies.us/lebanon/77.htm.

[13] Muqtadah al-Sadr, the extremist Shiite leader in Iraq, is a member of the same family. So was Ayatollah Muhammad Baqer al Sadr, perhaps the most influential Arab Shiite cleric of the past half century. The Sadr family led the attempts of Iraqi Shiite clerics to form a political movement. As many Iranian clerics studied in Najaf, the Iraqi city holy to Shiites, the Sadr family also served as an inspiration to scholarly movements in Iran.

Lebanon. This escalation, in turn, was caused by the growing Palestinian presence in the country.[14]

The Palestine Liberation Organization (PLO) was founded in 1964, redefining the Palestinian national struggle. Most Palestinians were Sunni Muslims, but the PLO was an organization of national liberation aimed at creating a nonreligious Palestine. PLO headquarters had been based in Jordan since the 1967 war with Israel. Following the events of the civil war known as "Black September" in 1970–1971, when Jordan's King Hussein violently evicted the organization from his country, it relocated to Beirut and Southern Lebanon. The PLO hoped to continue attacks against Israel from this traditionally Shiite area.[15]

In the following years, the Sunni community in Lebanon undermined their nation's fragile confessional politics. Lebanon's Sunni Muslim leaders attempted to dominate their nation and shake off the power-brokering arrangement of 1943. The Christian Maronites, supported by France and other Western countries (including Israel), could not ignore this challenge. Each of the parties began to form armed militias, expecting the imminent breakdown of the state.

In 1974, Musa al-Sadr formed the first Lebanese Shiite political movement in many years, *Amal*. The name was an acronym for *afwaj almuqawamah allubnaniyah* (The Brigades of Lebanese Resistance) but is also the Arabic word for "hope."[16] Sadr opposed the Palestinian presence in Lebanon, mainly because of what he termed the Palestinian "colonization" of the country's Shiite southern regions. The leftist factions within the PLO became the most secular elements of Lebanese society and they alienated the more religiously oriented Shiites. However, Sadr was also drawn to the Palestinians' revolutionary rhetoric. Ideologically, therefore, *Amal* mixed moderate political Islam, revolutionary oratory and Shiite tradition, drawing the youth of the urban, Shiite poor to the movement.

Following the 1982 Israeli invasion of Lebanon, a group of Shiite militants split from Amal and formed Hizballah ("the Party of God"). The formation of Hizballah was inspired by the fledgling Islamic Republic's efforts to export Khomeini's revolution from Iran to Lebanon. Hizballah presents itself as an organization devoted to the promulgation of Khomeini's *velayat-e faqih* (governance of the jurist), the doctrine which claims political authority for the Shiite scholars, and to the creation of an Islamic state in Lebanon.

Hizballah grew rapidly. Within a few decades, the organization became the dominant authority in Southern Lebanon. This was made possible with significant Iranian financial and military aid. The organization controls vast economic

---

[14] See Fouad Ajami, *The Vanished Imam: Musa Al-Sadr and the Shia of Lebanon* (Cornell University Press, 1992), especially pp. 159–90.

[15] See Shaul Mishal, *The PLO under Arafat: Between Gun and Olive Branch* (Yale University Press, 1986), pp. 15–20.

[16] See Ajami, *The Vanished Imam*, pp. 168–71.

resources in the south of the country, as well as other regions. Most notable is the *dahiya*, Beirut's Shiite neighborhood. Hizballah has become the primary caretaker of Shiite communal space in Lebanon. It commands a vast network of informal economic arrangements in the region. Hizballah also distributes vast funds to its Shiite constituents for a multitude of communal purposes such as education, housing, and the creation of jobs.[17]

The organization has been a major power player in the Lebanese political arena since the end of the civil war. The Ta'if agreement of 1989, signed by all parties involved in the civil war, made the Shiite political representation equal to that of the Maronites and the Sunnis. Still, Shiites believed that their representation was not commensurate with their demographic presence. Since 1989, Hizballah has been increasingly involved in the Lebanese political sphere so as to protect Shiite interests at the national level. Over the years, Hizballah has managed to make flexible and skillful use of political opportunities. These include the Israeli withdrawal of 2000, on which Hizballah publicly capitalized; the 2005 "Cedar Revolution" which enabled Hizballah to form its own political block; and the war with Israel in 2006.

As of the 2009 elections, Hizballah remains one of the main opposition parties in Lebanon. In the 128-member parliament, Hizballah is directly represented by 13 members. Hizballah also leads a parliamentary alliance consisting of fifty-seven members. It has orchestrated rallies against the government, mobilizing hundreds of thousands in the process. Still, Hizballah hesitated with regard to a violent takeover of power. Hizballah's alliances with Iran and Syria granted it significant status in the debate on Lebanon's political destiny.

Hizballah also acts beyond Lebanon's borders. It sees itself as a movement protecting both the religious interests of Shiites and the political interests of Arabs. Additionally, Hizballah's declared desire to challenge Israel is an indication of its self-perception as a transnational movement. Hizballah also views itself as an organ of the Islamic revolution inspired by Khomeini's ideology. During its 2006 war with Israel, Hizballah was often portrayed as the guardian of "Arab honor."[18]

The organization claimed to be responsible for ending the Israeli occupation of Southern Lebanon in 2000, thus succeeding where all other Arab regimes had failed. This self-presentation of Hizballah as the last truly Arab movement is a recurring motif that has been present in Lebanese Shiite vocabulary since the 1970s. This considerably broadens the political horizons of Lebanese Shiites.

Hizballah has the ability to act simultaneously in communal and institutional space as well as on the frontier. But what sort of presence does the organization exercise? What sort of legitimacy is it able to produce? An attempt to answer

[17] See, for example, http://www.foreignpolicyjournal.com/2011/02/03/hezbollah-a-state-above-the-state/.

[18] See, for example, http://www.boston.com/news/world/middleeast/articles/2006/07/19/hezbollah_inspires_pride_and_disgust/.

these questions requires parameters of tension and dilemma, rather than clear answers. Hizballah's leadership sees itself as a follower of Khomeini's message of worldwide Islamic revolution. Still, Hizballah has thrived in its outsider position. Diversity and flexibility play different roles for Hizballah's leadership than they do in the Iranian case.

In the Islamic Republic of Iran, the spatial diversity of Shiite leadership is meant to ensure the sustainability of the middle ground. It brings together the disparate identities, parties, and spaces at play in Shiite society and culture, creating durable dialogue and continuous engagement. It is this reality that highlights the balancing role of Shiite leadership.

In Hizballah's case, the leadership focuses on maintaining a perennial outsider's position. It is simultaneously embroiled in all three spaces, but it is also simultaneously removed from each. In other words, like its Iranian counterpart, the Hizballah's leadership's existence is founded on its ability to identify and exercise presence in communal space, institutional space, and the frontier. Hizballah sees itself as responsible for guaranteeing the continuity of the Shiite community in Lebanon. At the same time, the organization possesses real political clout on the Lebanese national scene, in both parliament and the Lebanese government. The leaders link Hizballah with Khomeini's revolution on the one hand, and do battle with Israel on the other.[19]

Hizballah's leadership remains both inside and outside communal space, institutional space, and the frontier. In communal space, it provides handsomely for the welfare of the community. In institutional space, it consistently challenges the Lebanese government but does not replace it in violent fashion. On the frontier, it can wage war against Israel, but also negotiate a cease-fire and observe international decisions regarding the conflict with the Israelis. Hizballah leadership is thus able to embrace its reality while maintaining a highly critical stance toward this same reality.

Missing Iraq

Iraqi Shiites differ from their Iranian and Lebanese brethren as well. In Iran and Lebanon, the Shiite community grew while bypassing the state. In Iraq, the state has been the most powerful political presence throughout the twentieth century. All three spaces – communal, institutional, and frontier – exist in Iraq, but their contours differ wildly from those described in the cases of Iran and Lebanon.[20]

In Iran, communal space is associated with the Shiite community of believers. This religious homogeneity precedes geographical, ethnic, and national divisions. In Lebanon, the Shiite community also exhibits a cohesive communal

---

[19] For repeated reiterations of these twin sources of identity, see Nicholas Noe (editor), *Voice of Hezbollah: The Statements of Sayyed Hassan Nasrallah* (Verso, 2007).

[20] For an innovative, comprehensive analysis, see William Polk, *Understanding Iraq: The Whole Sweep of Iraqi History, from Genghis Khan's Mongols to Ottoman Turks to the British Mandate to the American Occupation* (Harper Perennial, 2006).

solidarity. The Shiites of Iraq are different. They are divided into three main communal sections. These include the Shiite tribes in southern Iraq, the urban Shiite population and the religious scholars and professionals. This internal diversity is often incapable of supporting the sort of primordial attachment which bonds Shiites in Iran and Lebanon.

This lack of communal cohesion and social bonds creates an encounter with the state that also differs from Iranian and Lebanese patterns. In Iran and Lebanon, the Shiite communities could not be overlooked by the state. Shiites displayed a common identity, broad solidarity, and a joint sense of purpose that could not be denied, albeit in different forms.

Shiism has been present in Lebanon for close to a millennium. It has been the state religion of Iran for more than 500 years. During these periods, the Shiite community of believers emerged as the core of collective identity. It preceded the existence of a Lebanese state by centuries. In Iran, the community of believers grew within a state that forsook any claim to influence religious identity or thought. Gradually, the Shiite believers and scholars bypassed the nominally Shiite state to form an independent alliance. It is this alliance that served as the platform for the Islamic Revolution of 1979.

In Iraq, however, the internal diversity of the Shiite community did not encourage a common challenge to the state.[21] The tribes of the south were poor and spread over a vast amount of land. The scholars of the holy cities enjoyed nearly exterritorial status and were at the mercy of the state. The urban Shiite bourgeois did not overtly engage in state politics.

Iraq's Shiite tribes, based in the southern Iraqi desert, are fairly recent converts to Shiism, with the major waves of conversion occurring in the nineteenth century. It was during this period that many of the tribes settled down and adopted agriculture in the vicinity of the Shiite holy cities, Najaf and Karbala.

The two cities had risen to prominence in the eighteenth century, following the fall of the Safavid dynasty in Iran. Shiite clerics, who had enjoyed the backing of the Safavids, moved to Iraq and brought both students and economic clout. Najaf and Karbalah expanded their influence and became the dominant market centers of the region. The Sunni tribes came for the trade and gradually adopted Shiism.

The tribes that converted and those which remained Sunni conducted similar lives. Having accepted the Shiism promulgated by the scholars and students in Najaf and Karbala, tribal communities were very much defined by non-religious factors. The codes of the desert preceded Shiism significantly in influence over tribal society. With the founding of modern Iraq in 1921, the relationship between the Shiite tribes and scholars was manipulated by the Sunni authorities in Baghdad.[22]

---

[21] See Nakash, *The Shi'is of Iraq*, pp. 13–48.
[22] Ibid., pp. 49–74.

The Sunni rulers stripped the Shiite scholars of their status, denying them authority over the tribes and increasing the scholars' dependence on the state. The Sunni authorities also weakened the shrine cities' market dominance. This was carried out through the relocation of thousands of tribal Shiites to the rejuvenated urban centers, especially Baghdad. This increased the internal schisms within the three factions of Shiite society: tribal, urban, and scholarly.

Shiite middle ground politics flourish in political orders where the state is not the ultimate arbiter in matters pertaining to communal identity and belief. This prevents the dominance of state institutions over the community and the frontier. This pattern is discernible in the cases of Iran and Lebanon. Even during the heyday of Lebanese democracy in the 1930s and 1940s, the state was still based on multitraditional understandings and had no desire to meddle in the affairs of specific communities. In the Iranian case, the state did not attempt to intervene with communal dynamics until the twentieth century, and was then taken to task for its efforts.

In the Iraqi case, the state has enjoyed dominance over communities and the religious establishment. Following its founding, in 1921, the Iraqi state placed severe limitations on the authority of Shiite scholars, clearly demonstrating who maintained the dominant presence in Iraq. This state of affairs was compounded by a struggle over the leadership of the Iraqi community of scholars, when no single scholar managed to emerge as an acceptable leader. Shiites had no choice but to accept the authority of the new Sunni monarchy. Their internal divisions and the unimpeachable strength of the Iraqi government narrowed the chance for cultivating a fertile middle ground within Shiite society.

The dominance of the state was stressed even more significantly after the rise to power of the Ba'ath party in 1968. The major narrative of Iraqi discourse at the time, accepted by both Sunnis and Shiites, was Pan-Arabism. That is, sectarian differences were downplayed in the quest for a supranational Arab identity. Pan-Arabism was a pillar of Ba'ath social vision, and its promotion was considered an interest of the state. In fact, when Sunni-Shiite squabbles did occur, they often broke out because of Shiite anger over Sunni accusations that Shiites were not Arab or patriotic enough.[23]

Saddam Hussein's coup in 1969 abandoned Pan-Arabism for a totalitarian take on Iraqi nationalism. While incorporating Shiites into its regime, Hussein exercised absolute authority in the name of the state, leaving no room for other affiliations. Many Shiites signed on to this vision, fighting in the Iraqi army against their coreligionists from Iran. Still, Saddam was careful to nip any and all displays of Shiite opposition in the bud.

Such opposition began to form among the tribal chiefs, who resented Saddam's repressive policies, as well as among the Shiite scholars who feared for their authority and for the fate of religion. The scholars were also influenced by the

---

[23] For the definitive analysis of class relations in Iraq, see Hanna Batatu, *The Old Social Classes & The Revolutionary Movement in Iraq* (Saqi Books, 2004).

Iranian revolution of 1979. Attempts to develop an interpretative discourse did not succeed. Saddam executed the most prominent Shiite scholars and cracked down with a vengeance on the southern tribes. Following the U.S. invasion of 2003, Shiite scholars engaged in national politics but did not demanded Iranian-style authority. They seemed content to play an influential role in a political sphere that was formed around Western political conventions.

The power of the Iraqi state and the lack of religious cohesion are but two factors that demonstrate why Shiite leadership in Iraq did not formulate a middle ground reality. Shiite scholars in Iraq were as proficient as those in Iran and Lebanon at the craft of interpretation, as well as at the juxtaposition of spaces. Social circumstances and historical evolution impeded Shiite Iraqi middle ground initiatives.

In Khomeini's Footsteps

Shiite leaderships in Iran and Lebanon have challenged the authority of state rulers on matters regarding identity and community. The authority of the state in both countries did not extend to the shaping of Shiite identity. Shiite middle ground leadership grew from an alliance between communal space and the frontier. This alliance bypassed, for the most part, the institutional authority of the state. The scholars' authority emerged from direct communication and negotiation with the lay believers. Both the Islamic Republic of Iran and the Lebanese Hizballah apply this approach to their respective realities. The fact that one is constructive and the other subversive does not detract from their similarity.

The case of Iraq is different. Communal space and the frontier in Iraq were, throughout the twentieth century, divided and scattered. The Shiite tribes in southern Iraq were distinct from the residents of Najaf and Karbala, the two Shiite holy cities. It was the state that provided a sense of coherence to Iraqi society.

The similarities shared by the middle ground Shiite leaderships in Iran and Lebanon are as significant as their differences. Both are different from Shiite leadership in Iraq. Shiite middle ground leadership is a phenomenon influenced by history, geography, and politics as much as by religious affiliation. Attempts to explore this middle ground further should not end with dichotomous labeling. Appreciation for the complexity of middle ground leadership – its disdain for hierarchy, its multifocal perception of reality – requires that one examine the behavioral modes of Shiite leaderships of Iran and Lebanon. Such examination includes they ways in which Shiite leadership's strategies relate to domestic, regional, and global issues, and the dynamic of this leadership's decision-making process.

5

Forming the Middle Ground: Intra-Shiite Issues

The constitution of the Islamic Republic of Iran states that God is the sole sovereign. The body politic of the republic, however, is constitutionally composed of two parallel political structures. The parallel structures integrate difference into the core of the Islamic Republic's institutions. The first structure includes officials that are elected by the public, among them the president and the *Majlis* (the Iranian Parliament). These institutions are considered representatives of popular will. The second structure, which holds a significant share of executive power, consists of various institutions that are directly appointed by the religious-political leadership of Iran. These include the Supreme Leader, the Guardian Council, and the Expediency Council.[1]

The Supreme Leader is the head of state in the Islamic Republic. He is required to be pious, learned, and able to address the needs of his "flock." His post, however, is political and does not bestow religious authority that he has not attained through traditional means. The Guardian Council is an exclusive body of scholars, charged with ensuring that the laws passed by parliament are in accordance with the Shari'a, the Islamic law. The Expediency Council is a mediating body, created to settle debates arising between the "secular" interests of the state and the demands of Islamic tradition and law.

These bodies are arrayed so as to ensure conflicts between them. No branch of the Iranian regime enjoys complete separation from others. In fact, conflict between branches is consciously fostered, encouraging the intervention of third parties which regulate conflict and mediate a feasible solution. Following the 1979 revolution, there is no longer simply one way to go about the business of leadership. There are at least two ways, often contradictory. When these two ways find themselves in confrontation, it is the leadership's responsibility to

---

[1] The brief review of Iran's governing systems is drawn from the constitution of the Islamic Republic of Iran. These structures will be discussed in more elaborate fashion later in the study.

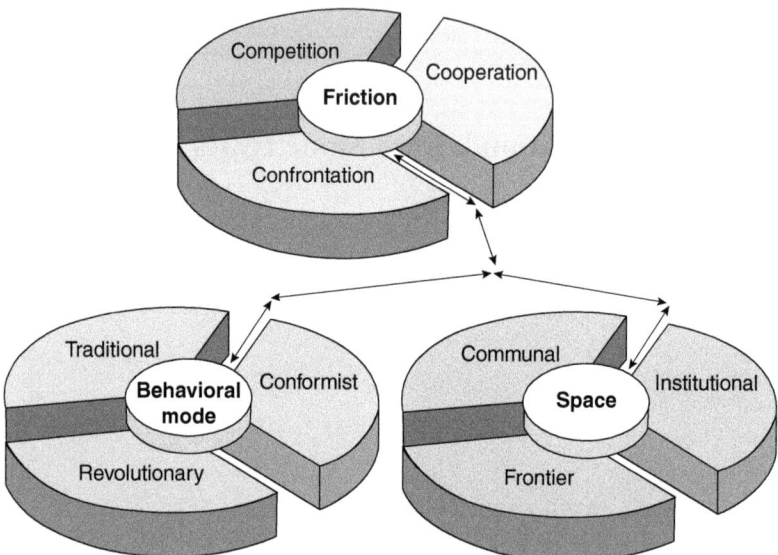

FIGURE 5.1. Toward middle ground practice: components.

introduce a third way, transforming exclusionary conflict into friction and a more desirable mode of action to challenge unsolvable issues.

Friction in the Shiite case is seen by many as consisting solely of conflict. Those who see Shiite leadership as the product of either strict, religious dogma or naked interests highlight the constant state of conflict these principles create. When Shiite leadership is presented as devoutly religious, the conflict is with secular modernity; when Shiite leadership is read as opportunistic, the conflict is with the core, universal principles of the international community such as human rights and international law. According to this view, conflict is about winning or losing. Winning allows the victor to impose his agenda on the loser, dismissing the latter for having lost. The struggle is undertaken in order to achieve this end (see Figure 5.1).

Contrary to this approach, Shiite leaderships see conflict as an anomaly. A clash of absolute truths, a dynamic based on mutual exclusion, is the least conducive state for Shiite leadership. We propose that friction in the Shiite style is driven by interaction between three dynamics – cooperation, competition, and confrontation. These three form a dynamic equilibrium that is the hallmark of Shiite leadership.

Friction is nearly volatile with potential. Success for a leadership operating within a friction-based system cannot be achieved through the dominance of one space or mode, but through the regulation of multiple spaces in the ensuing friction. This equilibrium is manifested in the daily practices of Shiite leadership in Iran, and later on in Lebanon. We refer to these practices as "friction management," which is another way of saying, "the behavior of middle ground leadership."

The Islamic Republic and Friction Management

Since the early 1980s, Iranian commitment to promote Islamic solidarity was frequently expressed by officials' statements and actions. Following the 1979 revolution, the new Islamic leadership acknowledged the need to balance between state interests and revolutionary ideals. Revolutionary principles required Iran to demonstrate its commitment to Muslims wherever they may be. Still, the new regime often preferred to subordinate the revolutionary vision to state interests.

Iranian leadership adopted, for instance, a balanced approach toward the conflict between Shiite Azerbaijan and Christian Armenia over the territory of Nagorno-Karabakh, which erupted in 1988. Iran assisted the Armenian war effort by serving as Armenia's main supply route. Iran feared that a successful secular Azerbaijan might encourage irredentist aspirations among its own substantial Azeri population, giving priority to domestic state interests over religious solidarity.

Such an approach does not mean that the radical vision that accompanied the 1979 revolution was abandoned. Large segments of the Iranian public turned to Islam as a means to promote solutions for their predicament. They believed that a society based on Islamic principles was capable of preserving communal values and the old, accepted beliefs.

Iranian popular traditions have continuously manifested Iran's national heritage.[2] Since the nineteenth century, a growing number of Iranian intellectuals, who had been exposed to Western politics and thought, began to assert that Iranian nationality preceded Islam and that Iranians were distinct from their Arab neighbors. This nationalist strain became officially identified with the Iranian state during the Pahlavi era (1925–1979).

Following the Islamic Revolution of 1979, attempts were made by the new regime to demonstrate the dominance of the Islamic identity over the Iranian national one. To a large extent, these efforts remained futile. The new Islamic regime tried to no avail, for example, to abolish the pre-Islamic traditions of Iranian New Year (*Norouz*) and the last Wednesday of the year (*Chahrshanbeh Souri*).[3] Iranian pre-Islamic legacy continues to be an integral part of Iranian identity. Despite growing Islamization, Iranian national sentiments continued to persevere. These were eventually used by the Islamic Republic as well.

---

[2] For a remarkable analysis of the link between politics and popular (religious) culture in Iran, see Ali Rahnema, *Superstition as Ideology in Iranian Politics: From Majlesi to Ahmadinejad* (Cambridge University Press, 2011).

[3] For a discussion regarding the Islamic regime's attempt to co-opt Mayday, as well as the examples mentioned, see Abrahamian, *Khomeinism*, pp. 60–87.

Iranian leadership turned to those sentiments to rally public support during the Iran-Iraq war of 1980–8. These sentiments were also utilized to increase the internal legitimacy of Iran's nuclear policy with respect to the international community since the early 2000s.[4]

These examples illuminate the friction-based, dynamic equilibrium for which Iranian Shiite leadership strives. Friction management in the Iranian case, we suggest, is undertaken through three distinct strategic behavioral modes – traditional, conformist, and revolutionary.

The traditional strategic mode is affiliated with communal space. Behavior in the traditional mode has a flexible, network-oriented perception of reality. Still, traditional behavior looks to the past for inspiration. Commonly held traditions or beliefs, a shared history, and the social bonds of family and community, all serve to provide context for traditional behavior. Behavior in the traditional mode favors negotiation and adaptation. Still, it is firmly grounded in broad definitions of identity, faith, and belonging.

The conformist strategic mode is affiliated with institutional space, usually that of the state. Most distinctly, this strategic mode occupies itself with the present. It does not negate its reality for the sake of an illustrious past or an even brighter future. This behavior is guided by the aspiration to reduce the disadvantages of the existing order. The grand idea of the conformist mode is the preservation of things as they are, avoiding significant change as much as possible while making the present constantly more habitable.

The revolutionary strategic mode is associated with the frontier and both its symbolic and physical borders. This mode represents proactive conduct, rejecting and negating present reality, placing its agents always "not here," "not now." The revolutionary mode refers to the desired state of affairs, or to the grand design of reality itself. Although the Shiite frontier leaned toward the metaphysical, it has undergone politicization over the twentieth century.

Friction between modes and spaces is the dynamic that drives Shiite society. Each of the strategic behavioral modes can ideally be identified with a single space, but – in fact – all three modes can be seen within the confines of each space. The role of Shiite leadership becomes the maintenance of the ensuing friction.

In this chapter, we examine this role in two cases that reflect the strategic behavior of Iranian leadership with regard to intra-Shiite issues. In the next chapter, we discuss Iranian Shiite leadership's behavior with regard to the non-Shiite world. The cases in both chapters include Iran's stance on parliamentary elections in Bahrain, issues of family planning, Iran's relationship with Venezuela and the issue of Iranian nuclear policy.

All the cases are characterized by a common, recurring pattern. Two of the three behavioral modes we describe engage in confrontation. The third mode

---

[4] For an example of the ongoing nature of this tension, see http://www.foreignpolicy.com/ articles/2011/04/29/is_ahmadinejad_islamic_enough_for_iran?page=0,1.

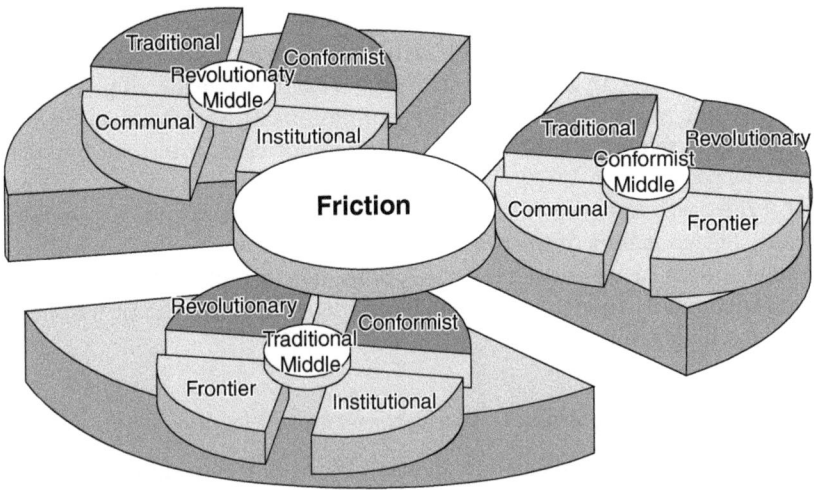

Modes of Behavior

Spaces

FIGURE 5.2. Toward middle ground practice: dynamics.

is then applied by the leadership, mediating between seemingly polarized absolutes. The resulting middle ground is formed in the third mode's image, making it possible to speak of "traditional," "conformist," and "revolutionary" middle grounds (see Figure 5.2).[5]

Three more case studies will be discussed in Chapters 7 and 8 – the Iranian presidential elections of 2009 and 2013 and the middle ground inhabited by Lebanese Hizballah. All three represent additional modes of middle ground behavior, not fully addressed by the tripartite relationship described previously.

The presidential elections represent the continuous conflict between the middle ground and the high ground, which we refer to as "middle ground radicalization." Whereas the middle ground does not reject the high ground, the high ground ultimately desires to abolish and subjugate the middle ground. This conflict will be demonstrated through a discussion of the 2009 elections and their aftermath. The 2013 elections will demonstrate the resilience of the middle ground within this conflict.

Lebanese Hizballah represents the variability of the middle ground. The plight of Lebanese Shiites was spatially and socially different from that of their

---

[5] The following cases focus on traditional and conformist middle grounds only. Traditional and conformist middle grounds apply types of logic – policy preferences, belief systems, and communal mores – more easily accessible within the conceptual framework we propose. This is unlike the revolutionary middle ground, which is often less familiar and requires an elaborate exposition that is beyond the scope of our study.

Iranian brethren. This, in turn, produced a type of middle ground different from the Iranian version. Khomeini's revolution sought the overt assumption of state authority by the Shiite scholars. Hizballah's leadership focuses on resistance. The organization resists the temptations of both state authority and revolutionary purism, maintaining a unique stance both inside and outside political conventions.

These three cases underscore the middle ground's multiplicity of possible expressions. The constants of the middle ground are friction and action, rather than absolute ideas or clear-cut power relations. The middle ground is to be recognized through its modes of behavior and their interactions, not by blind allegiance to a high ground vision.

The Traditional Middle: Bahrain's 2006 Parliamentary Elections

The case of Bahrain represents a confrontation between the revolutionary and the conformist modes in Iran's foreign policy. Bahrain's elections shed light on the friction between the Islamic Republic of Iran and its affiliation with Shiite communities outside Iran, as well as Iran's physical frontier. The Bahrain elections case confronts state and revolution. This confrontation is tempered by the cooperative and competitive influence of the communal mode.

Iran has historically claimed Bahrain as its territory since the island was under Persian rule (1602–1782). Between the eighteenth and the twentieth century, Bahrain was ruled by the British Empire. When Great Britain announced (1968) its intention to withdraw its forces from the Persian Gulf in 1971, Iran renewed its claim over Bahrain. Following a referendum carried out under UN supervision in 1970, when a majority of the Bahraini population voted in favor of independence, the Iranian Shah relinquished his claim.[6]

Following the 1979 revolution, Iran renewed its territorial demands over the Sheikhdom. Iranian leaders stressed the fact that the majority of Bahrain's population was Shiite. They argued that these Arab Shiites were suffering from persecution at the hands of Sunni authorities. Diplomatic claims, however, did not exhaust Iranian activities in Bahrain.

In 1981, Bahraini authorities accused Iran of supporting a coup attempt carried out by the Islamic Front for the Liberation of Bahrain to undermine the regime. In 1996, Bahrain revealed yet another plot to bring down the regime, allegedly organized by the Bahraini *Hizballah* movement in cooperation with the Qods Brigade of the Iranian Revolutionary Guards Forces.[7]

Mohammad Khatami's presidency (1997–2005) marked a significant improvement in relations between Iran and Bahrain. In 2003, Khatami became

---

[6] For a concise analysis of Bahrain's first five years of statehood, see Emile Nakhleh, *Bahrain: Political Development in a Modernizing Society* (Lexington, 2011).

[7] See http://www.nytimes.com/1996/06/05/world/bahrain-holds-44-it-says-are-tied-to-pro-iran-plot.html.

the first Iranian president to visit the country. The improved relations between both countries were apparent in the intensification of economic as well as commercial cooperation. Facing a growing conflict with the West concerning its nuclear program, Iran increased its appeasement efforts in the region. That was especially important because of the significance of its Gulf neighbors, whose cooperation was necessary to enforce international sanctions against Iran as well as to carry out a military assault against it.[8]

Iranian attempts to strengthen its relations with Bahrain continued after Mahmoud Ahmadinejad's election as president. In October 2006, the Iranian Foreign Minister, Manochehr Mottaki, visited Manama. During his meeting with the Bahraini Crown Prince, he expressed his satisfaction with the relations between the two countries and said that they should expand their ties in all areas. Mottaki stressed that the Persian Gulf states had to protect the security of the region and that Iran was ready to cooperate with its neighbors to safeguard regional security and make sure it would not be handed over to foreigners. In July 2007, the Iranian president met with Bahrain's new ambassador to Iran, Rashid bin-Sa'ad bin-Zafar al-Dusari, and pointed to Iran's willingness to expand its ties with its neighbors, including Bahrain.

Still, tensions between the two countries persisted.[9] Bahraini authorities still regarded Iranian involvement in the kingdom's Shiite opposition with suspicion. The U.S. military presence and joint maneuvers between Bahrain and the United States also tainted the relations between the countries.[10] Iran's national interest in maintaining stable relations with Bahrain was constantly challenged by the vision of a Shiite revolution and communal solidarity for Shiite brethren. Although the Iranians went out of their way to employ the conformist mode, the triggers of the revolutionary and traditional modes were apparent.

Iran and the Bahraini Elections

Iran interference in Bahrain's parliamentary elections was expressed during the 2006 parliamentary campaign. On November 25, the first round of elections for the forty-seat lower house of the Bahraini parliament took place. The elections were held for the second time since King Hamid bin-Issa al-Khalifa allowed restricted political reforms in 2001. For the first time since parliament was restored, Shiite opposition movements took part in the proceedings, led by the *al-Wifaq al-Watani al-Islami* (the Islamic National Accord) movement. *Al-Wifaq* won outright in all seventeen constituencies contested and became the biggest party in parliament. An alliance of Sunni Islamist candidates won twelve additional seats.

---

[8] See http://www.payvand.com/news/03/may/1048.html.

[9] For an informed analysis of Iranian-Bahraini relations, see this publication of U.S. diplomatic correspondence at http://www.guardian.co.uk/world/us-embassy-cables-documents/164906.

[10] For an analysis of Bahrain's geostrategic naval importance, see David F. Winkler, *Amirs, Admirals and Desert Sailors: Bahrain, the US Navy and the Arabian Gulf* (Naval Institute Press, 2007).

The elections in Bahrain placed the Shiite leadership of Iran in a dilemma. Iranian leaders intended to preserve good relations with Bahraini rulers, especially in light of the growing threat of a potential U.S. attack on Iran launched from Bahraini territory. Still, the elections were considered an opportunity for Iran to expand its influence in Bahrain through its allies among the Shiite opposition.

Prior to the parliamentary elections in Bahrain, several reports appeared in the media accusing Iran of bankrolling Shiite parties in Bahrain. These claims were strongly denied by Tehran. The Arab press reported that Iran tried to purchase real estate and property in the Bahraini city of al-Muharraq, meant for its supporters. Shortly before the elections, Bahraini officials also claimed that Iranian agents supplied Bahraini opposition leaders with rifles, money, and arms-training. Bahraini government officials also asserted that Iran had spent dozens of millions of dollars to ensure the victory of its Shiite allies in the elections. A senior government official said that there was evidence that agents employed by the Iranian Revolutionary Guards had formed sleeper cells in Bahrain in an attempt to break its strong ties to London and Washington.[11]

These claims were rejected after the elections by Sheikh Ali Salman, Secretary General of the Shiite opposition *Al-Wifaq* party. When asked about Iranian involvement in buying Bahraini property, in an interview with the Dubai-based *Al-Arabiyah* television station, Salman said that such involvement was merely a "media storm" related to the elections. He maintained that the people of Bahrain were protective of their political system and of Bahraini Arabism. Concerning Khomeini's doctrine advocating direct political authority for Shiite scholars (*velayat e-faqih*), he said that this concept did not extend beyond Iran to the people of Bahrain. The people of Bahrain, argued Sheikh Salman, had their own decision-making religious authority and were not tied to Khamenei, Iran's supreme leader. His own religious loyalty to Khamenei, he said, was not to Khamenei as the political leader of the Islamic Republic, but a loyalty to an authority (*marja'*) on Islamic Shiite thought. Salman also claimed that 80 percent of Bahrain's Shiites followed the Iraqi Ayatollah Sistani.[12]

The Shiite victory in Bahrain's elections was welcomed by Iranian conservative elements. Their reactions were conveyed in both traditional and revolutionary modes. The revolutionary mode was powerful in several articles published by the daily *Kayhan*, identified with the hardline conservative establishment in Iran. It closely covered the elections before election day and especially as the Shiite triumph became obvious. *Kayhan* referred to the election results as yet further evidence of the strengthening of Islam in the region and the ambition of Muslim nations to change the political status quo in their countries.[13]

---

[11] The Daily Telegraph, November 25, 2006.
[12] *Al-Arabiyah*, January 26, 2007.
[13] *Kayhan*, November 26, 27 and 28, 2006.

In an editorial published on November 28, 2006, the journalist Mohammad Imani considered the Bahraini election results as yet another failure of the wishes and plans of the "American, British and Israeli arrogant powers." While the world was invaded in the name of democracy, Imani said, the Islamists had come to power in certain countries such as Iraq, Palestine, Lebanon, and Bahrain through fully democratic and peaceful means. The crises in those countries were not domestic, religious, or ethnic wars. The issue was the awakening of the majority of Muslims who were ruled by leaders serving as mercenaries and lackeys of foreigners.

Principle-ism and Islamism had become a proud way of life in the region and a political movement in the motherland of Islam – Iran – had become the standard-bearer of that great movement. The vast armies of the faithful and active "principle-ists" would follow the same path as was described by the late Imam Khomeini as the mobilization of the oppressed and the global Islamic government.[14] Life in the revolutionary mode was thus recognized as the virtuous life. Dedicating oneself to transforming reality remained both the highest and the most effective calling in achieving a virtuous, justice-based world order.

Conformist Mediation

Despite vociferous revolutionary rhetoric, the relative silence of Iranian leadership toward the election results in Bahrain came across as pronounced. Iranian officials continued to reflect an appeasing approach toward Bahrain. They refrained from exploiting the election results and the Shiite achievements to raise revolutionary slogans and to call for a renewed attempt to export the Islamic Revolution to the Gulf States. Instead, they operated in the conformist mode.

The Expediency Council Chairman and Former President, Ali-Akbar Hashemi Rafsanjani, met with the Bahraini ambassador to Tehran in November 2006. Rafsanjani referred to the democratization processes in Bahrain as beneficial for the entire region. He also referred to the two countries' religious, cultural, and historical bonds and called for more extensive cooperation and utilization of all existing potentials and possibilities by the two sides.[15] Iran's national interest was to avoid conflict with its neighbors. Such squabbles could prove to be beneficial to the Western allies of Gulf Sheikhdoms in their confrontation with Iran over the latter's nuclear program.

Still, the official endorsement of the conformist mode did not impede use of the traditional mode as well. Iranian officials referred repeatedly to the Islamic kinship between Iran and Bahrain. However, they also emphasized that Iran was doing its best to reduce sectarian and religious tensions in the region, especially in light of the ongoing hostilities in Iraq.

---

[14] *Kayhan*, November 28, 2006.
[15] *Fars*, December 4, 2006.

Several months after the elections in Bahrain, the confrontation between the revolutionary and conformist modes became more evident following an editorial published by Hossein Shariatmadari, editor of *Kayhan*. In his editorial, Shariatmadari once again raised the claim that Bahrain was a part of Iran, having been separated from it through an illegal conspiracy between the Shah and the U.S. and British governments. Public opinion in Bahrain, Shariatmadari asserted, was in favor of returning this province to its motherland.[16]

The editorial sparked considerable tension between the two countries. Despite public and political uproar, Shariatmadari refused to back off his stance. In another editorial, he reacted to the severe criticism voiced in neighboring Gulf countries by saying that there was growing evidence that many people in these countries were dissatisfied with their governments and were willing to protest against them. When asked by *al-Sharq al-Awsat*'s reporter, whether his editorial reflected the views of Iranian senior officials and those of the Supreme Leader, Shariatmadari said that the leader was too exalted to express his views over an editorial in a newspaper.[17]

The political leadership's response to the crisis continued to reflect its preference for the conformist mode. As disquiet over the *Kayhan* article grew, the Iranian Foreign Minister Mottaki visited Bahrain on July 13, 2007 to meet his Bahraini counterpart and offer assurances of Iran's respect for Bahraini national sovereignty. In a joint press conference with his counterpart, he said that stable relations between the countries should not be affected by articles published in a newspaper. The minister did not present an official apology and said that if a Bahraini newspaper had published something against Iran, Iran would not have expected an apology from the Bahraini government.[18]

A stringent critique against Shariatmadari's editorial was also expressed in an article published by senior Foreign Ministry official, Javid Qorban Oqli, on one of the leading Iranian Web sites, *Baztab*. Oqli said that a newspaper associated with the Supreme Leader must not publish such articles that might be considered as representing an official Iranian view and cause tension and crisis in Iran's foreign affairs. Iranian official foreign policy, he said, was based on cooperation with neighboring countries and expanding the relations with them.

Articles such as Shariatmadari's might provide an excuse to certain countries incited by different elements to act against Iran and also to increase pressure on the Shiite majority in Bahrain. Promoting offensive foreign policy supported by the Supreme Leader did not justify igniting an unnecessary crisis under the circumstances.[19] Oqli's editorial reflects an effort to minimize potential confrontation highlighted by the article within a framework of friction.

[16] *Kayhan*, July 9, 2007.
[17] *Kayhan*, July 14, 2007.
[18] Associated Press (AP), July 14, 2007.
[19] Baztab.net, July 16, 2007; also quoted in yidwithlid.blogspot.co.il/2007/08/iran-wants-bahrain-back.html.

Iranian strategy toward Bahrain tended to favor the conformist mode. However, the confrontation initiated by traditional critics did not bring about active repression or a call to conformist dominance. Steps taken were usually pursued diplomatically, emphasizing cooperation and shared values. Iran's national interest was expressed in diverse forms throughout the period in question, constantly defined and redefined by the evolving equilibrium between the conformist, the traditional, and the revolutionary modes. Iran did not simply prefer conformist order to revolutionary fervor. Instead, the Iranian leadership simultaneously encouraged and repressed communal, institutional, and revolutionary sentiments.

Whereas advocates of the traditional mode tended to be more vocal than their rivals, this rivalry stood in inverse proportion to actual effect on the political situation. Similarly, proponents of the conformist mode hardly engaged in active confrontation with traditionalists. Vocal criticism provided them with the political room for maneuvering, necessary to protect the interests of the Iranian state. Confrontation was not replaced by cooperation or competition.

Sectarian tension in Bahrain was beyond the 2006 election. The events of the 2011 Arab Spring reignited civic unrest in the small kingdom. Demonstrators flocked to the Pearl (*lulu*) roundabout in Manama, the capital, demanding internal reform. Many of the demonstrators were Shiite Muslims, but they did not raise a sectarian banner. Instead, they claimed a desire to be more fully integrated into the Bahraini state, dominated by the Sunni royal family.

The demonstrators enjoyed the support of the Shiite political parties which had competed in the Bahraini elections. They were also endorsed by Sheikh Issa Qassim, the senior Shiite cleric in Bahrain.[20] External influences were dominant in attempts to portray the ensuing struggle as one between Sunnis and Shiites, despite the fact that both parties claimed their genuine Bahraini identity as the platform for their arguments and claims. The Bahraini authorities raised the specter of Iranian interference, and the Saudis followed suit in calling for a crackdown on dissent and "subversion."

The demonstrations, which raged for several months, resulted in a brutal campaign on the part of the Bahraini authorities against dissenters, many of them Shiite Muslims. Hundreds, perhaps even thousands, of Bahrainis have been detained with or without trial, and many have been tortured. Twenty Bahraini physicians and medical personnel were put on trial for assisting demonstrators in Manama.[21]

Saudi Arabia lent its military strength to the ruling Khalifa family, but refrained from irreversible, unilateral steps. At the same time, Iran refrained from overtly attempting to influence the outcome of the civic strife. In fact, the official commission of enquiry established to investigate the demonstrations and their aftermath concluded that no proof existed for Iranian involvement

---

[20] For example, see http://en.shiapost.com/?p=2441.
[21] See http://www.bbc.co.uk/news/world-middle-east-13966073.

in the events.[22] Bahrain's unique population mix, a somewhat disenfranchised Shiite majority facing a Sunni royal family, staunchly supported by Gulf allies and effectively endorsed by the United States, is conducive to the creation of a middle ground.

The volatile nature of the situation in Bahrain is a thorn in the side of Sunni Gulf monarchies concerned about both their international legitimacy and their Shiite minorities. The situation also increased the concern of the global financial community in regard to Iranian expansionism and the safety of maritime traffic (a large quantity of the world's oil) of oil in the Gulf. The large number of players involved in the Bahraini game, alongside its potential rewards and punishments ensure that Bahrain will draw the world's attention for a long time yet. In the following section we move to a domestic matter, regarding the tension between the conformist strategies and doctrinal tenets. The issue of family planning policy will provide us with yet another perspective on friction.

The Conformist Middle: Family Planning and the Islamic Revolution

In 1967, a National Family Planning program in Iran was established. The Family Protection Law, which was passed by the *Majlis* (the Iranian parliament) as part of the fourth five-year economic program (1972–7), was officially aimed at improving the physical, mental, and socioeconomic welfare of the Iranian family and to decrease the annual population growth rate. Its official aim was to reduce the population growth rate to an annual rate of 1 percent annually within twenty years. This program was advocated by recourse to the conformist mode, and focused on addressing the needs of the new, single-spaced Iranian state under the Pahlavi Shahs. However, for those left alienated by the Shah's rapid westernization, the program was also an act in the revolutionary mode, seeking to dismantle the irresponsible "old" world in favor of a more rational "new" one.

Following the Revolution of 1979, Ayatollah Khomeini issued a *fatwa* permitting birth control, provided that mother and child were not harmed. Abortion was excluded. The administrative council of family planning was nevertheless dismantled. Many of the family planning clinics were dissolved or downsized and contraceptive supplies remained limited.

With the outbreak of the war with Iraq in 1980, Iranian authorities began to present the large size of the Iranian population as a major source of military strength and national security. The government claimed that population size was an advantage and referred to the need to establish a "20-million Man Army" capable of defending the country against Iraqi aggression.[23]

---

[22] For the full description of events in Bahrain related to the Arab Spring, see the report of the commission gathered to study the events, see http://files.bici.org.bh/BICIreportEN.pdf.

[23] For a demographic review of population trends in Iran until 2000, see http://www.un.org/esa/ population/publications/completingfertility/2RevisedABBASIpaper.PDF.

The Regime's policy to strengthen family values by encouraging marriage as well as women's return to home-care led to a sharp increase in population growth in the first half of the 1980s. Data obtained from the national census held in 1986 indicated that the annual growth rate reached 3.9 percent. As the detailed results of the 1986 census became available, Iranian leaders began to realize the long-term economic and social implications of unbridled population growth. That is, the Iranian leadership began to realize that imposing no controls on population growth was bound to result in significant obstacles for economic growth and development.

In December 1989, a new revolutionary family planning policy was adopted. This followed a period of public debate. The policy was aimed at limiting the number of children in Iranian families. The Family Planning Law, which limited economic benefits to families having more than three children, was ratified by the *Majlis* in 1993. The national media and education system were entrusted with raising awareness on population issues and family planning. Clinics and medical centers were inaugurated to supply family planning services. State authorities also encouraged the use of contraceptives, including sterilization procedures for both men and women. Young couples were required to go through contraceptive tutoring before getting a marriage license. The renewed family planning program was highly successful and, in 2001, the population's annual growth dropped to 1.2 percent.[24]

In October 2006, President Mahmoud Ahmadinejad appeared to revalidate the revolutionary strategy concerning family planning. In a public statement, he rejected the notion that two children were enough. Iran, he said, had the potential to increase its population to 120 million. The West, Ahmadinejad said, was facing its own problems, and – as population growth in Western society was negative – it was afraid of the possibility that the Islamic society would grow and as a result would be able to overtake the West.[25]

Ahmadinejad's statement did not alter existing governmental policies. However, it poignantly highlights the mechanics of friction. No policy, or strategic mode, operates wholly without the context provided for it by other modes. There is no content without context and vice versa. Alongside the revolutionary mode, most frequently used in the late 1980s, the traditional mode was also favored among Shiite leaders in Iran. Iranian leaders turned repeatedly to Islam, especially in efforts to justify their changing approach toward family planning in the last two decades.

A Health Ministry report submitted by Iranian authorities to the 1994 Cairo International Conference on Population and Development stated that

the social laws in our country are based on religion. By studying the manifestation of life in our country it becomes clear that only those laws inspired and taken from the

---

[24] For a concise summary and analysis of Iranian family planning policies, see http://www.prb.org/pdf/iransfamplanprog_eng.pdf.

[25] Baztab.net, October 23, 2006.

spirit and essence of religion could be sustainable and this is a natural phenomenon ... it is necessary that the question of population programs be based on religion, otherwise they would not find popular acceptance.[26]

The traditional mode is here linked to religion. But what does adherence to religion mean in this case? What set of interests does religion promote?

During the second half of the 1980s, as the Iranian leadership revised its policy toward family planning, the authorities turned to religious jurists to obtain their support for the revival of the family planning program. In fact, Islamic approval of the family planning program was emphasized by the authorities during their campaign to promote the plan. The Health Ministry report to the Cairo Conference presented family planning as conforming to Islamic values.

The report argued that the monotheistic religions focused on expanding the population and restricting human influence on creation and procreation. Still, regard for the general welfare was a legitimate reason to adopt and apply other views. The Islamic community might require a multitude of believers at certain times and would thus encourage reproduction. At other times, owing to the existence of a massive work force and the reduction of employment opportunities, the community would be forced to set limits for population growth to promote social welfare.

The report also stressed the need to use legal contraception methods that were in conformity with the Islamic laws for implementation of fertility regulation. The report stated that the question regarding the use of contraceptives had been studied by religious scholars and jurists. They had come to the conclusion that preventing pregnancy while observing the principle of exigency and divine virtue was not only permitted but was even encouraged by religion.[27]

The Middle Ground of Family Planning

During the first decade of the twenty-first century, religious scholars continued to take part in the family planning campaign, explaining that Islam did not ban contraceptives. "Having a vasectomy or using a condom is not banned for the purpose of avoiding unwanted children or preventing individual or social harm," said a leading scholar in an interview.[28]

The traditional mode appears dominant in this exchange. The recourse to religion, which may seem to encourage a strict, dogmatic approach, reflects the sophisticated practice of interpretation. Respect for scripture is integrated with a flexible, informal understanding of the obstacles inherent in a life of faith. The basis for most religious rulings takes into consideration both the general interests of society and individual welfare.

The friction between the traditional and revolutionary modes is visible, as both make use of religious principles and popular belief. Although the modes

[26] National Report on Population, 1994, p. 13.
[27] National Report on Population, 1994, pp. 13–14.
[28] Interview with Ayatollah Hussein Mousavi Tabrizi, Associated Press (AP), June 6, 2002.

compete and confront, they also cooperate through the practice of interpretation. In other words, leaders' interpretative capabilities cannot exist effectively without some form of basic cooperation that is necessary for implementation when recourse to ultimate truth is not an option.

The middle ground politics of the Islamic Republic is not based on triumph or defeat. Each party to this middle ground knows in advance that attainable goals are rarely realized in full. Confrontation does not result in a clear preference of one mode over another. Cooperation does not resolve all difficulties, nor does it ensure that "everybody wins." Instead, the ultimate end of a middle ground order is the maintenance of friction. The struggle is often over what one relinquishes, rather than what one gains.

State officials and political figures realized that a policy of little or no regulation was harmful to the Iranian economy. They were joined by a significant number of religious leaders. By late 1989, a growing number of scholars were stating that it was an Islamic obligation to sacrifice the size of the Iranian family in favor of the common benefit and the interests of the state. The institutional dimensions of Islam bonded with the reliance on religious validation.

Economic and social aspects were also evident in the public campaign led by Iranian authorities. Efforts were made to convince the public that reducing population growth would be advantageous to both national and individual interests. Iranian authorities attempted to persuade the public that Iran's ability to feed its population and deliver its needs was significantly jeopardized by the high rate of population growth. Presenting the public with data concerning the shortages in education, housing, food supplies, and employment was meant to serve as a warning.[29]

The key position of the conformist dimension in Iranian strategy with regard to family planning was evident in the harsh criticism that followed President Ahmadinejad's remarks on the subject in October 2006. Questions regarding the President's remarks concerning Iran's capacity to hold a population of 120 million and his opposition to the two-child limit, received the following response. Mohammad Abbaspur, Chairman of the *Majlis* Education and Research Committee said that Iran possessed the necessary potential for such growth with regard to water supply, land, mines, and professional expertise. However, with Iran in the midst of a severe training and education shortage at all levels, the potential needed to be actualized first for population growth to become relevant again.[30]

The conservative press, which voiced the revolutionary or traditional strategic modes, criticized the President's remarks turning to Iran's national interests to justify its positions. The conservative daily *Resalat* claimed that economic

[29] For an analysis of the various factors at work in implementing Iranian population planning policy, see http://ase.tufts.edu/econ/events/neudcDocs/SaturdaySession/Session012/AHashemi FamilyPlanningProgramEffects.pdf.

[30] *Aftab-e Yazd*, October 28, 2006.

experts believed that increasing population growth without paying due attention to the economic conditions would lead to an increase in poverty as well as to widespread deprivation. According to those experts, *Resalat* reported, an expansion of population among the low-income groups would increase the economic pressures on the weaker strata of society. This would result in broadening the gap between rich and poor.[31]

An attempt on the part of one strategic mode to achieve dominance over the others is considered to be an anomaly. Effective leadership and middle ground reality gravitate toward a balance. Differences of opinion are recognized and encouraged, whereas pretenses to absolute truth are rejected. Shiite leadership is less focused on the realization of a single policy, and more engaged in promoting and regulating the reality of friction

[31] See http://www.terrorism-info.org.il/en/articleprint.aspx?id=17842.

6

Seeking the Middle Ground: Extra-Shiite Issues

Middle ground politics played an influential role in shaping the behavior of Iranian Shiite leadership when facing the world at large. In the cases of Venezuela and Iran's nuclear policy, two strategic modes battle for dominance. Ultimately, their confrontation is regulated by the entrance of a third mode, enabling a state of dynamic friction.

The Conformist Middle: The Case of Venezuela

The case of Iran's relationship with Venezuela examines a state of confrontation between the traditional and the revolutionary modes in the behavior of Iranian Shiite leadership. This confrontation is regulated by use of the conformist mode.

The final decade of the twentieth century saw the reemergence of the left as a leading political force in Latin America. One of the prominent representatives of the rising left is Hugo Chavez, first elected as president of Venezuela in 1998. Since his election, Chavez has acted to strengthen relations with various countries, including Iran.

It seems difficult to find commonalities between Chavez's radical socialism and Iran's revolutionary Shiism. Nevertheless, the ties between the two countries have been expanding in unprecedented fashion. Iran and Venezuela have enjoyed a lengthy and special relationship based on their mutual oil interests. The two nations were among the founding members of the Organization of Petroleum Exporting Countries (OPEC) and have been working for years to guarantee their common economic interests. Still, it was Chavez's rise to power that heralded a new era in relations between the two countries. This became evident through dozens of mutual cooperation agreements signed in a variety of fields, mutual presidential visits, and delegation exchanges.

Ahmadinejad's election to the presidency in the summer of 2005 expanded relations further. One of Ahmadinejad's main goals was to initiate a lasting change in Iranian foreign policy. Since World War II, Ahmadinejad claimed, the world had been dominated by the United States and its allies. He sought to rectify this "historic injustice" by calling for reforms in the UN that would annul the veto privilege given to the five permanent members of the Security Council.[1] Ahmadinejad's commitment to the transformation of global reality assumes the revolutionary mode. Ahmadinejad's worldview greatly resembled Chavez's revolutionary vision, thus contributing to the establishment of a strategic alliance between the two countries. This alliance was based on mutual interests as well as on a joint revolutionary fervor.

During his first two years as president, Ahmadinejad visited Venezuela twice, and Chavez held three visits to Iran. During his first visit to Venezuela in September 2006, Ahmadinejad referred to Chavez as his "revolutionary brother." He also referred to the common thoughts and interests between the two countries and urged the need for unity. While acknowledging the geographical distance between the two countries, their hearts and minds, he said, were very close.[2] Ahmadinejad's use of the traditional mode, emphasizing the informal kinship of a community of peers, demonstrates the intricate friction of modes that exists in all spaces occupied by Shiite leadership.

There is no better way to present this friction than through the conference organized by the Islamic Students Association of Tehran University in September 2007. This conference, titled: "Che like Chamran," which was also attended by children of the South American revolutionary, Ernesto Che Guevara, sought to strengthen the link between Iran's Islamic Revolution and the Socialist Revolution in Latin America. The title of the conference was chosen for the alliteration in the names of the two revolutionaries: Che Guevara and Mostafa Chamran. Chamran, who helped to found the *Amal* movement in Lebanon in the 1970s, was appointed as Defense Minister following the Islamic Revolution. He led paramilitary forces during the early phase of the Iran-Iraq war and was killed in battle in the southern Iranian province of Khuzistan in 1981.

Mortaza Firoozabadi, Secretary of the Islamic Pro-justice students' movement at the university, was quoted as saying that his movement and Che Guevara's children, as well as the Latin American countries, share two common traits: no fear of death and a willingness to free the oppressed, thereby restoring the rights of all peoples of the world.[3]

In a message sent by President Ahmadinejad to the conference participants, he stressed the common struggle of all revolutionaries who represented the

---

[1] For President Ahmadinejad's speech in the UN General Assembly (September 19, 2006), see *The Washington Post*, September 20, 2006.
[2] *Associated Press*, September 17, 2006.
[3] Inter-Press Service, October 3, 2007.

"downtrodden" to establish world justice and to fight oppression. He drew a parallel line between the revolutionaries in Latin America struggling for independence and the Islamic Revolution led by Ayatollah Khomeini.[4]

The Iranian conservative press, reflecting the line adopted by the mainstream religious establishment, embraced the revolutionary mode with gusto. In a series of articles dealing with Iran's relations with Venezuela, the common ideological foundation between Iran and the Latin American left was highlighted, as well as the common ambition shared by Iran and Venezuela to form a new world order. The revolutionary mode thus served to fortify the dominance of the frontier.

The emphasis on the negation of reality in the revolutionary mode was, however, tempered by the immediate link to the traditional mode and communal space. The sympathizing attitude by the conservative Iranian establishment toward the renewed South American Left was evident in an article concerning the rising Latin American left in recent years, published in *Kayhan* daily by Abdol Hamid Shahrabi. Shahrabi highlighted the main principles adopted by neo-Marxists in Latin America, such as safeguarding Latin America's independence regarding imperialism and establishing social justice. He elaborated the measures taken by President Chavez, which manifested principles of allocating financial resources in favor of the poor and defending the rights of the oppressed social stratum. The public and the social activists, Shahrabi claimed, mobilized to support Chavez because they believed that he was committed to carry out basic changes for the benefit of the suppressed and to establish advanced values of social justice.[5]

Revolution and Tradition Compete

The cooptation of the traditional and the revolutionary was a calculated strategy meant to address the gap between Chavez's secular socialism and Iran's espousal of Islam. This was made possible by interpreting Chavez's worldview as being consistent with the official religiosity of the Iranian leadership. Chavez was referred to by President Ahmadinejad not only as a revolutionary but also as "worker of God and a servant of his people."[6]

Criticism in regard to the attitude toward Venezuela, voiced by political groups and individuals outside the Iranian ruling circles, also reflected the traditional mode. Those elements were not persuaded by the "religious presentation" of the neo-Marxist regimes in Latin America, and instead focused on the ideological and cultural gaps between the Islamic Republic and the Latin American regimes. Other sources praised Chavez and Fidel Castro for protecting Islamic clerics and preachers operating in their countries.[7]

---

4 *Fars*, September 25, 2007.
5 *Kayhan*, March 8, 2007.
6 *El-Universal*, July 31, 2006.
7 *Rasa* News Agency, September 15, 2007.

The "Che like Chamran" conference, organized to show the common ground between Iranian and Latin American revolutionaries, actually exacerbated the differences between dogma and ideology. Shortly after the opening of the conference, Che Guevara's daughter protested what she considered a distortion of her father's thought. She said that Che had never talked about God and knew there was no absolute truth. Following her speech, other participants also started to mention the differences between the Iranian revolutionary Chamran and the South American revolutionary Che Guevara.[8]

Other adherents of the traditional mode, specifically those who wished to see it become politically and culturally dominant, attributed more importance to the gap between Islam and Latin American Socialism. One member of this school, the editor of the ultra-conservative blog *Nesl-e Khomeini* (Khomeini's Generation), criticized the "Che like Chamran" conference. He suggested that the conference was a mistake made jointly by the Iranian Foreign Ministry and a group of overly enthusiastic students. The Foreign Ministry, representing the conformist strategic mode, sought to expand political and economic relations with Venezuela. The blogger suggested, however, the one mode that true followers of Khomeini should apply is the traditional mode in its most dogmatic, institutional variant. The separate and independent identity of the revolutionary Islamic movement led by Khomeini was linked neither to the West nor to the East.[9]

Iranian officials have referred often to the economic and political benefits Iran has accumulated through its special relations with Venezuela. During the first decade of the twenty-first century, nearly 200 cooperation agreements were signed between Iran and Venezuela in a variety of fields. These include oil and energy, industry, commerce, housing, education, culture, agriculture, mines, petro-chemistry, and aviation.

Attempts were made to link the conformist and revolutionary modes. The Iranian leadership highlighted its efforts to promote economic cooperation with Venezuela in certain fields, which could allegedly assist in the fight against Western hegemony and implement a new and just world order. Iran and Venezuela agreed, for instance, to invest billions of dollars in development of joint projects in "Third World" nations.[10]

The traditional mode was also invoked by emphasizing the promotion of joint humanitarian projects, such as building 7,000 houses in Venezuela. Through these special projects, Iran could demonstrate that its relations with Venezuela exceeded the customary perceptions in international relations and were based not only on political or economic interests but also on the principle of justice and solidarity.

---

[8] *IPS*, October 5, 2007.
[9] *Nesl-e Khomeini*, October 7, 2007.
[10] See http://foreignaffairs.house.gov/112/HHRG-112-FA-WState-NBailey-20120202.pdf.

The conformist mode reflected criticism of the government's foreign policy toward Venezuela as harmful to Iranian national interests. The reformist daily, *Kargozaran*, for example, severely criticized President Ahmadinejad for the agreement he signed with President Chavez to establish the joint fund to assist "anti-imperialist" countries. It claimed that it was not justified to invest 1 billion dollars out of the national budget in that fund, while it was not clear which benefit it had for Iran and which those "anti-imperialist" countries were.

No one could oppose assisting economically weak countries, *Kargozaran* asserted. Yet, one may wonder, whether it was wise to give such assistance at a time when a senior official in the Iranian Ministry of Health was claiming that its budget was not sufficient to collect contaminated garbage from the hospitals and while seniors in the Education Ministry estimated the Ministry's budget deficit at 1 billion U.S. dollars.[11]

Iranian relations with Venezuela provide a glimpse of Shiite friction and its various constitutive elements. Confrontation rages between the traditional mode and its communal, local knowledge and the revolutionary mode with its transcendent grand vision. However, this confrontation-based understanding can be very limited. Three modes of behavior are clearly discernible, but neither achieves supremacy, nor does any one manage to oust any of the others. Friction is balanced through the definition of confrontation and its defusing by cooperation and competition. The resulting middle ground acknowledges the distinctions between strategic modes, but allows constant communication and engagement.

All three strategic modes employ distinct rationales and justifications. Yet it is their interaction and friction that provide coherence and sustainability. The truth value of these modes emerges from the friction they produce in tandem, not from their independent claims to dominance. This state of affairs demonstrates the distinct nature of friction-based leadership. In more conventional polities, the success of leaderships is often associated with their ability to adhere to a defined goal. In the case of the Iranian leadership, success is indicated by the maintenance of competing goals and dynamic preferences.

Deconstructing the Conformist Middle: Iranian Nuclear Strategy

As the world attempts to make sense of Iran's nuclear policy, emphasis is often placed on questions of resolution. Will Iran get the bomb? Will the Iranians use the bomb? Scholars and policymakers are engaged in trying to provide clear-cut answers to these direct questions. Focusing exclusively on these questions is misguided. As we have shown in diverse cases, Iranian strategy, both domestic and foreign, seems geared mainly toward friction management – that is, striving for dynamic equilibrium, maintaining difference, and seeking the middle

[11] *Kargozaran*, January 15, 2007.

ground. Examining the friction within the conformist mode on the nuclear issue demonstrates the creativity and dynamism of Shiite leadership.

Iranian nuclear policy since 2003 has become one of the major issues on the Iranian agenda. It is, perhaps, the most influential factor affecting Iran's relations with the international community. In the terms of our discussion, the nuclear issue represents a dilemma. Iranian nuclear strategy is created and promulgated in what might be termed "double friction." That is, the friction within Iranian society, is complemented by the friction created through engagement with the international community. Double friction serves as a platform for "equilibrium in progress," based on various uses of the conformist mode by diverse Shiite leaders in Iran. In other words, the conformist mode, similarly to the traditional and revolutionary modes, is itself a creature of friction.

Since an opposition group revealed the location of secret Iranian nuclear sites in August 2002, the Iranian leadership has been forced to acknowledge the existence of an Iranian nuclear program. Iranian leaders justified the nuclear program as an inalienable right under the Non-Proliferation Treaty (NPT). Still, they were willing to negotiate with the international community and to make provisional concessions, aimed at reassuring the West that this program was meant for civilian use only.

In October 2003, Iran agreed to suspend its uranium enrichment process, albeit temporarily, and to sign the additional protocol of the NPT, which allowed for unannounced International Atomic Energy Agency (IAEA) inspections at nuclear sites. This conciliatory policy, which lasted until the summer of 2005, reflected the Iranian leadership's reluctance to provide its enemies with grounds for attack. Nuclear development was presented to the world as a part of the Iranian national interest. Iran's nuclear capabilities were not meant to serve a revolutionary agenda or even a traditional one. Nuclear development targeted the needs and future plans of the Iranian state and not the promotion of Shiite revival or the dominance of Islam.

Hassan Rouhani, the current president of the Islamic Republic and former secretary of Iran's Supreme National Security Council (SNSC), reflected the conformist strategy adopted by the Iranian government since 2003 in an interview to the *Jam-e Jam* daily in December 2007. The Iranian decision to freeze the uranium enrichment process, he said, reflected Iran's concern over the political developments in Iraq and Afghanistan. Iran feared significant UN interference in its nuclear program, as well as a possible U.S. attack. This concern resulted, according to Rouhani, in Iran's decision to suspend its nuclear activities and to sign the additional protocol to the NPT.[12]

Iran seemed to change course during the summer of 2005. In June Iran declared its intention to resume conversion activities. It rejected an incentives package proposed by the EU and renewed its nuclear activity in August 2005. Following the installation of Mahmoud Ahmadinejad's administration in the fall

---

[12] *Jam-e Jam*, December 10, 2007.

of 2005, Iran adopted an approach even more focused on confrontation. Despite growing threats made by the IAEA to refer its nuclear case to the UN Security Council (UNSC), Iran returned to enrichment research in January 2006.[13]

Still, despite its apparent change of policy and the adoption of a more combative pose toward the international community, Iranian leaders did not abandon the conformist mode. Iran's leadership continued its negotiations with the West despite the referral of its nuclear issue to the UNSC. Negotiations continued even after three rounds of sanctions imposed by the Security Council against Iran since December 2006. Conservative political elements in Iran vociferously demanded withdrawal from the NPT in reaction to the UN response. Iranian leaders, however, continued their talks with the EU and avoided breaking the rules and suspending cooperation with the international community as well as withdrawing from the NPT.

In the summer of 2007, Iran began a process of negotiations with the IAEA, The agency implied that these negotiations were meant to clear up outstanding questions regarding its past nuclear activities. In June 2007, amid discussions held by the UNSC concerning a third round of sanctions, Iran agreed to devise an action plan with the IAEA aimed at resolving relevant issues regarding its nuclear ambitions. Such seemingly contradictory measures are often construed as a cynical ploy meant to buy time for the Iranian program. We argue, however, that proceeding with negotiations while simultaneously continuing to acquire nuclear knowledge and expertise, demonstrates the logic of friction. Irreversible actions, such as either signing a deal with the West or fully promoting a military nuclear program, go against the grain of a friction-based rationale. A marriage between negotiations and self-arming is, therefore, an optimal strategy for the Iranian leadership.

Revolution within Conformist Strategy

Iranian negotiations on nuclear regulation are often described as a diversion, meant to draw attention from Iran's nuclear development. Still, examining the behavior of the Iranian leadership provides a different explanation. Iranian policy is at its most committed when it is also able to walk a parallel path.

Public statements on the part of Iranian leaders present the spectrum of friction within the conformist mode. Iranian leaders, from Supreme Leader Khamenei to the government energy experts continued to reassure the international community with regard to the civilian nature of Iran's nuclear program.[14] Iranian officials argued that Iran was developing nuclear energy to generate electricity, to master the fuel cycle, and to become a supplier of nuclear fuel in the future. Iran justified its interest in nuclear technology by referencing the need for diversifying its energy sources. Leaders also claimed

---

[13] See http://articles.cnn.com/2012–03–06/middleeast/world_meast_iran-timeline_1_nuclear-program-iran-signs-iran-s-natanz?_s=PM:MIDDLEEAST.

[14] See: http://news.sky.com/story/928077/irans-supreme-leader-no-nuclear-weapons.

they wished to keep abreast with a technology often identified as a hallmark of scientific progress.[15]

We have defined the conformist mode as related to the institutional space of the state. In the nuclear issue, these dimensions take on diverse forms. They uphold a vision of Iranian sovereignty focused on national strength and independence. Still, they reflect a solid relationship with the world and a commitment to its shared values. The conformist mode is itself in a constant state of friction, each of its divergent elements recognizable when juxtaposed against others.

The inner friction of the conformist mode is further demonstrated by the fact that Iranian national interests were emphasized both by proponents of the Iranian nuclear option and its small minority of critics. Those who argued against the nuclear program claimed that such a policy would be detrimental to the national cause. In an open letter sent to the Supreme Leader, prominent reformist journalist, Ahmad Zeidabadi, claimed that the price Iran had to pay to achieve nuclear capability was too high. If realizing an economic or scientific achievement endangered Iran's existence or its security and national assets, he said, it was not justified to insist on achieving those goals. The negative implications caused by the imposed sanctions and the possibility of a military attack against Iran were much more significant than the advantages of producing nuclear fuel.[16]

Ahmad Shirzad, a former MP, also questioned the reason behind Iran's nuclear program. In an interview with the Spanish daily *El Pais* in September 2007, he claimed that the Iranian nuclear program was too costly if it entailed putting all other national projects off for a decade or so. The program, he said, cost 4–5 billion dollars, and this sum might have been invested in building gas and oil power stations.[17]

The proponents of Iran's nuclear program emphasized Iranian state interests as well. This was true especially following the combative statements made by President Ahmadinejad. Former-President Ali-Akbar Hashemi Rafsanjani reflected this approach when arguing on several occasions in favor of diplomacy and against using slogans. In a Friday sermon given in Tehran, he suggested that Iran's current situation requires wisdom, negotiations, and extensive diplomatic activities.[18] This criticism of Ahmadinejad's revolutionary statements demonstrates that, within the friction-based Shiite leadership, a claim to absolute dominance on the part of a single mode of behavior serves as a threat of imbalance and crisis. The way out of this anomaly lies in the management of friction toward a dynamic equilibrium.

---

[15] Ibid.
[16] *Advar* News, April 10, 2007.
[17] *El Pais*, September 18, 2007.
[18] *Fars*, September 30, 2005.

The Iranian approach to the nuclear issue also reflected a more confrontational side. The nuclear issue extolled goals and values commensurate with the revolutionary vision. Specifically, nuclear power symbolized the influence necessary for Iran to attain its self-perception as a world leader. Western opposition to Iran's nuclear technology, stated President Ahmadinejad at a conference in Tehran, was not a mere objection to Iranian technological know-how and industry. Instead, it was a challenge offered by what he defined as "the potentials of global arrogance" and the political executive potentials of the Islamic Revolution. Iran's enemies, he stated, had no concern about uranium enrichment in Iran. They were actually worried that they might yield to conviction of the Islamic Revolution and lose their dignity because of Iran's access to nuclear technology.[19]

The revolutionary voice within the conformist mode grew more pronounced following Ahmadinejad's election to the presidency in 2005. The new Iranian government adopted a more belligerent tone. Shrugging off stronger resolutions from the IAEA threatening to refer the nuclear issue to the UNSC, Iran resumed its enrichment research in January 2006. It continued its nuclear activities after a series of resolutions were adopted by the Security Council to impose sanctions on Iran. In February 2008, Javad Vaidi, Deputy Secretary of the SNSC was quoted as saying: "We are running a new generation of centrifuges."[20] The Iranian announcement came just a few days before the UNSC was due to meet and consider a third round of sanctions against Iran.

Another expression of this revolutionary voice within the conformist mode was Iran's insistence on self-sufficiency regarding its nuclear program. International proposals that Iran would import enriched uranium from abroad rather than rely on a domestic product, were rejected by the Iranian leadership insistence on retaining the full fuel cycle. This revolutionary voice was frequently offset by a traditional voice. Islam, however, was used also by revolutionary proponents of the Iranian nuclear military option. A hard line cleric, Mohsen Gharavian, was quoted in February 2006 as saying that the use of nuclear weapons might not constitute a problem according to *shari'a*. He suggested that when the entire world was armed with nuclear weapons, it was permissible to use those weapons as a countermeasure.[21]

Shiite leaders supporting nuclear development also used Islamic sentiments to mobilize their public. In a meeting with citizens from the northern city of Tabriz, held in Tehran in February 2008, Khamenei referred to U.S. President Bush's call to maintain the pressures over Iran. The Supreme Leader declared that the Iranian people would stand up for its rights and would protect them in light of the continuing pressures and propaganda, because God would reprimand the Iranian people if they did otherwise.[22]

---

[19] Reuters, February 25, 2007.
[20] *Associated Press*, February 25, 2008.
[21] *Rooz*, February 16, 2006.
[22] Iranian television, Channel 1, February 17, 2008.

The Nuclear Issue and the Future of Middle Ground Politics

The beginning of the twenty-first century's second decade saw no change in Iranian middle ground policy with regard to its nuclear capabilities. Iran's leaders openly courted conflict, opening the Russian-built reactor in Bushehr in late August 2010. They also announced the production of 20 kilograms of 20 percent enriched uranium, which is considered weapons-usable. In response, several rounds of sanctions were imposed on Iran, each tougher than its predecessor. The United States unilaterally imposed sanctions on Iranian petroleum products in July, 2010.[23]

Simultaneously, Iranian leaders have engaged the international community on the nuclear issue. Iran has expressed readiness to allow IAEA inspectors into its facilities, and is also a signatory to the Additional Protocol of the Nuclear Proliferation Treaty. A significant demonstration of Iranian engagement came in May of 2010. On May 17, 2010, Iran signed a declaration, brokered by Turkey and Brazil, in which Iranian leaders agreed to send 1,200 kilograms of low-enriched uranium (LEU) to Turkey in exchange for 120 kilograms of fuel for the Tehran research reactor within one year.[24] The notion of exchanging uranium for fuel had been on the table for several years. The joint declaration represented an original and fresh effort to restore Iran's standing as a member of the international community. The Iranian-Brazilian-Turkish initiative ultimately fizzled out. It did not receive the support of the United States or the IAEA. Still, the idea exhibits the potential of middle ground politics to challenge the current global order.

Following the attempt to forge a tripartite agreement, international reaction to Iran's acquisition and development campaign grew much more stringent. Severe economic sanctions were imposed on Iran by the global community, including a removal of Iran's banks from the global clearing system and various measures targeting Iran's oil and financial industries.[25] Several rounds of negotiations between Iran and the P5+1 (the United States, China, Russia, France, Germany, and the UK) took place, with no clear results.[26] Additionally, the Israeli leadership mounted an intensive campaign for constant consideration of a military strike against Iranian nuclear facilities. The campaign reportedly,

---

[23] For a detailed chronology of Iran's nuclear policy from its inception in the 1950s, see http://www.nti.org/e_research/profiles/Iran/Nuclear/chronology.html.

[24] See http://www.guardian.co.uk/world/julian-borger-global-security-blog/2010/may/17/iran-brazil-turkey-nuclear.

[25] For a timeline of sanctions placed on Iran, see http://www.mapreport.com/citysubtopics/iran-p-o.html. For an interesting analysis of the effect of sanctions on Iran's economy, see http://www.lepointinternational.com/it/economia-e-finanza/medio-oriente/867-how-sanctions-affect-irans-economy.html.

[26] For an illuminating example of Iran's policies and negotiation tactics on the nuclear issue, see the following article and its reference to an Iranian position paper demanding "long term cooperation" and other middle ground measures: http://www.atimes.com/atimes/Middle_East/NG07Ak03.html.

included assassinations of nuclear scientists inside Iran,[27] as well as cyber-attacks against computers servicing Iranian reactors.[28] Israel publicly set tough conditions for reengaging Iran, including shutting down certain facilities and effectively relinquishing much of Iran's civilian technology.[29]

The election of Hassan Rouhani to the presidency of the Islamic Republic brought with it sweeping change. Five months after Rouhani's election, on November 24, 2013, an interim agreement was signed in Geneva between Iran and the five permanent members of the UN Security Council, with Germany as co-signee (P5+1). The agreement came after several rounds of intense negotiations, and seems to be an indication of a conformist, pragmatic worldview shaping policy in both the United States and the Islamic Republic of Iran.

The interim agreement[30] and the rapprochement preceding its signing took the world by storm. Presidents Rouhani and Obama spoke on the phone. Business firms from all over the world – oil, commodities, finance – waited eagerly for permission to operate in the lucrative Iranian market. Pundits and observers issued ominous warnings, as did Israel's Prime Minister and his entire cabinet.[31]

For the purposes of our discussion, the agreement demonstrates the inherent dynamism of Iranian middle ground politics. Yesterday's unmentionables become today's inevitables in the blink of an eye. Effectiveness begins with respect for one's rivals, an understanding of difference as a social and political cornerstone. Such understanding is most immediately expressed through a politics of moderation, an acceptance of another's right to be an other. The costs of ignoring difference and the opportunities offered by its embrace is made clear in the next chapter, considering the 2009 and 2013 presidential elections.

Policy and Middle Ground Strategy: Concluding Note

The reality of the middle ground requires its own language of thought as well as its own modes of behavior. We have demonstrated that the middle ground in

---

[27] For coverage of the assassinations speculating about Israeli involvement, see, for example, http://www.csmonitor.com/World/Middle-East/2012/0112/Was-Israel-behind-Iran-nuclear-scientist-s-assassination, http://www.time.com/time/world/article/0,8599,2104372,00.html, and http://www.haaretz.com/news/diplomacy-defense/sunday-times-mossad-agents-behind-iran-scientist-assassination-1.407593, among others.

[28] For various analyses of cyber-attacks on Iranian reactors, see http://www.juancole.com/2012/06/behind-the-usisraeli-cyberattacks-on-iran.html,http://islamnewsroom.com/news-we-need/1877-obama-cyberattacks-iran-nuke-plant, and http://www.nytimes.com/2012/06/01/world/middleeast/obama-ordered-wave-of-cyberattacks-against-iran.html?pagewanted=all.

[29] For one example of a list of conditions, see http://www.jpost.com/IranianThreat/News/Article.aspx?id=264839.

[30] See full text of the agreement at: http://english.farsnews.com/newstext.aspx?nn=13920903000397.

[31] See: http://www.haaretz.com/news/diplomacy-defense/.premium-1.559781.

practice is a kaleidoscope. The myriad entities within the middle ground exist distinctly, but all form a larger, more intricate image.

This larger image is often a subject of struggle and strife. The Shiite middle ground is not monolithic. In the Shiite case, this middle ground underwent a rapid process of politicization during the second half of the twentieth century. In fact, the political history of the Islamic Republic of Iran consists mainly of clashes between differing visions and perceptions of the middle ground. None of the parties, competing within the Islamic Republic, consider this competition to be a zero-sum game or clash of destinies. Victory and defeat are not absolute. Struggle is a part of middle ground reality. A political life within the middle ground is a hotbed of durable conflict and prolonged tension.

7

The Struggle for the Middle Ground: The 2009 (and 2013) Presidential Elections

The Iranian presidential elections held in June 2009 present a deliberate attempt to perform a profound shift from the friction-based logic we have so far identified as a key principle of post-1979 Shiite leadership. The politics of the middle ground, the Khomeini-inspired political tradition of the Islamic Republic, came under attack. This attack was perpetrated by a movement that, while closely intertwined with the politics of the middle ground, views the latter as a sign of social weakness and ideological deviance. Incumbent president Mahmoud Ahmadinejad was the figurehead for this movement, which included prominent scholars, the establishments of the Revolutionary Guards, and the *Basij* militia, as well as well-known politicians. This movement has, ultimately, become persecuted in its own right. However, for the purposes of our discussion, it will fulfill the role described earlier.

We refer to this movement as middle ground radicalization. It originates and grows in diverse systems tending toward the dynamic patterns of the middle ground. Members of this movement accept middle ground practices as the default social practice. They do not, however, perceive the middle ground as inherently virtuous. Middle ground radicalization sees the middle ground worldview as a means, rather than an end.

For Khomeini, the middle ground was the cornerstone of his worldview. For Ahmadinejad, the middle ground was a necessary evil. Khomeini believed in a distinction between the absolute and the human. He saw the middle ground as the preferable option for a meaningful, virtuous life available to fallible man in the absence of God's absolute truth. Ahmadinejad saw the middle ground as devoid of inherent value. He envisioned a direct link between the absolute and the human. After addressing the UN General Assembly in 2005, he spoke of feeling the Vanished Imam's presence at his side:

"Ahmadinejad said that someone present at the UN told him that a light surrounded him while he was delivering his speech to the General Assembly. The Iranian president added that he also sensed it.

"He said when you began with the words 'in the name of God,' I saw that you became surrounded by a light until the end [of the speech]," Ahmadinejad appears to say in the video. "I felt it myself, too. I felt that all of a sudden the atmosphere changed there, and for 27–28 minutes all the leaders did not blink." Ahmadinejad adds that he is not exaggerating.

"I am not exaggerating when I say they did not blink; it's not an exaggeration, because I was looking," he says. "They were astonished as if a hand held them there and made them sit. It had opened their eyes and ears for the message of the Islamic Republic."[1]

The middle ground is presented as the existing, convenient way for Ahmadinejad to hasten the Mahdi's return. Nowhere was the tension between these two interpretations clearer than in the case of the Iranian presidential elections held on June 12, 2009.

The 2009 Elections

The tenth presidential election of the Islamic Republic or Iran was held on June 12, 2009. Incumbent President Mahmoud Ahmadinejad was running against two reformist challengers (Mir Hossein Mousavi and Mehdi Karroubi) on the one hand, and a conservative competitor (Mohsen Rezaee), on the other. Two rounds of voting were expected to be held, as no single candidate was seen as able to cross the 50 percent threshold that guarantees immediate victory. Ahmadinejad, however, was declared the victor with more than 65 percent of the vote after a single round. The results surprised Iranians and the world. Although there is no clear-cut proof, most Iran experts seem to agree that, contrary to previous elections in the Islamic Republic, the results of the 2009 elections were forged.[2]

Understanding the stakes of this challenge requires a brief review of the Islamic Republic's political system. This review is written with the well-known story of the blind men and the elephant in mind.[3] The tale places several blind men in a room with an elephant. Each of the men is asked to touch the elephant and recount his impressions. As each man feels only a part of the beast, they cannot reach agreement regarding the true nature of the elephant. Middle ground politics are somewhat similar to this elephant. Their ongoing friction and their rejection of a binary approach make attempts to provide a comprehensive description of the middle ground futile. The following discussion, drawn from the constitution of the Islamic Republic of Iran,[4] presents the complexity of Iranian middle ground politics through its various political institutions. Each institution highlights a significant feature of the middle ground, yet their interaction creates middle ground politics as a whole.

[1] See http://www.rferl.org/content/article/1063353.html.
[2] See http://fpc.state.gov/documents/organization/125709.pdf.
[3] For the version presented by the famed Persian poet Rumi in the thirteenth century, see: http://www.khamush.com/tales_from_masnavi.htm#The%20Elephant
[4] http://www.iranchamber.com/government/laws/constitution.php.

The Polity of the Islamic Republic

The regime of the Islamic Republic is an intricate and complex construction with elements of democratic procedure alongside unprecedented attempts to create a modern Islamic theocracy. The Iranian constitution states that the Islamic Republic derives its legitimacy from popular will:

Article 1 [Form of Government]

The form of government of Iran is that of an Islamic Republic, endorsed by the people of Iran on the basis of their longstanding belief in the sovereignty of truth and Koranic justice, in the referendum of 29 and 30 March 1979, through the affirmative vote of a majority of 98.2% of eligible voters, held after the victorious Islamic Revolution led by Imam Khumayni.

However, it also recognizes the exclusive sovereignty of God:

Article 2 [Foundational Principles]

The Islamic Republic is a system based on belief in: 1) the One God (as stated in the phrase "There is no god except Allah"), His exclusive sovereignty and right to legislate, and the necessity of submission to His commands.[5]

Sovereignty is the cornerstone of proper government, but – as it lies with the Divine – the status of human leadership is somewhat different. This difference and resulting friction motivate the Islamic Republic's quest for dynamic equilibrium.

Human leadership is charged with the interpretation of God's legislative prerogative. God creates laws and men apply them, but only once the laws have been properly interpreted and contextualized. The most qualified interpreter is the *faqih*, or Supreme Leader, of the Islamic Republic. This constitutional position was initially articulated in Khomeini's lectures on *velayat-e-faqih*, the governance of the jurist. The *faqih* regulates an intricate matrix in which the branches of the state (legislative, executive, and judicial) interact, each commanding diverse powers but none enjoying total, exclusive dominance (Article 110).

The Supreme Leader

The first Supreme Leader of the Islamic Republic, the man for whom the position was created, was Ayatollah Ruhollah Khomeini. His chosen heir, Ayatollah Sayed Ali Khamenei, was appointed Supreme Leader in 1989. He is the ultimate regulator, formulating the interests of the regime and making sure all its disparate elements are able to interact within a framework of dynamic friction. The Supreme Leader is selected by the popularly elected Assembly of Experts.

---

5 The Constitution of the Islamic Republic of Iran, available online at http://www.servat.unibe.ch/icl/ir00000_.html.

The constitution states that the criteria on the basis of which the Supreme Leader is to be chosen:

Article 109 [Leadership Qualifications]

(1) Following are the essential qualifications and conditions for the Leader:
   a. Scholarship, as required for performing the functions of religious leader in different fields.
   b. Justice and piety, as required for the leadership of the Islamic Ummah.
   c. Right political and social perspicacity, prudence, courage, administrative facilities, and adequate capability for leadership.
(2) In case of multiplicity of persons fulfilling the above qualifications and conditions, the person possessing the better jurisprudential and political perspicacity will be given preference.

The supreme leader must combine the qualities of a highly capable politician with an impeccable scholarly reputation. Article 109 was amended after Khomeini's death in 1989, so as to place a much larger emphasis on political and administrative skills than as previously stated. Khomeini was the original *faqih*, the one whose presence grounded the entire system. After his death, no equal heir could assume the position, and allowances made the transformation of the position into a much more process-based (rather than presence-based) existence.

The President

The Iranian president holds the highest popularly elected office in the republic, and is subordinate only to the Supreme Leader. The president serves for a maximum of two consecutive terms of four years each. Candidates running for the Presidency must be approved by the Guardian Council on the basis of satisfying the following criteria:

Article 115

The President must be elected from among religious and political personalities possessing the following qualifications:

- Iranian origin;
- Iranian nationality;
- administrative capacity and resourcefulness;
- a good past record;
- trustworthiness and piety; and
- convinced belief in the fundamental principles of the Islamic Republic of Iran and the official madhhab [religion] of the country.

According to the constitution, the president is the head of the executive and acts simultaneously as coordinator of the three branches of government – legislative, executive, and judicial. These terms are used loosely, and are not at all identical with Western definitions of government branches. This coordinating responsibility was eventually removed from the president and transferred to the Supreme Leader when that position required additional political prowess. The president's responsibilities include the signing and supervision of laws passed by the *Majlis*, administration of the national budget, the signing of international agreements ratified by the *Majlis*, the appointment and endorsement of ambassadors, and acts as head of the Supreme National Security Council.

Parliament

The Iranian Parliament, the *Majlis,* is a legislative body responsible for introducing and passing legislation, ratification of international treaties and agreements, and approval of the national budget as put forth by the president. According to the constitution, laws passed by the *Majlis* must be approved by the Guardian Council on the basis of accordance with Shari'a law. This state of affairs highlights the elements of friction within the regime. Legislation is legitimate once it is interpreted, and various modes of behavior interact and form a single, dynamic whole.

The Guardian Council

The Guardian Council is, perhaps, the most influential body in Iran. This influence is a result of the council's singular prerogative as stated in Article 4 of the constitution:

All civil, penal financial, economic, administrative, cultural, military, political, and other laws and regulations must be based on Islamic criteria. This principle applies absolutely and generally to all articles of the Constitution as well as to all other laws and regulations, and the wise persons of the Guardian Council are judges in this matter.

The council is the topmost supervisory body in the Islamic Republic of Iran. The Supreme Leader is the nucleus of the system, the presence required to imbue it with charisma and personal legitimacy. The Council of Guardians embodies the collective, operative logic of the friction-based middle ground. Among the council's duties are the supervision and certification of elections, including also the approval of candidates both to the Assembly of Experts, the Presidency, and the *Majlis.*

The council is made up of twelve members, half of whom are prominent Islamic jurists, with the rank of Ayatollah, appointed by the Supreme Leader. The other half of the council consists of jurists specializing in different areas of law who are nominated by the judiciary and approved by Parliament. Parliament is, in many ways, dependent on the council's approval. The council must approve all bills passed by the Majlis and has the power to veto them, which leaves Parliament stranded in the absence of Guardian support. It is not accidental that such overriding powers were granted to one of the bodies in the Islamic Republic with the express mandate to interpret the law, rather than apply it.

The council's significant role within middle ground politics is not the result of ideological affinity. Middle ground politics are a continuously negotiated order. This is a significant trait of Iran's Shiite leadership. Its distinct components often operate according to a high-ground agenda, seeking attainment of specific goals and the promotion of grand principles. The middle ground is created from the interaction between these components, placing their different overriding goals into a relative, dynamic framework.

Thus, when Supreme Leader Ali Khamenei asked the Guardian Council to investigate claims by reformists of the 2009 elections having been rigged,[6] the council's affirmation of the results came as no surprise. The council repudiated the opposition's arguments and, ultimately, certified Ahmadinejad as the winner.

The Expediency Council

The Expediency Council is a thirteen-member body with policy-making, supervisory, advisory, some limited legislative power, and adjudicating functions. This council was established in 1988 when the original Islamic constitution was revised by referendum. It is engaged almost completely with the regulation of friction. Its members include prominent and influential thinkers on matters of religion, society, and politics.

The Council was created to manage the resolution and settlement of disputes between the *Majlis* and the Council of Guardians and to serve as an important and influential advisor to the Supreme Leader. In a way, the council expands the *faqih*'s personal authority into the diverse spaces that comprise the Shiite middle ground.[7]

The Assembly of Experts

The Assembly of Experts is responsible for the election, supervision, and dismissal of the Supreme Leader of Iran. In September 2007, former president Hashemi Rafsanjani was elected chairman, and he is the one who presides over the eighty-six directly elected Islamic scholars – *mujtahids* – that comprise the Assembly. For the purposes of our discussion, the Assembly of Experts highlights the fact that no decision made within middle ground politics is irreversible. In other words, maintaining the critical edge of interpretation, its

---

[6] See, for instance, *The New York Times*, June 15, 2009, online at http://topics.nytimes.com/topics/reference/timestopics/organizations/g/guardian_council_iran/index.html.

[7] For a useful discussion and visualization of Iran's political system with a particular emphasis on the Expediency Council, see http://news.bbc.co.uk/2/shared/spl/hi/middle_east/03/iran_power/html/expediency_council.stm.

constant challenge to established conventions is one of the elements of middle ground virtue.[8]

The Elections Examined

The presidential elections of June 12, 2009, produced a profound crisis for the Islamic Republic. This crisis is somewhat counterintuitive for outside observers. The winners, Ahmadinejad, and the radical circle he represents, were seen as attempting to preserve the rule of an extremist religious establishment. The protesters, on the other hand, were perceived as seeking reform or advocating a second revolution culminating in the overthrow of religious rule. This is a misguided view. The protesters were the ones fighting for the integrity and preservation of middle ground politics, the system put in place by the Islamic Republic in 1979. The president's supporters were attempting to force a far-reaching innovation in Iranian politics – that is, the adoption of what we have defined as middle ground radicalism.

Immediate Consequences

On June 13, 2009, the day following the record-high turnout for the Iranian Presidential Election, incumbent president Mahmoud Ahmadinejad was declared the winner with approximately 63 percent of the vote. The believed-to-be winner and the incumbent president's main adversary, former prime minister and reform advocate Mir Hossein Mousavi, received approximately 34 percent of the vote. Speculations suggesting that the elections had been tampered with on a massive scale immediately began to circulate. Mousavi denounced the election results, calling for their invalidation so as to restore people's trust and the legitimacy of the state.[9]

The Opposition Responds

On June 14, opposition candidate Mir Hossein Mousavi presented the Guardian Council with a formal request to annul the election results. Meanwhile, mass protests, which had erupted on June 10, spread from the streets of Tehran to the cities of Rasht, Orumiyeh, Zahedan, and Tabriz.[10] The scope of the protests was remarkably large, with hundreds of thousands marching in Tehran on June 15. The protesters wore green. This was the color of Mousavi's Campaign that was adopted by the post-election protest movement. The fact that green is the color traditionally identified with Islam reinforces the protesters' allegiance to the Islamic regime. They were equipped with signs reading "Where's My

---

[8] Ibid.

[9] For an example of analysis supporting this conclusion, see Mehdi Khalaji, "Khamenei's Coup," *The Washington Post*, June 15, 2009 at http://www.washingtonpost.com/wp-dyn/content/article/2009/06/14/AR2009061401758.html.

[10] See "Timeline: Iranian Election and Aftermath," Reuters News Agency, online at http://www.reuters.com/article/worldNews/idUSTRE55H3TE20090618.

Vote?,"[11] "The Government of Coup D'état: Resign, Resign,"[12] and "Mousavi we support you!"[13] State security forces responded by stepping up the violence and firing their weapons above and into the crowd, leaving at least seven people killed on June 15 alone.

The Twitter Revolution

Despite the state's attempts to strangle bandwidth and restrict Internet access, the Internet became a vital window to the world. On June 16, The Guardian Council declared that although it was willing to approve a partial recount of the vote, it would not consider annulling the election results. Restrictions on foreign news correspondents and the state's jamming of mobile and telephone networks, led to the occurrence of what has been labeled "The Twitter Revolution." The blogosphere, Twitter, YouTube, and Facebook became critical channels of communication and coordination among protesters on the ground. These words and images inspired tangible worldwide sympathy for the opposition's cause. [14]

On June 17, the protest movement held an enormous silent march in Tehran to mourn those killed over the past days. National soccer team players wore green armbands in protest of the elections when taking the pitch for an official match. The players were banned for life from the Iranian national team.

On June 18, demonstrations were held to mourn slain protesters. The Guardian Council began to review complaints submitted regarding the election results. On June 21, the relatives of Hashemi Rafsanjani, former president and, at the time, head of both the Expediency Council and the council of Experts, were arrested.[15]

Rafsanjani was one of the more vocal critics of the elections and their results. He was seen as the focal point of the opposition, much more so than the candidate Mousavi. Applying pressure to a political figure through relatives is not uncommon in the annals of Iranian political history. Still, in our case, this act merits specific mention. It reflects the single-minded thoroughness applied by the middle ground radicals. They did not choose to pursue Mousavi actively, but attempted to nip the opposition at the bud in an overriding manner. The

[11] See *The New York Times* Editorial, "Behind the protests, Social Upheaval in Iran," June 23, 2009, online at http://roomfordebate.blogs.nytimes.com/2009/06/23/behind-the-protests-social-upheaval-in-iran/.

[12] Syma Sayyah, "Photos and Report: Tehran's Great Green Silence March," Payvand Iran News, June 16, 2009, online at http://www.payvand.com/news/09/jun/1163.html.

[13] BBC News Online, "Iran protesters defy rally ban", online at: http://news.bbc.co.uk/2/hi/middle_East/8099952.stm.

[14] See, for instance, Trita Parsi, "Who's Fighting Who in Iran's Struggle?" in *Time Magazine*, June 16, 2009, online at: http://www.time.com/time/world/article/0,8599,1904989-2,00.html; Evgeny Morozov, "Iran Elections: A Twitter Revolution?" in *The Washington Post*, June 17, 2009, online at http://www.washingtonpost.com/wp-dyn/content/discussion/2009/06/17/DI2009061702232.html; Ari Berman, "Iran's Twitter Revolution," in *The Nation*, June 15, 2009, online at http://www.thenation.com/blogs/notion/443634.

[15] See http://news.antiwar.com/2009/06/21/clerical-rift-widens-as-rafsanjani-relatives-arrested/.

overriding objective, taking control of the country and leaving no room for other voices, was clear at the outset. The end justified the means, whether they included shooting in the streets or the arrest of opposition members' relatives.

On June 26, the Guardian Council declared that the elections were the "healthiest" ones held since the revolution. On June 29, the Guardian Council certified the election results. During demonstrations held on June 30, a young Iranian woman, Neda Aqa-Soltan was shot and killed by a *Basij* militiaman. As the video of her death spread across the globe, she immediately became a symbol, a face of the protests. Her name, Neda, is the Persian word for "voice," "calling," or "divine message." This has led to her being referred to as the "voice of Iran."

The significance of Neda's death, however, was soon diminished. During the 1979 revolution, civilian deaths in demonstrations were a major motivating force behind the protesters. They provided the civil unrest with a temporal axis. The Shiite mourning cycle for the dead is forty days long. At the end of each forty-day cycle, the demonstrations erupted once more. This was not the case with Neda, once more indicating that the protesters were less inclined toward revolution and more toward preserving a political order they viewed as functional and virtuous.[16]

Police and government security forces became increasingly violent against protesters. They raided and ransacked student dormitories around Iran overnight and beat, threatened, and arrested their inhabitants. They were dressed in civilian clothing and infiltrated the protesters, once again exhibiting a convicted determination which had not been seen on the Iranian political scene since the riots preceding the 1979 revolution.

The Scholarly Debates

Although the streets of Iranian cities had seemingly quieted down several weeks after the elections, the situation grew more intense behind the scenes. Ahmadinejad received vocal support from leading scholars occupying public and political positions. At the same time, many scholars outside the state leadership began voicing their discontent over the elections and the ways in which the president and the supreme leader had seemingly distorted results.

Ayatollah Montazeri, once Khomeini's chosen heir, issued a *fatwa* against the sitting regime. Commenting on state-ordered or sanctioned individual and public offenses committed against the protesters, he stated: "[These offenses entail] the most severe punishment, in this world and in the world to come, since in addition to the evil sins of fraud and of distancing [people] from the religion, they also corrupt [the very principles of] justice and law."[17]

---

[16] See http://www.nytimes.com/2009/06/23/world/middleeast/23neda.html.

[17] Ayatollah Montazeri as quoted by Memri in "Iranian Ayatollah Montazeri Issues Fatwa Against the Regime", July 12, 2009, No. 2439, Special Dispatch – No. 2439; online at the Web site of the late Ayatollah Montazeri, (Iran), July 10, 2009, www.khandaniha.eu.

Although not explicit, this criticism was directed at the Supreme Leader, Ali Khamenei. Khamenei, who did not previously affiliate himself with the radicals, remained aloof when the controversy was at its peak. Such indecision in the face of a profound crisis proved very much decisive. The public was quick to associate him with the radical cause.

The Supreme Leader was also criticized for neglecting his duties as an arbiter and adjudicator of conflicts and for siding with president Ahmadinejad. Khamenei's eldest son was a prominent member of the radical camp, and he was accused of attempting to secure this son, Mojtaba, as his heir. Having done so, Khamenei's behavior was seen as self-aggrandizing and deceitful, willing to sacrifice the integrity of the friction-based regime. Even the conservative candidate running in the 2009 elections, Mohsen Reza'i, criticized the government, warning "that the political and social rifts opened by the disputed June 12 vote and subsequent crackdown could lead to the nation's 'disintegration.'"[18]

The transgression committed by Ahmadinejad and his supporters reflected their fundamentalist outlook. This was the cause of growing discontent among some senior scholarly leaders. These leaders perceived themselves as witnessing the disintegration of the very system they founded and relied on. This understanding led members of the senior religious establishment both to call the incumbent government brutal and illegitimate and to voice serious concern regarding the future of the Islamic Republic. Many senior religious scholars saw it as their duty to restore the regime to its middle ground base, after seeing the regime take an unwanted turn toward radicalism at the hands of Khamenei and Ahmadinejad.

Criticism from the reformist candidate Mir Hossein Mousavi echoed that of the scholars. Mousavi warned that if the charges of election fraud were not resolved appropriately, Khomenei's doctrine of *velayat-e faqih*, the ideological underpinning of the Islamic Republic, would be compromised. In a letter requesting that new elections be held, Mousavi wrote: "If the large volume of cheating and vote rigging, which has set fire to the hay of people's anger, is expressed as the evidence of fairness, the republican nature of the state will be killed and, in practice, the ideology that Islam and republicanism are incompatible will be proven."[19] Opposition leaders also pointed to the risk that voters, having lost their trust in the regime, will not come to the polls next time around.

In his Friday sermon on July 17, 2009, former president Hashemi Rafsanjani denounced the government's violent crackdown against protesters and demanded the release of those detained. Instead of suppression, he said, the government should address the concerns Iranians have over the legitimacy of the vote. Rafsanjani's criticism revealed a fundamental split between hardliners

---

[18] Michael Slackman, "In Iran, a Struggle Beyond the Streets," *The New York Times*, July 8, 2009, online at: http://www.nytimes.com/2009/07/08/world/middleeast/08clerics.html.

[19] See http://iranfacts.blogspot.co.il/2009/06/my-translation-of-mousavis-latest.html.

and reformists over the importance of democratic rules and procedures in the Iranian political order.

Middle Ground Transformation

Two leading forces collided in the 2009 elections. First, the presidential incumbent, Mahmoud Ahmadinejad, represented various groups – both within and outside the religious establishment – that were dismayed with the delayed gratifications offered by the Islamic Republic. The open-ended practice of politics inspired by Khomeini had lost its attraction for those who saw the Islamic Republic as a divinely ordained necessity. This radical mode did not fully reject the dynamics of middle ground politics. Still, the middle ground radicals sought to emphasize that these dynamics were means to an end – the establishment of a virtuous society living in strict accordance with God's law.

Ahmadinejad had many followers among blue-collar Iranians. Moreover, he reflected the rise to institutional dominance of the Iranian Revolutionary Guards Corps (IRGC), its veterans, and other affiliates. The IRGC was the political cadre of the Islamic revolution. In recent years, the IRGC has become one of the most prominent organizations in the Islamic Republic, controlling vast economic wealth as well as pursuing both extensive military and domestic interests.[20]

The second force, represented by spurned presidential candidate Mir Hossein Mousavi, considered its members to be defenders of the Khomeinist middle ground. Mousavi condemned the imbalance perpetrated by Ahmadinejad throughout his first term and in the election campaign. Mousavi perceived Ahmadinejad and his circle as attempting to alter the balance between the various elements of the middle ground. Mousavi's Green Movement suspected that Ahmadinejad's rhetoric and actions were to pave the way for a radical takeover.

In a declaration issued on January 2, 2010, Mousavi provided a description of the political situation in Iran six months after the 2009 election. Comparing Iranian politics to a flowing river, Mousavi succinctly presented the challenge of middle ground radicalism and the reply he hoped to provide:

I think that the solution to the current problems and the present crisis is as follows. Today the situation of the country is like an immense roaring river where massive floods and various events have led to its rising and then caused it to become silted. The solution to calm down this great river and clear its water is not possible in a quick and swift action. Thinking of these kinds of solutions that some should repent and some should make deals and there should be some give-and-take to solve this great problem is in practice going off the track.

I consider letting streams and springs of fresh clear water into this river to be the solution that will slowly and gradually improve the water and the river. I also believe that it is still not too late and our establishment has the power to accomplish this important

---

[20] See http://www.rand.org/pubs/monographs/MG821.html.

task, should it have insight and a respectful and kind view toward all of the nation and its layers.[21]

Mousavi does not seek to negate Iran's current reality. He does not reject this reality, nor does he wish to replace it. His middle ground exists in the heart of reality. The optimal state of this reality is one of flow. The most serious threat to the existence of this reality is the cessation of motion. Mousavi, who sees himself as charged with care for this river, considers maintenance of the river's flow as his main responsibility.

This flow is to be ensured through diverse, dynamic, and less-than-radical measures. No single action, such as diversion of the river's channel or a centralized augmentation of the river's volume will suffice. This demonstrates the relationship between high-ground extremities and middle ground practice. Mousavi does not challenge the reality of the river's flow. In fact, his notion of effective action begins and ends with ensuring this flow.

Still, the flow itself is not dependent on Mousavi. His options for effective action are tangential to the flow. His middle ground politics was based on mutual sustenance established between the river and its side channels. Ahmadinejad's middle ground, on the other hand, was based on the potential for clash between flow, silt, and side channels, and on the possibilities for a clear-cut decision in favor of one element over the others.

True to the dynamic nature of the middle ground, Ahmadinejad's stance did not remain ideologically rigid. Elements loyal to the president severely curbed Mousavi's public appearances, as well as those of his ally, Mehdi Karroubi. In mid-February 2011, the two were put under house arrest and separated from their families. They have reportedly spent time in jail as well. Still, after this clear-cut victory, It was Ahmadinejad's fortune which quickly changed.

After 2009

Ahmadinejad's success bolstered several of his supporters, who had long doubted the need to favor orthodox Shi'ism over other aspects of Iranian identity. Prominent among these was Esfandiar Rahim Mahshai, Ahmadinejad's close advisor and vice president for one week. He was removed from the post by the Supreme Leader, Khamenei, who accused him of "deviance." Mahshai was accused of supporting and advocating for nationalist causes at the expense of loyalty to state Shi'ism above all else.[22] Additionally, Mahshai was accused of plotting against the office of the Supreme Leader, a plot which included illicit wiretapping.

Ahmadinejad, Mashai's patron, soon received the same suspicious attitude from the Supreme Leader and his conservative supporters. In fact, Khamenei

---

[21] Translation of speech quoted from http://enduringamerica.com/2010/01/02/iran-document-mousavis-5-stages-to-resolution-statement-1-january/.

[22] See   http://www.enduringamerica.com/home/2011/4/22/iran-and-wikileaks-2010-esfandiar-rahim-mashai-a-key-advisor.html.

spoke publicly about a desire to do away with the (elected) presidency, so as to strengthen the Islamic Republic by strengthening the office of the Leader.[23] Ahmadinejad's lower-class base, fiercely nationalistic while sharing their standard-bearer's messianic beliefs, became a middle ground constituency. The president's followers became a threat to the fiercely pragmatic coalition of conservative scholars and top Revolutionary Guards brass.

This coalition, which focused mostly on remaining in power at all costs, saw the combination of messianism and social radicalism as its new enemy, and actively targeted Ahmadinejad and his supporters. The middle ground had been shattered by a radical surge, but quickly reformed and reestablished its presence.

Still, archconservatives dominated public discourse and assumed political power during Ahmadinejad's second term. The 2009 elections revealed that the most thorough challenge to middle ground politics stems directly from the middle ground itself. The confrontational potential of the middle ground nurtures the possibility of self-destruction. The catalyst is a state of middle ground crisis, when one extreme attempt to dominate the myriad voices engaged in friction. The conviction that faith is exclusively linked to the attainment of an ultimate goal undermines one of the primary tenets of Shiite Islam – the existence of the void created by the vanishing of the Twelfth Imam. The Shiite middle ground, as we have described it, defines faith as the struggle to create meaning from the void. Middle ground radicalization, on the other hand, uses faith to fill the void.

The 2013 Elections

The presidential elections of 2013, which brought Hassan Rouhani to the post, were, effectively, a referendum on the appeal of middle ground radicalization. Several prominent candidates had been disqualified prior to the election by the Council of Guardians. One of them was Mashai, Ahmadinejad's heir apparent. Another, unthinkably, was Hashemi Rafsanjani, one of the most powerful in Iran who had already served as president and was the perennial head of the Expediency Council. The official reason for his disqualification was his age, which would prevent him from effectively discharging the duties of the president.

Unofficially, the country was rife with rumor. Rafsanjani was known to have been critical of the violent repression exercised after the 2009 elections. His daughter, Faezeh, had been tried and found guilty of spreading propaganda against the Islamic Republic.[24] Many had spoken of Rafsnajani as the only candidate who could save Iran from the extremism of the radical leadership.

---

[23] See http://www.nytimes.com/2011/10/27/world/middleeast/in-iran-rivalry-khamenei-takes-on-presidency-itself.html.

[24] She would later be arrested to serve the sentence; see http://www.presstv.ir/detail/2012/09/24/263358/hashemi-rafsanjani-daughter-arrested/.

Upon news of his disqualification, on the eve of the campaign, it seemed certain that the radicals were about to cement their hold on power.

This gloomy forecast was compounded by the slate of candidates approved to run. There were seven candidates, and all but one had impeccable conservative credentials. Representing the most hardline, messianic elements was Said Jalili, who entered the campaign as Iran's chief nuclear negotiator with the international community. His opinions left no room for compromise on the nuclear issue, or on any other issue for that matter. Various pundits both inside and outside Iran claimed Jalili was the candidate favored by Supreme Leader Khamenei. Although the leader himself made no public display of sponsorship toward any candidate, Jalili's campaign grew louder and brasher after these predictions were made.

The only candidate with known Green Movement affiliations was Mohammadreza Aref, who had served as vice president in the administration of reformist president, Mohammad Khatami. The most dynamic opposition to Jalili came from the conservative and IRGC-affiliated mayor of Tehran, Mohammad Baqer Qalibaf. Whereas Jalili was seen as a conservative ideologue (particularly because he had no tangible political experience), Qalibaf was seen as a successful technocrat. He was considered a highly effective mayor, transforming the public vistas and city administration of Tehran. Qalibaf himself catered to the technocratic image by spreading mixed messages depending on his audience. He bragged to an IRGC audience about his participation in government suppression of various demonstrations, including the ones following the elections of 2009.[25] To a more provincial audience, he extolled his management credentials and his commitment to restoring "[t]ranquility and stability" to the country.[26]

After a heated campaign, which saw a debate and criticism among the candidates themselves reaching unprecedented levels, the winner came as a surprise. Although the commentators had noticed the candidacy of Hassan Rouhani, practically no one expected him to emerge triumphant. Among those who may have entertained the thought, no one foresaw a first-round victory, negating the need for a runoff generally thought unavoidable.

Rouhani seemed a known quantity. He was a *faqih*, a religious-legal scholar of junior rank, who also sported a PhD from Glasgow Caledonian University. He had served for many years as first secretary on Iran's Supreme National Security Council, and – after leaving the post – remained the Supreme Leader's personal representative on the council. Rouhani had also served as Iran's nuclear negotiator between 2003 and 2005. In 2011, he published an extensive memoir describing his nearly two years as negotiator, revealing much about

---

[25] See http://www.iranhumanrights.org/2013/05/ghalibaf_tape/.
[26] See http://beforeitsnews.com/alternative/2013/05/qalibaf-vows-to-solve-problems-in-2-yrs-2652428 .html.

the decision-making process involved and establishing him as a thoughtfully moderate conservative.[27]

Despite these stable, familiar credentials, his campaign proved to be an act of middle ground subversion. He took great care not to alienate any potential backers, most importantly the Supreme Leader. Often, his silences were as effective as his words. His rallies were a relatively safe haven for students and younger activists, who called publicly for the release of Green Movement leaders and political prisoners. (Rouhani did not join the cries, nor did he suppress them in any way.)

Still, his words spread a pronouncedly critical middle ground message. He spoke against the heightened security atmosphere all over the country, saying that as president he would expand Internet access, meddle less in affairs of public modesty, and strengthen Iran's contact with the world.[28] When other candidates attacked Jalili's conservative statements, Rouhani remained positive, stressing the need to solve the nuclear standoff through intense dialogue with the West. He stressed this commitment during his first press conference as president-elect.[29]

Rouhani's victory was stunning in breadth and depth. Kevan Harris describes it in the following words:

Rouhani won 50.7 percent of the more than 36 million votes cast (a turnout of 72.7 percent). The second-place candidate, Tehran mayor Mohammad Baqer Qalibaf, garnered only 16.6 percent. The patterns make plain the scale of the victory. In 19 of Iran's 31 provinces, Rouhani collected a higher percentage of votes than in Tehran. He won all the major provincial cities, including hometowns of rivals, and drew massive support from ethnic minorities. He took 81 percent of the vote in the small Kurdish county of Baneh on the Iraqi border and 86 percent in the Baluch county of Sarbaz adjacent to Pakistan. He had spoken of ethnic pluralism at his rallies, and people noticed. Meanwhile, though he was the sole cleric in the contest, Rouhani did relatively poorly – 38 percent of the vote – in the Shi'i seminary city of Qom. If his victory marked a "return to clerical power," as some American analysts tweeted, the theological center did not seem ecstatic about it.[30]

A thorough analysis of the 2013 elections is beyond the scope of this book. Their relevance for our discussion lies in their effective demonstration of the Iranian middle ground resilience. President Rouhani is not easily labeled a "reformist" or a "hardliner." Rouhani is committed to a constant engagement and communication of Iran's environment, rejecting isolation and closure. He

---

[27] For an instructive discussion of the memoir, see http://www.iranfocus.com/en/index. php?option=com_content&id=27907:what-will-irans-new-president-do-his-memoir-offers-some-clues&Itemid=32.

[28] See http://www.reuters.com/article/2013/07/03/us-iran-politics-idUSBRE9620AZ20130703.

[29] See http://www.reuters.com/article/2013/08/06/us-iran-rouhani-nuclear-idUSBRE9750LD20130806.

[30] See Harris's succinct, enlightening analysis of election results at http://www.merip.org/mero/mero071913.

is committed to similarly constant engagement and friction among the citizenry of the Islamic Republic, firm on reducing state control of social contact. Most importantly, he described his victory in clear-cut terms when he called it a "Victory for Moderation."[31]

Many Iranians considered boycotting the 2013 elections. Their decision to embrace Rouhani was seen by opponents of the Islamic Republic as at best a forced choice among poor and poorer options, and at worst a sham.[32] Their argument, voiced also by such dignitaries as Israel's PM, was that the Supreme Leader calls all the shots in the nondemocratic Islamic Republic, and that he chose to put a moderate face on Shiite fanaticism.

The 2013 elections serve as an effective demonstration of middle ground leadership and politics. Iranians rejected radical extremism, but did not opt for different extremism as a remedy. They overwhelmingly voted for a man who called for change from the inside. Moreover, his call for change was inspired by a desire for return to equilibrium, rather than the creation of a new system ex nihilo. His sense of moderation was mostly focused on discovering anew the bonds of Iranian and Shiite community. He dared to speak of "the world" not as a demonic entity which hates Iranians, but as a middle ground, an arena dependent on friction and contact for survival. Evaluated through the perpetual motion of the middle ground, Rouhani is a link in a chain rather than a "revolution." He demonstrates the maturation of the Shiite middle ground in Iran, and not its brutal suppression or its inevitable dissolution.

How does the middle ground resonate in different social and political circumstances? How might they be seen by non-state Shiite entities? The following chapter demonstrates how these ideas fare in a different political climates and social environment, that of Lebanese Hizballah.

---

[31] See http://www.reuters.com/article/2013/06/15/us-iran-election-idUSBRE95C1E120130615.
[32] See http://washingtonexaminer.com/linda-chavez-another-sham-election-in-iran/article/2531901.

8

Middle Ground as Resistance: Lebanese Hizballah

Lebanese Shiites have several "faces," but none is more prominent than that of Hizballah. Hizballah commands thousands of citizens as part of its armed militia, and sends representatives to the parliament and other government institutions in Beirut. Although Shiites have become a part of Lebanese politics, however, their political identity is grounded in tension between national affiliation and their communal heritage.

Much of this tension is embodied in the activities of Hizballah's leadership. Hizballah underwent a process of "opening" (*infitah*) in the early 1990s. The organization's visibility, especially that of Hassan Nasrallah, its General Secretary, has become significant. Still, the deliberations and activities of the organization's leadership are mostly covert. Observers estimate that at the highest level, key decisions are discussed by the seven-member *Shura* (Consultative) Council. Most of the Council's members have religious credentials. All of them are graduates of the Najaf religious seminaries, in Iraq, where they studied Khomeini's innovative perception of Shiite leadership.

The Shura Council is elected for life by the Central Council, which consists of nearly 200 religious and political leaders. Among them are also Hizballah's elected representatives to the Lebanese Parliament. Each of the *Shura* Council members is also the appointed head of the high administrative and decision-making bodies of Hizballah, such as the Political Bureau and the Military Commands. In turn, these senior officials select the members of these bodies, usually from the ranks of the Central Council.[1]

Hizballah's leadership, with its lengthy communal heritage of persecution and exclusion, is different from its Iranian counterpart. Iranian leadership operates within a coherent environment. All of the different spaces and strategic modes at work within Iranian society interact continuously because

[1] See Naim Qassem, *Hizbullah: The Story from Within* (Saqi Books, 2005), pp. 129–31.

they share a single framework defined and regulated by friction. In the case of Hizballah, this environmental coherence does not exist. Hizballah's environment is fragmented. Its power is not fully invested in the Lebanese state. The organization faces a major threat from Israel, and is often treated as an enemy by Lebanese security forces. In this state of affairs, the most accessible path to self-determination is resistance. Challenging the prevailing orders, in other words, becomes essential for the positive definition of identity. Resistance is not a means to a political end. It is the essence of survival.

Iranian leadership is present in all of the constituent spaces of Shiite society. This presence shapes community, state and frontier, and allows for dialogue between the three. Friction is practiced as dynamic consent. The presence of Hizballah's leadership is different. Hizballah's viewpoint on its environment is extraneous. A history of marginalization combined with a highly politicized communal consciousness seems to suggest an activist, aggressive strategy on the part of Lebanese Shiites toward the Christian Maronite and Sunni communities. This strategy, however, does not reflect total rejection. Hizballah cannot afford and does not wish to enter into a full confrontation with the state. Lebanese Shiites willingly adopt the civil identity common to all Lebanese citizens. Although this state of affairs may seem contradictory, it is the reality of Shiite life in Lebanon.

The necessity of neither fully rejecting nor totally accepting its environment creates for Hizballah what we define as a strategic mode of resistance. This mode originates in Hizballah's "primal" state – irresolvable tension between change and continuity. Both dynamics are necessary for Hizballah's survival. Therefore, the organization simultaneously applies the traditional strategic mode, affiliated with continuity, and the revolutionary strategic mode, affiliated with change. This simultaneity seems immanently paradoxical or anomalous. When applied together, both modes appear mutually exclusive. The organization, for example, has entered negotiations with Israel regarding prisoner exchanges. In Hizballah's case, this is revolutionary strategic behavior. At the same time, Hizballah carried out an armed attack on Israeli personnel, which amounts to traditional strategic behavior for the organization.

How is it that Hizballah does not succumb to the temptation of adopting a single strategic mode? After all, Hizballah seems cut from the most extreme of cloths. Hizballah's diverse worldview seems to provide an answer. The strategic preference of one mode over the other is the main threat to Hizballah's existences. Grand strategy is a privilege denied to minorities. If they win, they risk losing their distinct identity. Should they lose, the minority stands a good chance of being obliterated.

It is the conformist strategic mode, the mode associated with minimizing the drawbacks of the existing order, which becomes the most effective form of resistance against the sway of radical action and ideology. Contrary to conventional wisdom, Hizballah does not reduce its difficulties by striving for harmony. It is resistance which alleviates the organization's most pressing concerns. Neither wholly accepting nor fully rejecting the traditional and revolutionary logics, the conformist mode prevents Hizballah from capitulating to the demands of ultimate visions. The conformist mode enables the existence of friction, that is, simultaneous confrontation, cooperation and competition. Hizballah's leadership is, thus, able to apply strategic resistance without comprising its integrity and influence on reality.

Throughout the twentieth century, the Shiite community in Lebanon emerged from its relative marginalization, gradually entering the political fray and becoming one of the most significant parties in the political arenas of the Lebanese state, the Arab world, and the Middle East. We will briefly follow this process, highlighting critical junctures and focusing on the emergence of Shiite leadership.

The Shiite Awakening

During the first half of the twentieth century, Lebanese Shiites faced two notable obstacles – the composition of the Lebanese government and the weakness of the Shiite scholars. Lebanon was initially formed as a political entity under a French mandate, following World War I and the collapse of the Ottoman Empire in 1923. An independent Lebanese state was created in 1943. Officially, it was ruled by a multi-confessional National Accord, designed to maintain the relationship between the various religious communities. Informally, Lebanon was ruled by an alliance of the Maronite Christians – protégés of the French – and the Sunnis.[2] Lebanese institutional space was dominantly nationalist. Religious politics were generally shunned.

The ongoing struggle between Israelis and Palestinians added to the difficulties of the Shiite community. Several thousand PLO activists, deported from Jordan in 1971, settled in Southern Lebanon and transformed it into their base of operations.[3] Thus, many clashes between Israelis and Palestinians took place on Lebanese soil. The Lebanese Civil War, which began in 1975, uprooted many Shiite communities. Toward the end of the 1970s, the Shiite population in Lebanon concentrated in the Beqa'a Valley in the south of Lebanon and in the *Dahiya* neighborhood of Beirut.

Perhaps, the most important political leader of the Shiite community at the time was Musa al-Sadr. Al-Sadr, scion of a prominent scholarly family, was born and educated in Iran.[4] He came to Lebanon in 1955 as an attempt by the scholarly leaders to revitalize communal structure. Al-Sadr was the first Shiite

---

[2] To add to the frustration of the Shiites in Lebanon, this system did not take into account the Shiites' real portion of the population, nor did it provide an adjustment mechanism facing future demographic changes; the Shiites were therefore forced to accept a representation system that discriminated against them and which they could not possibly change by political means.

[3] See Mishal, *The PLO under Arafat*, p. 15.

[4] See Ajami, *The Vanished Imam*, pp. 29–51.

leader to address the plight of Lebanese Shiites in political fashion. In 1974, he formed "The Movement of the Disinherited," a broad social movement aimed at creating political impact.

In 1975, al-Sadr formed *Amal*, the first Shiite activist political party, which attempted to rally the Shiite community behind two banners. The first was a reform of the Lebanese state by elevating the political status of the Shiite population. The second was a reform of community affairs by challenging the land-owning elite. However, al-Sadr did not adopt exclusionary rhetoric. Rather, al-Sadr chose to forge an alliance with the Maronite Christians.[5]

His leadership drew authority from his religious credentials. Yet, al-Sadr focused his efforts on increasing Shiite influence within the Lebanese state. Built on the foundation of acknowledged difference, al-Sadr felt that disregard for Shiite interests served as the only bonding agents for Sunnis and Christians. He was determined to change this state of affairs. Al-Sadr led mass rallies and attempted to initiate parliamentary legislation meant to improve the living conditions and political clout of Lebanese Shiites. He drew his power from the unique combination of religious scholarly skills and familial prestige alongside acute political awareness.

In 1978, while on a visit to Libya, al-Sadr disappeared. He was apparently kidnapped by henchman of the Mu'ammar Qaddafi, the Libyan tyrant. Following Qaddafi's removal from power in 2011, it was revealed that al-Sadr had spent long years in a secret Libyan prison, finally succumbing to illness and the harsh conditions of his incarceration. Al-Sadr's successor, Nabih Berri, could not claim al-Sadr's unique qualities or credentials. His political demeanor and agenda were not religious. Those within *Amal* who felt the need for a stronger link to Iran's Islamic Republic split with the movement in 1982 to form Hizballah, the Party of God.[6]

The period beginning in 1978 was one of critical instability and flux for Lebanese Shiites. The civil war, the disappearance of al-Sadr, the Israeli incursion of 1978 and the 1979 Islamic Revolution in Iran all brought the Lebanese Shiite community to the brink of disintegration. The Lebanese state was incapacitated by the fighting on several fronts simultaneously. The rise of Khomeini in Iran emphasized the obstacles faced by Lebanese religious leaders. Whereas these Iranian were engaged in local political pursuits, Khomeini led a movement committed to forging anew the bridge between the community and the frontier.

Against this backdrop, Hizballah made its claim to leadership. Unlike its Iranian antecedents, Hizballah did not identify itself with the existing structure of the state. Instead, it chose a path of challenge and resistance. Exploring case studies dealing with Hizballah's relations with Syria, Israel, and the Lebanese state, we demonstrate the ways in which Hizballah applies conformist behavior to maintain a position of resistance.

[5] Ibid., pp. 85–122.
[6] See Qassem, *Hizbullah*, pp. 14–19; Norton, *Hezbollah – A Short History*, pp. 20–2.

Syria

Syria practically ruled Lebanon for almost twenty years, following the end of the Lebanese civil war in 1989. During this period and until the withdrawal of its forces in 2005, Syria's power allowed Hizballah to prosper. Since the Syrian withdrawal, Hizballah has remained the principal pro-Syrian element in Lebanon. This state of affairs is complemented by the fact that Syria is Iran's most prominent state ally in the Middle East. Most of Iran's military aid to Hizballah is transferred by Syrian means. Hassan Nasrallah, who became the leader of Hizballah in 1992, expanded the relations between Syria and his organization.

Syria continued to support Hizballah in the face of considerable international condemnation and possible ostracism. When tested, however, Hizballah applied both traditional and revolutionary strategies toward Syria, and this application was regulated by conformist resistance. The first significant test came with the assassination of the Lebanese PM, Rafiq Hariri, in 2005.

The Assassination of Rafiq Hariri

The sequence of events which led to the assassination of Prime Minister Rafiq Hariri and the withdrawal of Syrian forces from Lebanon, both in 2005, demonstrates Hizballah's strategy of resistance. UN Security Council Resolution 1559, adopted toward the end of 2004, called on the Lebanese government to disband and disarm all militias. Its approval was followed by a heightened awareness and involvement in the Lebanese-Syrian issue by the international community.[7]

Lebanon's Prime Minister at the time was Rafiq Hariri, a billionaire construction tycoon with powerful Saudi contacts. Hariri staunchly opposed Syrian involvement in Lebanese affairs. His opposition to Syria and support for Resolution 1559 allegedly cost him his life. He was assassinated in a bombing attack on February 14, 2005. His death was followed by vociferous international protest, calling for the establishment of an investigative tribunal under UN auspices.

Following the assassination, a massive popular protest formed against the Syrian presence in Lebanon. The political coalition which arose from this popular movement called itself the "March 14" alliance, and was backed by international support.[8] This coalition negotiated a historic withdrawal of Syrian troops from Lebanon. The debate concerning the implementation of Resolution 1559 and the establishment of the international tribunal were the two most acrid political issues in Lebanese politics. Syria's allies opposed both issues.

---

[7] For a description of the evidence gathered with regard to the assassination, as well as ongoing cases, UN documentation, and other materials, see the Web site for the Special Tribunal for Lebanon: http://www.stl-tsl.org/.

[8] See http://www.14march.org/.

Hizballah had good reasons to oppose Resolution 1559, which effectively meant its disarmament. Without Syrian military presence in Lebanon, the organization was far more vulnerable to a political alignment which could lead to its marginalization. This scenario seemed quite possible, taking into account the criticism propounded by many March 14 leaders regarding Hizballah's possession of arms and its independent activity against Israel.

The pullout of Syrian forces presented Nasrallah with a major challenge. He was no longer obligated to upholding Syrian interests. Denied Syrian protection, he had to redefine Hizballah's identity within the new political system. Nasrallah's considerations were influenced by Syria's growing isolation, the result of Syrian aid to Lebanese militias and Syria's close relations with Iran.

In 2005, Hizballah was presented with the opportunity to politically support the causes dear to Syria, most pressing among them the issue of the international tribunal for the investigation of the murder of Hariri and Security Council Resolution 1559. Although the political debate was divided on the question of support for Syria, Hizballah did not directly declare its support for any of the parties. The organization sided with the Lebanese government, calling for a withdrawal of Syrian forces.[9]

This signified a change in Hizballah's strategic behavior. Until then, the organization had vocally criticized the Lebanese government. Following the election of 2005, Hizballah agreed to enter the March 14th government and accept ministerial positions. At first glance, such policy appears to cater to immediate needs. Still, we suggest these actions indicate that Hizballah's rationale was being transformed. From an immediate endorsement of Syrian causes, Hizballah's leadership began to apply a strategy we have defined as conformist resistance

In the early months of 2007, Hizballah's supporters held mass rallies and rioted in the middle of Beirut. The riots, initiated in response to the anti-Syrian and anti-militia initiatives of the March 14th government, were seen by many as an attempt at a coup d'etat. However, the violence ceased after several days. It was Hizballah's leadership that had initiated the unrest that stopped the riots and called off the demonstrators.[10]

How can one explain these seemingly contradictory policies, with one hand striking violently and the other held out in reconciliation? Some observers understood this behavior to be inconsistent. That is, Hizballah's behavior was deemed devoid of strategic coherence. According to our argument, these events demonstrate Hizballah's worldview of conformist resistance.

In the fragile state of Lebanese politics following the 2005 Syrian withdrawal, Hizballah could not afford to adopt a clear-cut strategy which fully

---

[9] For an analysis of Hizballah's strategy following the 2005 Lebanese elections, see http://emperors-clothes.com/archive/hez.htm.

[10] For an on-the-scene description of the riots, see http://www.michaeltotten.com/archives/001369.html.

accepted or completely rejected the emerging political order. This state, in turn, called for a working formula based on a calculated rationale of resistance. Although a position of resistance was not new for Hizballah, post-2005 Lebanon represents the first time this resistance was applied in a conformist manner. To maintain authority and sustainability, Hizballah's leadership acknowledged the existing order in limited fashion. One might say that the integrity of Hizballah's political affiliations, be they to the Lebanese state or to the Syrian regime, became dependent on the organization's potential for simultaneously subverting these orders.

In the case at hand, this is discernible with regard to both Syria and Lebanon. When Hizballah joined the call for Syrian withdrawal in 2005, it appeared to affirm the new Lebanese administration. Hizballah, however, did not renounce its pro-Syrian attitude. Thus, when it entered the Lebanese government, Hizballah was in a position to promote Syrian interests from the heart of Lebanese power. One cannot ascribe to Hizballah an overriding commitment to either of these ends. Both strategic ends were inextricably linked. Neither could exist alone.

According to this logic, Hizballah's leadership needed to become a part of the Lebanese state in order to subvert it. Similarly, the leadership needed to express reservations regarding Syrian interests in order to advance them. Hizballah thus both affirmed and negated its political reality. This juxtaposition of the traditional and revolutionary strategic modes, simultaneously endorsing both change and continuity, was regulated by resistance in the conformist mode. One tends to think of resistance as being directed against an existing order, in support of an alternative vision. In the case of Hizballah, life in the middle ground takes the form of conformist resistance.

Israel

Hassan Nasrallah, Hizballah's General Secretary, had the following to say with regard to Israel: "As for Israel, in our opinion and planning it will remain an illegal entity, illegitimate, temporary, and cancerous ... therefore we will join with other elements opposed to normalization with this entity since the struggle against normalization will hinder Israel's transformation into a regional superpower."[11] The struggle against Israel reflects a wide array of issues. These include armed conflict, strategic arms build-up, support for the Palestinian struggle and tacit understandings with Israel meant to stabilize the Israeli-Lebanese border.

Hizballah adopts competing policies on diverse issues. It is motivated by the middle ground logic of neither fully accepting nor totally rejecting existing

---

[11] Nasrallah's interview in *Al Ahram* (February 16, 2000) as cited in Daniel Sobelman, *New Rules of the Game: Israel and Hizbollah after the Withdrawal from Lebanon* (Jaffee Center for Strategic Studies, Tel Aviv University, Memorandum 65, 2003), p. 27 (in Hebrew).

orders. Similarly to the Syrian case, resistance here is not aimed toward extreme goals. Instead, Hizballah's approach toward these issues in juxtaposition affirms and maintains the sustainability of middle ground reality.

We present Hizballah's relationship with Israel as a spectrum, stretching between military conflict and diplomatic negotiation. We discuss the political and military effects of the 2000 Israeli withdrawal and the 2006 war between Lebanon and Israel on the Israeli-Hizballah relations. We also discuss Hizballah's middle ground politics as they were reflected in the negotiations between Israel and the organization regarding prisoner exchanges during the 2000–2008 period.

Border Clashes

Hizballah's military operations against the Israeli army were originally meant to force the latter to leave Lebanon. Once this goal had been accomplished in 2000, Hizballah's leadership deepened its strategy of conformist resistance. The organization intensified its two seemingly contradictory strategies. First, Hizballah engaged in direct military conflict with Israel along the international border. Second, Hizballah sought to continue acting along the lines of the tacit understandings first reached with the Israeli authorities in 1996. These understandings included agreements to cease armed hostilities according to accepted limits. However, both sides interpreted the understandings in self-serving ways.

Following the 2000 withdrawal, Hizballah launched numerous operations against Israel.[12] The organization undertook considerable effort to justify each attack. The most popular justifications included the attacks' contribution to the affirmation of Lebanese sovereignty. That is, Hizballah claimed that its attacks serve Lebanese national interests on various fronts ranging from the liberation of disputed territory to punishing Israel for having its fighters fly through Lebanese airspace.

Between 2000 and 2006, Hizballah also increased its military deterrence potential by acquiring a wide range of "strategic weapons." Among these were medium-range rockets such as the Iranian *zilzal* and *fajr* missiles, Syrian-improved "extended-range" Katyusha, modern anti-tank weapons systems, and so on.[13] The fact that the organization possessed weapons able to reach cities in northern Israel, certainly added to Hizballah's deterrence factor in this conflict.

Simultaneously, Hizballah and Israel continued to operate according to a series of tacit understandings first formulated in April 1996. The ground rule of these understandings was that no side may attack civilians. Still, Hizballah maneuvered to identify causes for its military actions against civilians and soldiers alike, so as not to appear in breach of the understandings. Such was

---

[12] See http://www.meforum.org/499/the-return-of-hizbullah.

[13] For a full list, see Andrew Exum, "Hizballah at War," Policy Focus #63, The Washington Institute (December 2006), p. 63; available online at http://www.washingtoninstitute.org/policy-analysis/view/hizballah-at-war-a-military-assessment.

Hizballah's need for legitimacy, that it cited Israeli treatment of the Palestinians in the West Bank and the Gaza Strip as its motivation for military actions.

Hizballah's strategy of conformist resistance was very much apparent between 2000 and 2006. According to Ahmad Hamzeh, The organization launched more than 5,000 operations.[14] Faced with the Israeli occupation of Southern Lebanon, Hizballah was fully committed to all-out armed resistance with a clear goal – remove the occupying forces. When the political order changed with the 2000 Israeli withdrawal, however, Hizballah could not completely reject the new territorial reality, just as it could not wholly accept it. Therefore, while Hizballah continued its military attacks, their number decreased significantly. The attacks no longer sought simply to occupy territory or kill Israeli troops. They were now carefully planned, executed, and justified so as to appear legitimate and warranted. Hizballah remained on the attack, but without committing exclusively to the military path.

Conversely, Hizballah's tacit understandings with Israel, initially reached before the withdrawal, remained permanently less-than-comprehensive. The rules established were seen by Hizballah as milestones meant to be surpassed. Hizballah's leaders maintained a continuous dialogue with Israel via the services of international mediators, but were still willing to breach the understandings when legitimate opportunity and motive presented themselves. Hizballah did not resolve itself to full negotiations with Israel, acknowledging the importance of understandings while simultaneously destabilizing them through military action.

It was conformist resistance which allowed Hizballah's leadership to regulate this tension. The organization could not afford a full-fledged war with Israel, nor could it survive the public image of an appeaser. Maintaining both attacks and dialogue with Israel became feasible strategy. This state of affairs could exist when both strategies were applied and subverted simultaneously.

The 2006 War and Its Aftermath

Following the Israeli withdrawal, Israel assumed that Hizballah would not use its rocket and missile arsenal unless it felt existentially threatened. The organization declared 2006 to be "the year of the prisoners." Hizballah then kidnapped two Israeli soldiers in order to ransom Lebanese prisoners kept in Israeli jails. In stark contrast to Hizballah's assessment, Israel invaded Lebanon, specifically targeting Hizballah personnel and installations with all its might. The Israeli Air Force quickly destroyed the organization's long-range missiles. Later on, Israeli planes systematically demolished the *Dahiya*, Beirut's Shiite neighborhood and Hizballah stronghold.[15]

---

[14] See Ahmad Nizar Hamzeh, *In the Path of Hizballah* (Syracuse University Press, 2004), pp. 89–99.

[15] For two opposing views of the bombing, and particularly of Israel's "Dahiya Doctrine" regarding potential destruction of civilian areas in retaliation for attacks on the Israeli civilian heartland,

Israel's response was seen by the organization as threatening its very existence. Still, Hizballah's leadership held to the strategy of conformist resistance while adapting it to the changing circumstances. The reality of war seemed to demand one of two possible outcomes. Hizballah could win, for example, by forcing Israel to cease hostilities. The organization could also lose, for example, by being driven from its strongholds in Southern Lebanon or by being eliminated as an influential actor on the Lebanese stage. Hizballah's leadership, however, refrained from making such a dichotomous choice. Hassan Nasrallah defined victory as a combination of attrition and survival.[16] How was this definition realized on the ground?

The organization's leadership translated its rocket arsenal, so far used as deterrence, into actual military power. Hizballah wished to cause attrition among Israeli troops, but also on the Israeli home front. The organization assumed that such domestic attrition would pressure Israel's leaders to end their military actions. During the war, Hizballah's strategic goal was to deny Israel any real achievements. In fact, this denial was defined by the organization's leadership as victory. Hizballah was thus able to resist the Israeli initiative without clearly defining victory or failure.

This strategy characterized Hizballah's war tactics as well. The organization's regular paramilitary forces denied the Israel Defense Forces (IDF) territorial gains as much as they could. At this stage, the Shiite fighters typically melted away into the countryside, their fortified bunkers or "nature reserves." The organization's tactical performance mirrored the leadership's commitment to conformist resistance. Hizballah's units fought in a decentralized manner. Each unit was given a similar mission of defending specific territory. Typically, this was the village from which most of the unit's fighters hailed. Fighting units were also provided with the resources required for this mission. The unit was then left to determine the exact timing and tactical choices best fit for this mission. The situational logic inherent in conformist resistance, rejecting superimposed notions of victory and defeat, is reflected in this tactical insight.[17]

Following the war, conformist resistance took on yet another form. In his first speech after the end of hostilities, Nasrallah declared victory in brief, cursory fashion: "First of all, I do not want to assess or discuss in detail what we are currently witnessing, but I want to say briefly and without exaggeration that we stand before a strategic and historical victory for Lebanon – all of Lebanon, for the resistance, and for the whole nation."[18] The great majority of his speech was devoted to Lebanon's reconstruction efforts. He demanded that

---

see http://www.jpost.com/Features/FrontLines/Article.aspx?id=167167 (pro-Israeli) and http://electronicintifada.net/content/israels-dahiya-doctrine-comes-gaza/8006 (anti-Israeli).

[16] See http://www.opendemocracy.net/article/the-hizbollah-project-last-war-next-war.

[17] For an analysis of Hizballah's tactics during the war, see http://www.jamestown.org/single/?no_cache=1&tx_ttnews[tt_news]=860.

[18] Quote drawn from http://arabist.net/archives/2006/08/16/nasrallahs-speech-full-text/.

such efforts begin immediately, and defined the victory of the resistance in its survival.

Prisoner Exchanges

During the period discussed (2000–2008), Hizballah and Israel carried out several rounds of negotiations regarding Palestinian and Lebanese prisoners held in Israeli jails, as well as Israelis captured by Hizballah.[19] The strategy of negotiation stands opposed to the organization's repeated armed clashes with Israel along the Lebanese-Israeli border. The adoption of competing strategies enabled Hizballah's leadership to occupy its position of conformist resistance. Whereas the Lebanese and Arab environment seemed to seethe with confrontation, Hizballah's leadership advocated negotiations. It could thus present itself as caring genuinely for the interests of common Lebanese. Still, when Arab regimes sought understandings with Israel, Hizballah could continue to pursue aggression, thus presenting itself as the guardian of Arab dignity.

The two most significant peaks in the negotiations between Hizballah and Israel were the 2004 and 2008 prisoner exchange deals. These deals were the culmination of lengthy, elaborate negotiations. The deals were preceded by three Hizballah attacks in which five Israeli soldiers and one civilian were kidnapped. The attacks served the organization's aggressive strategies, but were also perpetrated in order to enable a channel of negotiations. Both strategic ends, armed struggle, and understandings, were served. Still, neither was clearly preferred over the other.

The 2004 deal followed two kidnapping operations in 2000. Hizballah kidnapped three Israeli soldiers near the border and later snatched Elchanan Tennenbaum, a retired Artillery Colonel, while he was on business abroad. By 2004, the negotiations led to the release of 436 prisoners by Israel, including 400 Palestinians, 23 Lebanese, a German Muslim, and several other Arab nationals, as well as the remains of 59 Lebanese soldiers. Hizballah turned over the remains of three Israeli soldiers it kidnapped in 2000 and released Tennenbaum. The most remarkable achievement of this deal for Hizballah was the release of Sheikh Abdul Karim Obeid and Sheikh Mustafa Dirani, two of Hizballah's most senior members, who were kidnapped by Israel in 1989 and 1994, respectively.[20]

The sizable difference between the price paid by Hizballah and that paid by Israel represented, for the organization, the fruits of conformist resistance. The efficacy of Hizballah's attacks was demonstrated in the extent of its diplomatic achievements, rather than in Israeli casualties or territorial losses. The exchange, so significantly in Hizballah's favor, demonstrated the benefits of constantly challenging the powers that be.

---

[19] For an interesting analysis of the negotiations, see http://www.opendemocracy.net/article/the-israel-hizbollah-prisoner-deal.

[20] See http://www.jewishvirtuallibrary.org/jsource/Society_&_Culture/prisonerswap012904.html.

The exchange itself took place on January 30, 2004. Ten days prior to the deal, while the negotiations were taking place via German mediation, Hizballah attacked an Israeli bulldozer that allegedly crossed the border (the "Blue Line") and killed one IDF soldier. These events demonstrate another aspect of conformist resistance. At its most effective, conformist resistance abandons conventional modes of thought and action. It is applied in tension with conventional wisdom. This tension expands the scope of Hizballah's maneuvers and allows it to remain both in and out of its environment.

The second prisoner deal, in 2008, followed the 2006 war between Israel and Hizballah. The war was sparked by a Hizballah attack on an Israeli patrol. Two Israeli soldiers were kidnapped, and eight died in the attack and retaliation efforts on the same day. The two kidnapped soldiers apparently died soon after the attack. Hizballah held their corpses for two years, waiting for a suitable deal. After prolonged negotiations, the organization exchanged the corpses for Lebanon's longest-serving prisoner in Israel, Samir Quntar. Quntar had been in jail since being apprehended after a terror attack in 1974. The organization also received several Palestinian prisoners, as well as Hizballah fighters captured during the 2006 war.[21]

The prisoner exchange of 2008 reflects the communal origins of conformist resistance. The radical transformation of the Shiite community in Lebanon – from marginalization to significant political influence – strengthened the role of communal practices in Shiite political conduct. The community's innate ability to encapsulate contradiction alongside its informal structure of authority made the politicized communal space of Lebanese Shiites remarkably conducive to conformist resistance.

This was the dominant theme in Nasrallah's speech upon receiving the prisoners. At the beginning of his speech he welcomed all Lebanese and Iranian dignitaries "to this wedding ceremony." Later, the speech was interspersed with expressions of communal solidarity and belonging:

We remember the perseverance of our people, those whose homes were destroyed; those who had to leave their homes; those who suffered a lot ... this perseverance is the main factor, the biggest factor which contributed to achieving this prisoner swap.... In addition to these, the families of the detainees and the martyrs, the honorable families who put their trust in us, who had confidence in us. These families helped and contributed.... This victory is your victory, it is your achievement.[22]

Hizballah received some political criticism from Lebanese politicians after the prisoner deals: "How is it that some of us have the right to conduct negotiations ... with Israel, while the state ... is accused of collaborating with the enemy?" asked Walid Junblatt, a Druze leader of the March 14 governing

---

[21] For a thorough analysis of the deal, see http://electronicintifada.net/content/israel-hizballah-prisoner-deal/7619.

[22] Quoted in: MEMRI special dispatch, July 17, 2008

faction. It is this critique that leads us to another arena in which Hizballah applies conformist resistance – the politics of the Lebanese state.

Lebanese State Politics

Lebanese politics were reinvented in 1989 after the end of the civil war. The Ta'if agreement, which marked a new era for relations between the diverse religious communities of Lebanon, also heralded a new beginning for Hizballah. Prior to the agreement, the organization rejected the political and social system of the country, and its strategy could largely be described as revolutionary, in the sense of actively striving to bring about regime change. During the period between its foundation in 1982 and the end of the civil war in 1989, Hizballah operated under direct Iranian supervision and identified itself much more with the Islamic Republic than with the Lebanese state. Since 1989, Hizballah has increasingly promoted itself as Lebanese and Arab.[23]

Even before the end of the civil war in 1989, there were voices within Hizballah that called for greater involvement in Lebanese politics. The end of hostilities bolstered these voices. As soon as Lebanon's state institutions became more viable and functional, Hizballah sought a greater role in the political system.

The 2000 elections in Lebanon ended with Hizballah becoming the largest block in Parliament and dominating most municipalities in Shiite areas in South Lebanon and the Beqa'a valley. This came as a direct result of the Israeli withdrawal that same year. The Lebanese public credited Hizballah with direct responsibility for the Israeli withdrawal. This increased the organization's popularity outside the Shiite community as well. Hizballah did not fight Israel as a Lebanese national force, but as a sectorial guerilla organization. Still, the results of this struggle were Hizballah's ticket to a place of prominence in Lebanese politics. The organization simultaneously pursued two competing ends, each destabilizing and affirming the other. This was a position of conformist resistance.

Once acknowledged as a legitimate political entity, Hizballah's criticism against the government wore the face of anti-Western rhetoric. This platform allowed the organization to forge multiple and changing alliances with other political forces in the country. Hizballah joined the labor unions of Shiite *Amal*, the Socialist party, and the Maronite Christian and Sunni factions in denouncing foreign and sectarian involvement in trade relations.[24] These domestic alliances were not meant to promote a particular agenda. Hizballah was primarily concerned with weakening the existing order without committing itself to a unilateral struggle that may endanger its other activities.

---

[23] For a timeline of Iran-Hizballah relations, see http://www.irantracker.org/military-activities/iran-lebanese-hezbollah-relationship-tracker-2012. For a concise discussion of Iranian-Lebanese relations, see http://iranprimer.usip.org/resource/iran-and-lebanon.

[24] *Ahd Al-Intiqad*, April 22, 2005.

The necessity of maintaining tangible tension as a part of conformist resistance is reflected in Hizballah's behavior toward the Lebanese political establishment. Hizballah's street rallies in late 2006 and early 2007 are a case in point. At these rallies, Nasrallah called on his supporters to besiege the government compounds in Beirut, after the national government attempted to limit Hizballah's power and popularity, which grew significantly after the war with Israel. Hundreds of thousands responded to his call. Still, Nasrallah pointedly forbade any expression of violence and called for full cooperation with the army.[25]

Within Lebanese politics, tension was preserved by a display of Hizballah's rapid mobilization and mass political commitment. When directed at Israel, the policy of maintaining tension took the form of lethal attacks in the midst of peace negotiations. In both cases, the organization's ability to carry out the unexpected without bringing about the collapse of the existing order helped maintain its position of conformist resistance.

The strategy of conformist resistance is far from an instrumental one. Conformist resistance has become Hizballah's second nature, the common thread linking Hizballah's behavioral patterns. The organization holds true to conformist resistance even when discussing its most precious asset, the very thing which allows it an independent existence – its weapons and military presence in Lebanon. Hizballah's declarations regarding its weapons have made it clear that the organization understands its armed status to be non-negotiable.[26] On other issues, Hizballah is ready to compromise and acknowledge the limits imposed by the Lebanese polity, particularly when it is favorable to him.[27] Still, Hizballah appears ready to engage other parties in negotiations concerning its military capabilities, although the scope of these negotiations is not clear. While still denying any intent to disarm, Nasrallah declared in 2005 that "we agreed that the resistance, its weapons and its role will be subject to internal national dialogue" on a basis of a discussion on "all fundamental issues."[28] Nasrallah has expressed his impassioned commitment to conformist resistance in many speeches and declarations. His words from May, 2008, demonstrate the extent to which conformist resistance has become the principal tenet of Hizballah's worldview:

In the July [2006] war … our most important power element was the command and control, since the communications between the leadership, the posts and the battle sites in the field were safe.… [In their decision on the illegitimacy of Hizballah's network] they used the same words of the American Foreign Ministry. They are their followers and committed to their orders.… This decision, first and foremost, is a declaration of war and opening of war from the part of the government of Walid Junblatt … for the

[25] See http://www.english.moqawama.org/essaydetailsf.php?eid=722&fid=11.
[26] See http://www.aljazeera.com/news/middleeast/2012/01/20121154542742500.html.
[27] See http://www.rohama.org/en/news/3977/sayyed-hasan-nasrallah-hails-new-lebanese-government.
[28] *Ahd Al-Intiqad*, April 15, 2005.

American and Israeli interest.... I am not declaring war here; I declare a decision for self-defense.... Whoever wants dialogue, we are ready for dialogue.[29]

Hizballah and the Diversity of the Middle Ground

Following the war with Israel in 2006, Hizballah has kept firmly on the path of conformist resistance. The organization has seen its parliamentary delegation decrease in numbers after the June 2009 elections. Still, its power and influence have hardly been damaged. Hizballah has only two ministers in the Lebanese cabinet, but in early December 2009, the Lebanese parliament established a National Unity Government which allowed Hizballah to keep its weapons.[30] This ensures Hizballah's autonomy and allows its leadership room for diverse activity bypassing the Lebanese state. The organization has taken part in squabbles between Shiites and Sunnis, yet it has maintained and even enhanced its image as a national Lebanese movement. Hizballah's national status has deteriorated since the organization began its participation in the Syrian conflict. Hizballah's aid to the Assad regime has not been received well by Sunni and Christian Lebanese.

Hizballah draws it's organizational and political viability from the long-term application of conformist resistance in different situations. The evolving Shiite order in Lebanon simultaneously challenges and draws inspiration from the Islamic Republic of Iran. The distinct strategies of friction management in Iran and Lebanon – by participation and assembly and by conformist resistance – are expressions of the new Shiite politics of the middle ground. Both strategies became politically active in response to the dominant state visions promulgated by the Pahlavi Shahs in Iran and by the Maronite-Sunni coalition in Lebanon.

The difference between Shiite middle ground politics in Iran and in Lebanon is rooted in widely divergent historical circumstances. Born with the Safavid Empire in the early sixteenth century, the Shiite religious establishment in Iran enjoyed the support of the state. As the state rose in power and authority, both identities continued to exist simultaneously. During the twentieth century, the Pahlavi Shahs of Iran attempted to disrupt this balance in favor of the state.

In the 1960s, the Iranian state under Mohammad Reza Shah Pahlavi mounted a monolithic challenge to the parallel nature of Iranian society. Mohammad Reza Shah sought to eliminate competing centers of power and to subjugate them to his monarchy. This challenge forced prominent religious scholars to recast their Shiite identity in a political mold. Many scholars chose to support the Pahlavi state. Still, the vision that prevailed considered Shiism

---

[29] See Nasrallah's speech of May 8, 2008 (authors' translation): http://www.youtube.com/watch?v=6hRwn3kJ_xE.

[30] For additional information on this issue, see http://www.nytimes.com/2009/12/11/world/middleeast/11lebanon.html?_r=1&ref=hezbollah.

redefined as middle ground politics as a viable alternative to the state logic of the Pahlavis.

Middle ground politics in Iran were based on mutual recognition by disparate elements and an attempt to regulate a dynamic equilibrium between them. Although the Islamic Republic has led a tumultuous existence, for the most part it has practiced and sought friction. In fact, the demonstrators who took to the streets following the presidential elections of 2009, perceived themselves as the defenders of the middle ground against a radical attack.

In Lebanon, Hizballah's political reality was quite different from the Iranian case. Lebanese Shiites did not consider themselves to be full participants in the Lebanese polity. Moreover, they perceived the Lebanese state as transient at best. This state of affairs was conducive to a politics of resistance.

The Lebanese Shiite community traditionally played a marginal role in Lebanese history. It willfully isolated itself, and its members were often poor and disadvantaged. Lebanese Sunnis oriented themselves toward the Islamic world, and Lebanon's Maronite Christians were closely linked to Europe. The Shiite community, however, remained removed from the core of power even after the Lebanese state had been established. Shiite communal solidarity did not grow alongside the state.

This pattern continued after the founding of Lebanon in 1943. While the Shiites were citizens of the Lebanese state, the community was still led by local, semi-feudal nobles. During the period between Lebanon's foundation and the breakout of civil war in 1975, however, Lebanese politics grew turbulent. The fragile balance between religious denominations was destabilized and the traditional division of power was challenged. Lebanese Shiites responded to this challenge by undergoing a rapid process of politicization in the 1960s and early 1970s. The new Shiite political movement was directed at radically altering the existing social order.

The attempts of Lebanese Shiites to gain influence were motivated by a desire to look after their communal interests. At a later stage, especially during the Lebanese civil war (1975–1989), Lebanese Shiites presented themselves as caretakers and defenders of "Arab dignity." This claim rose again following Israel's withdrawal from Lebanon in 2000 and the war with Israel in 2006. The relationship of the Lebanese Shiite community with the Lebanese state remained negotiable.

The radicalization of Lebanese politics in the 1960s and 1970s encouraged Lebanese Shiites to join the political fray. The state challenged the Shiite community to reinvent itself. The Shiite response was one of defiance and criticism, rather than consent and compliance. Iranian Shiite leaders made the conceptual leap from community to state without much effort, as their authority and legitimacy equaled or surpassed those of the existing state. In Lebanon, however, the political authority of Shiite leaders was built on their defiance of the state and on their ability to safeguard the interests of the Shiite community while in conflict with the state.

Still, the close affinity between Iranian and Lebanese Shiite leaders remains apparent. Iran has backed Hizballah since the latter's foundation in the early 1980s. Hizballah, in turn, continues to express its loyalty to the Khomeini's doctrine of *velayat-e faqih* (the governance of the jurist). Hizballah's members were trained by Iranians and operate Iranian armaments. Hizballah has often been treated as an Iranian proxy, realizing Tehran's will to directly take on Israel in military fashion.[31] This interpretation sits well with an attempt to portray Iranian Shiite leadership as possessing and applying a coherent plan of regional domination and ideological struggle.

However, as the middle ground will, reality offers diverse, seemingly contradictory conclusions. An interview given by Nasrallah in February 2012 surprised many pundits in Israel and abroad. In the interview, Nasrallah acknowledged his consultations with Iranian leaders, but claimed with conviction that such instructions were not binding instructions in any way. Nasrallah further suggested that he, and his leadership, would be the ultimate decision makers, in case of an Israeli strike on Iran or Lebanon.[32] Such an approach could be seen as a wedge between Iranian and Lebanese Shiite leaderships.

It is this affinity that grounds their complicated relationship with each other and with the world at large. Both Iran and Hizballah express a radical challenge to conventional political wisdom. Their practice of friction management and understanding of the world as a middle ground distances Shiite leaders from the high-ground logic of democratic orders.

Iran and Hizballah's conduct is a mix of historical processes, acute political instincts and a distinctly religious vision of the world. The fact that these components do not necessarily adhere into a clear-cut, dogmatic or interest-based strategy often leaves many mystified. It is this internal diversity that marks the Shiite logic we have been following as a true force to contend with on the global stage.

---

[31] See, for example, http://www.tnr.com/article/politics/the-iranian%E2%80%93israeli-war.

[32] See, for example, the following coverage of the interview: http://english.alarabiya.net/articles/2012/02/08/193327.html http://theiranproject.com/blog/2012/02/08/sayyed-nasrallah-stressed-irans-supports-of-hezbollah/.

9

HB and the Temperate City

Life in the Shiite middle ground is in a state of becoming. Things collide and disperse, approach and withdraw. Absolute truths serve as unattainable, yet tantalizing horizons. Still, the existence of the middle ground is a struggle against the desire for perfection.

Conventional wisdom encourages clear-cut decisions. One party wins and the other loses. Within the Shiite middle ground, this is hardly an acceptable conclusion. Winners and losers keep interacting. Acknowledged difference becomes the origin, the stability of middle ground life. Less comprehensive solutions than difference are treated as provisional measures.

This interaction is the lifeblood of the Shiite middle ground. When interacting, one does not know what the other might say. The unexpected might happen, opinions may change, and new insights about oneself or one's surroundings may be garnered. The limits imposed by interaction – the need to speak, addressing another, replying to another's words – have a liberating effect on the ideas expressed. When one is forced to adapt one's words to social context, those words cannot ring hollow.[1]

The middle ground emerges through personal participation, much more so than through external observation. The individual occupying the middle ground is in a process of becoming. He or she may believe in perfection, but not as an attainable goal. Perfection is the source of inspiration and the object of desire, an unrequited passion. Perfection is a horizon, not a destination. To appreciate this becoming, we need to reject a binary categorical view and enter the fray. When we look through the eyes of the other, it is likely that we will see ourselves in an unexpected light.

---

[1] For a philosophical expression of this idea, see Heinrich von Kleist, *On the Gradual Production of Thoughts Whilst Speaking*. ed. and trans. by David Constantine (Hackett Publishing, 2004).

Our imagined Shiite other is Hossein B. (HB). He has emerged from our encounter with the Shiite reality of the last two generations. He is a denizen of the middle ground, familiar with both the yearning for the absolute and the necessity of living in the here-and-now. Hossein is an Iranian whose life has been linked to the tumult of the Islamic Republic. He ushered it in as a young man, and reflects on it in midlife. For HB, what conventional wisdom sees as contradictions – between utopia and pragmatism, faith and reality – are equally solid building blocks for Hossein.

Early Hopes, Current Agonies

HB is in his fifties. He sports a well-trimmed beard and wears an oxford shirt, buttoned at the collar, beneath a modest sports jacket. Hossein B, is leaning back in a lawn chair, on the porch of a little hostel in the Alborz Mountains, overlooking Tehran.

The Islamic Revolution broke out when HB was in his early twenties. He was a student at a Qom *madrasa* at the time, and demonstrated with his friends against the Shah's regime. His family had always been religious, and his father thought HB might forge useful connections at the *madrasa*. Still, it was always clear that he would go into the family television business. Over the years, they have also added a lucrative sideline of satellite dishes.

HB studied at a state high school and then pursued more advanced religious studies at a *madrasa*. Later, he persuaded his parents to let him study international relations at Tehran University. HB wanted a few more years of freedom, telling his father that contacts outside Iran would come in handy when one made a living from technology. During his time at university, Hossein B. read the classics of political philosophy. Mill's "On Liberty" seemed almost Iranian to him. The concepts of *azadi* (liberty) and *'adl* (justice) had been the cornerstones of Iranian public protest throughout the twentieth century.

Tocqueville's "Democracy in America" also sounded familiar. HB thought a great deal about the book's description of religious communities in the United States and their influence on national politics. He still goes to a tradeshow in Germany once a year. Sometimes he vacations in Turkey.

When he was growing up, Hossein had a Jewish friend. They met in high school and later took a few classes at university together. HB's friend also came from a devout family. His grandfather had been a rabbi, and one of the family traditions was to sit and study on Saturday mornings. HB remembers how astounded he was by the points of resemblance he found between the Talmud and the Shiites texts he studied at the *madrasa*. Both were occupied with a profound problem – how to make the best of our life in this world, as opposed to a perfect world. Hossein B. recalls his amusement when he learned that Jews, just like Shiites, thought that one could never wholly understand God's priorities. Any truth one acquired was always partial, fuzzy and liable to change.

In fact, HB remembers one particular story he studied with his Jewish friend. In the story, a non-Jew came to visit the two Jewish sages of the age, Hillel and Shamai. The non-Jew asked both sages to teach him the Torah while he stood on one foot. Shamai kicked him out. He wasn't willing to speak with anyone who thought religion was frivolous enough to be approached on one foot. Hillel, on the other hand, told him that the entire Torah could be summarized with the phrase: "Don't do to others what you hate having done to you." The rest, said Hillel, was commentary.

HB has often thought about this story. Hillel seemed so Iranian to him. For Hillel, religion is, first and foremost, about personal contact. Having faith means trying not to turn anyone away, no matter how obnoxious he or she is. Faith is the basic element of community, another truth to be found in Hillel's words. A religious life is formed in the interaction between two different persons, both unique individuals, who find the strength to maintain their difference with respect.

His Shiite school friends have dispersed. Some of them live in Europe and the United States. One teaches chemistry at Yale; the last HB heard, he had been shortlisted for a Nobel. Another friend runs a hi-tech empire in the Silicon Valley. HB sometimes watches the talk shows broadcast on the satellite from Los Angeles. His friend is often mentioned as a patron of the Iranian community there. A third friend is a philosopher in Germany. Even the dailies sponsored by the regime interview him on occasion, asking for his opinion on politics and culture. HB's first girlfriend from junior high school is now an international correspondent for a global news site.

Several of his classmates joined the Revolutionary Guards, and today they are immensely rich. One of them is stationed in Lebanon, reportedly training Hizballah troops. Another friend works for *Hatem Al-Anbi'aa'*, the economic corporation handling the global activities of the Guards. He is a construction engineer, specializing in roads and bridges. HB recalls hearing that he is stationed in Tanzania now.

HB corresponds with his friends living abroad, mostly via emails but also through IM chats. He is an avid Internet user, reading the foreign press and downloading films and music. His recent contact with his friends in the Revolutionary Guards is not as frequent, but they still talk. One of his classmates, a provincial governor, just called him about a government contract regarding communications equipment; HB promised he would look into it. Still, it was a strange experience. He knew this was his friend on the phone, but it felt like the conversation was taking place across a great divide.

HB is troubled. He celebrated his birthday in August 2009, two months after the elections. He realized then that something was wrong. His generation thought the world was their oyster. They were going to change it for the better. What had the times come to?

HB does not delude himself. He knows Iran is not a democracy. Still, he thought his vote would mean something. HB remembers the heady days of the revolution in the late 1970s. Khomeini spoke to the people in tapes about the Shah's reforms. He said the Shah was evil, which HB found amusing. Then he said something that made more sense to HB. Khomeini claimed that the Shah was trying to impose a way of life which was foreign to Iranians. HB and his friends saw Khomeini's point. The Shah claimed to be the source of all authority. The new school books suggested that the loyalty of Iranians was to Shah, God, and Country, with the Shah occupying the place of primacy.

Iranians were used to something different. For nearly 500 years, power in Iran had been informally shared. The country was ruled by Shahs. Their rule depended on the consent and support of the religious scholars, the major landowners, the rich merchants and other powerbrokers within society. The notion that one person could simply claim to be the source of authority seemed frivolous at best, dangerous at worst.

HB attended the lectures of several prominent religious figures advocating change. He often recalls the visit of Ali Shariati to Tehran University.[2] Shariati, who combined a religious upbringing with a predilection for French existentialism, was an intellectual firebrand, most beloved by students and young people. He spoke of Shiism as the first revolutionary party in human history, beginning with Ali, the first Imam. He declared Shiite commitment to equitable redistribution here and now, alongside a fiery faith in God and the eschatological justice of the Twelfth Imam.

HB remembers another revolutionary hero, the assassinated heir apparent to Khomeini, Mortaza Motahhari. Motahhari was an exceptional product of the traditional Shiite system of higher religious education. He studied the classics of Islamic philosophy and was an enthusiastic reader of translations into Persian from the great writers of the Western canon. Whenever HB read one of Motahhari's numerous articles or books, he was struck by the man's pragmatic worldview. Motahhari was always willing to debate his rivals. He never shied away from an argument. He always said that arguments were the whole point of religious life. Motahhari's Islam was focused on participation, on leading a meaningful life in this world rather than the next.[3] HB had always thought of his religion as a synthesis between Shariati's passion and Motahhari's pragmatism.

HB recalls the Khatami victory in the 1997 presidential elections. Khatami, a Shiite scholar who had spent several years in Germany, advocated a need for improving Iran's relations with the world. He called for a dialogue of civilizations. The religious establishment threw its weight behind a different candidate then, but the people voted in Khatami with a landslide. Khatami had

---

[2] For a detailed historical and intellectual biography of Shariati, see Ali Rahnema, *An Islamic Utopian: A Political Biography of Ali Shariati* (IB Tauris, 2000).

[3] For an intellectual history of Motahhari's thought, see Mahmood Davari, *The Political Thought of Ayatollah Murtaza Mutahhari: An Iranian Theoretician of the Islamic State* (Routledge, 2005).

the common man at heart and seemed to speak truth to power. HB thought Khatami could steer the country onto a different path. The Khatami presidency was a major disappointment.

When Ahmadinejad was elected president in 2005, HB was not sure if the new president was a fanatic or just energetically conservative. Before Ahmadinejad, HB had never seen an Iranian national leader who emerged from such humble surroundings. The president's father was a blacksmith, and he grew up in a poor suburb of Tehran with his seven siblings.

His first term did not bode well. Newspapers were closed and individual liberties curtailed. Still, it was not until the presidential elections of 2009 that HB considered Ahmadinejad's policies as an attack on the pragmatic Iranian middle ground. This attack, thinks HB, was dangerous because it was carried out by members of the fold, not by outsiders. Khomeini's rule was highly repressive, but it was far from rigid. Khomeini rejected instant gratification. He equated national interest with religious interest, and he spoke of constant, never-ending struggle as the mark of a virtuous society. Those who hijacked the 2009 elections were different.

HB thinks of Ahmadinejad as the spoiled teenager of the family, longing to rebel against almost everything as long as he has his comfortable room and a sizable allowance. Ahmadinejad and his followers appreciated the pace and energy of the middle ground, but only as means to their end. They could not stomach the delayed gratification so central to the middle ground system. They were convinced that their authentic religious convictions granted them the ability to understand God's will and to enact it on Earth. Then, of course, the hunter became the prey. They should have known the Supreme Leader would turn on them in a heartbeat. Was it worth all that trouble?

HB had a big fight with his daughter, Afsaneh, after the 2009 elections. Afsaneh announced that she and her friends were joining the Green Movement demonstrators on the streets. He was worried. He shouted, threatened, and cajoled, but to no avail. HB had heard about the roughness with which the militias and the revolutionary guards treated demonstrators. He was mortally afraid for his daughter. In the end he gave up. In his heart of hearts, HB was proud of her, and a little envious.

When Afsaneh had gone to university, she came back one day and read him a poem, in English. He did not remember the entire poem, as it was quite long, but he recalled the poet reminding his reader that "the fire and the ice are never more than one step away from the temperate city."[4] That expression, "the temperate city," resonated in his heart. That was what he wished for his daughter. He did not want her to become a revolutionary, moving past the point of no return. He wished her to always reside in the temperate city, and was pleased with her willingness to defend it.

---

[4] Se: W.H. Auden, "The Sea and the Mirror" in *Collected Poems* (Modern Library, 2007), p. 401.

He thought that it was his daughter who was acting like a responsible adult, and not the goons in power. She and her friends had mature goals. They did not call for the abolition of the regime, but wanted their votes to count and the Islamic Republic to prosper. Still, Hossein B. knew that it simply was not this easy. He knew that the battle with the radicals would be intense. Although HB had real differences of opinion with them, he could not completely reject them. Nothing was more bitter than a "family" squabble.

HB has heard about the "mid-life crisis" and thinks that he is a textbook case. He feels a burning need to sort out his life, to take stock. He wants to know who his allies are. He wants to know who he could count on and to be sure who will turn him down. And so, HB decides to look outward. He was brought up in the schools of the Pahlavi Shahs. He was taught that Iran was a world power, and that it should strive to take its proper place among the strongest nations in the world. When he was a young man, he heard Khomeini speak about Iran's uniqueness, about its commitment to defend religion all over the globe. Those words still resonated deep inside him.

HB felt that the 1979 revolution brought something unique into the world – an attempt to change the conventions of state and society. There was no reason to accept the conventional gospel of the imperialists, or the coercion of the free-market gods. The Iranian Revolution would provide a lesson for oppressed societies – to return to themselves, to seek out authentic forms of political and cultural expression.

He is older and savvier now. HB knows that a political revolution thrives off slogans and simplistic truths. He realizes the revolution's leaders manipulated his generation. The ardor of twenty-somethings is a real asset for someone with a clear political agenda. Still, Hossein B. is convinced he was wrong about the intensity, but not about the principle. He feels he should not abandon this commitment to justice.

Iran, he feels, has lost its diversity. The Islamic Republic was once naughty, but it was – well – cool. Its leaders presented real alternatives, they were a third way. HB need only consider the ridiculous response of the authorities to the events of the 2011 Arab Spring to realize that the coolness is long gone. Iran's leaders frequently claimed that the revolutions in the Arab world were simply a continuation of Khomeini's revolution. No one listened, and certainly no one agreed. Such statements earned nothing but the scorn of the west.[5] One can only be for the regime or against it.

HB wants that diversity back. This was the reason he found himself volunteering to get out the vote for Hassan Rouhani in the 2013 presidential elections. The field of candidates was not optimal, to be sure. There were a lot of

---

[5] For examples of such scorn, see http://www.thenational.ae/thenationalconversation/comment/invoking-the-arab-spring-iran-rewrites-its-own-history; http://www.nytimes.com/2012/02/03/world/middleeast/effort-to-rebrand-arab-spring-backfires-in-iran.html?pagewanted=all; and http://www.foreignpolicy.com/articles/2012/01/24/supremely_irrelevant.

personal and factional rivalries, and most of them were hidden from the eyes of ordinary citizens. No one could be sure who was behind each candidate, and the candidates themselves thought better of proclaiming reformist affiliations. A lot of people in Iran and in the West said that Khamenei, the Supreme Leader, favored Said Jalili, who was extremely conservative and inexperienced.

Rouhani was the sole candidate who spoke consistently about issues that HB thought were important. In fact, HB was impressed not just by what Rouhani said, but by the way he spoke. Rouhani seemed to stand for moderation. He said, time and again, that the atmosphere of the country was getting too polarized, too extreme. There were too many security people in the streets, too many limitations on the lives of ordinary people.

Rouhani was far from a liberal. He did not support rapid westernization. He praised the revolution and expressed his loyalty to the Supreme Leader. He has been an insider since the 1979 revolution; he is very senior in the national security establishment. Still, he claimed that the true creed of the revolution was moderation. Rouhani believed in interaction and communication. He said that the solution to Iran's problems lay in constructive dialogue with the West, not in the hardline statements of Jalili. Rouhani did not speak about the house arrest of Mousavi, yet abstained from silencing the students who publicly called for the release of political prisoners at his rallies.

No matter what Rouhani said, the true revolution for him was one that did not lose sight of the middle ground. He was smart about his campaign, taking care not to alienate the conservatives but making sure to reach out to diverse audiences – youth, professionals, junior clerics, and many others. Rouhani spoke about Iran and the revolution as a spectrum, a whole based (dependent, in fact) on its internal pluralism and difference-based dialogue.

When Rouhani won, HB was thrilled. He felt a joy he had not felt since 1979, and this time it was a hope for the future. The spectrum's existence, the room for debate and participation, are important. HB has always suspected absolute convictions. He had been taught that a person of faith accepted the answers he was given, after having asked his own questions. The ongoing interplay between question and answer is the engine of Shiite religious life, a life of virtue. Iran under Ahmadinejad, he feels, lost this interplay.

HB understands that the middle ground is not simply an ideology to be espoused. Furthermore, the middle ground is not the opposite of the extremity Iran is now occupying. The opposite of one extreme is another extreme. The middle ground is different. It is the epitome of concrete reality, yet it is also in a process of becoming. Life is about the here-and-now. History is not defined by movement in a single direction. Redemption is for the future, rather than the present. Those who seek redemption in the present are left without both.

HB Ponders the World

When he attended school under the Shah, Hossein B. learned that Iran had always looked to the world. The Persian Empire was the first to strive for world domination. In modern times, Iranian politics and culture engaged both Asia and Europe repeatedly. Under the Islamic Republic, Iran remained involved in world affairs. HB has heard often about Iran's stand as a defender of the oppressed all over the globe.

Feeling that his Iran has lost its middle ground bearings, Hossein B looks to the world hoping to find them. Can he find an inspiration, a source of identification and support, for Iranians? If so, he might be able to reignite his own faltering flames, to find again the passion and struggle of life in the middle ground.

Iraq and the Arab Vicinity

HB begins with Iraq. Fatemeh and Ali, his sister and brother-in-law, live in Iraq. Ali is an aspiring Shiite religious scholar. He is based in Najaf, the most holy of Shiite cities. Students from all over the world flock to its seminaries. Iraq has generally adopted a more Western style of public life since the U.S. occupation of 2003. Censorship of the Internet or the press is rare. One can buy just about anything, and Western culture is consumed by many, often in the open.

Hossein B. remembers his visits there. His brother-in-law took him to the seminary, where HB felt thirty years younger. He was impressed with one thing that remained constant during Saddam Hussein's reign and after the U.S. invasion of 2003. Whether they were Shiite or Sunni, Iraqis always considered themselves to be Iraqis first and foremost. Under Saddam, Shiites certainly had reason to grumble. Still, they were grumbling about being left out of the state, not about wanting to secede from it. They thought their marginalization was unfair, when they were such loyal Iraqis.

The state has been the dominant element in Iraqi society over the last century or so. In Iran and Lebanon, the Shiite communities maintained a strong, independent identity. The state did not play a part in the formation and maintenance of this Shiite identity. There was often cooperation, and the notion of state power was not repugnant in the eyes of Shiite scholars and laypersons. The Shiite religious communities in Iran and Lebanon, however, enjoyed autonomous authority on broadly diverse issues, including private law and public education.

The situation in Iraq is different. One might say that three Shiite communities exist in Iraq.[6] These include the tribesmen of the south, the scholars of the holy cities, and the urban population of Iraq's great cities, first and foremost Baghdad. These three communities are quite distinct from each other. The tribesmen living in the deserts and marshes of southern Iraq, are fairly new converts to Shiism. They converted after the rise to prominence of the holy cities, Najaf and Karbalah, in the eighteenth century. The two cities became centers of finance and trade. The conversion of the tribesmen was motivated, among other factors, by the desire to enjoy the new-found economic prosperity of the region.

[6] See Nakash, *The Shi'is of Iraq*, pp. 13–48, 75–108.

The scholars of the holy cities are a community unto themselves. Shiite students from all over the Islamic world come to study and live in the seminaries of Najaf and Karbalah. This community is charged with the spiritual welfare of Shiites worldwide, in communities all over the world. Yet, the scholarly community of the holy cities is a distinct entity, pursuing its own interests and agendas. The religious scholars in Iraq, for example, have a history of supporting the Iraqi state. They became critical of it under Saddam Hussein, when the state began to target religious leaders. However, under the regime elected following the U.S. occupation of 2003, Grand Ayatollah Ali Sistani, the most popular Shiite authority in the country, holds a highly influential role in the administration and legitimacy of the government.

The urban Shiites are a diverse community. Many of them possess secular state education and a national Iraqi identity. These Shiites grew up under the fervent ideology of Pan-Arab and Iraqi nationalism. They saw incorporation into the state as a desirable goal. Many of them became civil servants. Following the U.S. invasion of 2003, urban Shiites hold significant positions of power in post-2003 Iraqi politics, including the prime-ministership.

Shiite communal solidarity has been crucial in the formation of middle ground politics. This has been true in Iran and in Lebanon. The Shiite communities in both countries were able to bypass the state and create alternative visions of society and polity. All Iraqi Shiites share allegiance to the same scholarly leaders. Still, each community has its own agenda, as well as its own unique reality and practices. The Iraqi state has proven strong enough to bridge many of these gaps.

Outside the immediate neighborhood, Egypt has possessed a national consciousness since the mid-nineteenth century. North African Arab leaders are committed to nationalism as well. Kaddafi created his Libyan republic by uniting tribes. Hassan II of Morocco brought together the Arab, French, and Berber under his monarchy. Algeria's national identity was powerful enough to drive out the French in 1962. The state was also powerful throughout the Persian Gulf monarchies, where it is tied to the authority of the ruling families.

HB realizes that the Arab Sunni state comes at the expense of religious and ethnic solidarity. This state of affairs, he thinks, is hardly compatible with the middle ground politics for which he longs. Arab leadership is centralized and hierarchical, removed from the heterogeneous and diverse structure of Shiite leadership. HB also understands something crucial about his fellow Arab Shiites. He was taught to consider them his brothers. He now recognizes that while this may be true with regard to issues of faith, it does not mean much with regard to politics. The notion that all Shiites – Arabs and non-Arabs – share a single outlook or one set of political convictions is out of touch with reality. Visions of a Shiite political bloc are a projection of Western fears about an Islamic takeover. When the West cannot afford to criticize Sunnis, thinks HB, it unloads on the Shiites.

The modern Iranian state took form under European tutelage. When Bush had America on the rampage, it was Europe which acted as a force for mediation around the world. Muslim presence in Europe is growing, and European states display a fair amount of tolerance towards Islam. The continent is coming into its own as a global power. Could Europe prove to be HB's salvation?

Europe

Hossein B. has always had a taste for Russian literature. When he came to this mountain guesthouse he brought along the new Persian translation of Dostoevsky's "The Idiot." Sitting on the porch during the early hours of the morning, his eyes caught Prince Mishkin's thoughts:

[Mishkin] ... remembered that during his epileptic fits, or rather immediately preceding them, he had always experienced a moment or two when his whole heart, and mind, and body seemed to wake up to vigor and light; when he became filled with joy and hope, and all his anxieties seemed to be swept away for ever.... That there was, indeed, beauty and harmony in those abnormal moments, that they really contained the highest synthesis of life, he could not doubt, nor even admit the possibility of doubt. He felt that they were not analogous to the fantastic and unreal dreams due to intoxication by hashish, opium or wine. Of that he could judge, when the attack was over. These instants were characterized – to define it in a word – by an intense quickening of the sense of personality. Since, in the last conscious moment preceding the attack, he could say to himself, with full understanding of his words: "I would give my whole life for this one instant," then doubtless to him it really was worth a lifetime.[7]

For HB, Mishkin reflects the spectrum of European culture. Europe became the breeding ground of the most influential big ideas in modern history. European history is full of social movements which turned into "isms." Socialism, Capitalism, Darwinism, and Calvinism are four prominent examples. They encompass and process the social world. They affect a hierarchy between idea and practice. The formative ideas come first, and they inspire and shape action.

European tradition, thinks HB, is affiliated with the abstract, the ideal that ought to exist, to be an attainable future of present-day reality. Leaders are expected to expand present reality in order to fit the big idea. Facilitating the transformation of reality justifies the existence of societies and leaders.

HB is well aware of the different legacies left by Socialism and Fascism. Still, he thinks that in both cases a nearly transcendental perception of history is accompanied by belief in a manifest destiny. The purpose of this form of leadership is to help society move toward this future. Such big ideas seek to strip away the detrimental layers of present reality until the idea-infused core is revealed and the promised future is once more attainable. For HB, moments when everything comes together, when reality is transformed by the big idea, are moments of grace, not goals to be pursued.

---

[7] Translation drawn from http://www.gutenberg.org/files/2638/2638-h/2638-h.htm.

The Islamic Republic of Iran is built on the notion that God is its sole sovereign. Still, God's commandments are to be applied through laws made and enforced by human beings. Hossein B. suspects that the boundary between the Divine and the human is significantly blurred in the European tradition. Where he is used to friction as a means for regulating conflicts and disagreements, European idealists seem to him to seek emotional certainty and harmonious order. Once the big idea is established and demarcated, the commitment to this idea becomes an obligation. HB's notion of a virtuous life originates in the irresolvable tension between knowing that perfection exists and being unable to attain it.

HB is aware that the West portrays Iran as a country run by insane mullahs who demand full obedience. Still, his experience of religion under the Islamic Republic is based much less on absolute truth than on his daily reality. Europeans think their big ideas give them direction in life. Big ideas tell them where to go, as well as how to get there.

Where HB thought he would see freedom in idea and practice, he discovers the existence of big ideas as burdens. This is not a cross he is prepared to bear. What sets him apart, as a person of faith in a faithless world, is the knowledge that his world is defined by meaning which exceeds his grasp. HB's notion of a good life consists of striving toward an ideal. Were he to reach the ideal, he could no longer strive. Only God does not strive. He alone is perfect.

HB considers turning to Russia or China for assistance. Russia is in the midst of reverting to autocracy, the form of government with which it is most familiar. The notion of one man building a country in his image is something HB remembers from the Pahlavi years in Iran. For centuries, leadership in Iran had been exercised through an alliance between kings, scholars, rich merchants, and landowners. The Pahlavi Shahs sought to change this multifocal structure and ground all power in their monarchy. HB sees himself as the product of Khomeini's revolution against Pahlavi rule. He cannot imagine himself fraternizing with the Russian national vision, so antithetical to the middle ground.

Israel as Europe?

Israel is an experiment in devotion to a big idea.[8] This is one of the reasons the very existence of Israel seems so wrong to the leaders of the Islamic Republic. It is built on the notion that adherence to Zionism can reshape Jewish heritage and alter existing geopolitical reality. At times, HB concludes that Israeli leaders are prisoners of their ultimate vision. How could the Israeli leadership lose the middle ground quality of living between longing and reality? Hossein B. wonders if this has happened because Israel has forsaken its Jewish heritage in favor of Zionism.

---

[8] For a discussion of big ideas and foreign policy in an U.S. context, see Stefan Halper and Jonathan Clarke, *The Silence of the Rational Center: Why American Foreign Policy is Failing* (Basic Books, 2007), pp. 21–48.

When he studied with his Jewish friend, he was sure that Jews experienced the world very much like Shiites. They shared the outlook of a minority striving to make things right while acknowledging the inherent injustice of the world. Both traditions originate from life in the middle ground. They are both interpreting and adapting, understanding friction as the norm rather than anomaly, keeping one step ahead of the majority in order to survive.

HB has heard much from the Iranian media about Israel's plans to attack Iran. He thinks that Israel's brashness demonstrates how far it has strayed from its religious beginnings. HB has no doubt that the Islamic regime is using the Israeli threat in manipulative fashion to distract the Iranian public from the problems at home. He has heard some vicious anti-Semitic rhetoric coming from Iranian leaders. He has also, however, heard from many Iranians that the government of the Islamic Republic should refrain from getting involved in the Israeli-Palestinian conflict. HB has yet to hear an Israeli spokesperson express anything but fear and contempt for Iran.

HB finds this disturbing. He is no stranger to war. Many of his peers died during the war with Iraq. It is the single-mindedness which bothers him. Does Israel have no problems other than the Islamic Republic? If this is the case, then Israel has lost its middle ground bearings. Should there be some truth in what the regime is saying, Israel is a loose cannon. HB finds it difficult to reconcile this with the Judaism he remembers from his childhood. Looking at Israel and Europe, HB finds it difficult to identify a middle ground. In Iran, big ideas drive reality. They do not coerce it.

Hossein B. is now at a loss. He thinks he might do well to look for support in the most unlikely place. For more than thirty years, he has been taught that the United States is the source of all evil. It is said to be Islam's enemy, Iran's nemesis, and a threat to the entire world. Because his intuitions have all failed him so far, is it realistic to find reverberations of the middle ground in the heart of the "Great Satan"?

The United States

Several years ago, HB went to Germany for a business exhibition. Getting to Tempelhof airport quite late for his flight to Tehran, he discovered he had forgotten his book. The duty-free bookstore did not have anything in Persian, and had little to offer in English. His flight was about to leave, and HB grabbed the first big book he found. At worst, he thought, he would have a chance to practice his English.

When his plane took off, HB took the book out of his briefcase finding he had purchased an anthology of famous speeches. Nelson Mandela, Mahatma Gandhi, John Kennedy – their words of inspiration were produced in large, inviting font. HB never finished reading the book, but one speech he had not heard about previously has remained with him since. This is Theodore Roosevelt's "Man in the Arena" speech, delivered at the Sorbonne on April 23, 1910. The passage HB has often thought about is actually Roosevelt quoting

Abraham Lincoln. The history textbooks of the Islamic Republic praise Lincoln as an enemy of imperialism. Ever since he read this quote, HB has thought that Khomeini's affection for Lincoln runs even deeper:

I think the authors of the Declaration of Independence intended to include all men, but they did not mean to declare all men equal in all respects. They did not mean to say all men were equal in color, size, intellect, moral development or social capacity. They defined with tolerable distinctness in what they did consider all men created equal-equal in certain inalienable rights, among which are life, liberty and pursuit of happiness. This they said, and this they meant. They did not mean to assert the obvious untruth that all were actually enjoying that equality, or yet that they were about to confer it immediately upon them. They meant to set up a standard maxim for free society which should be familiar to all – constantly looked to, constantly labored for, and, even though never perfectly attained, constantly approximated, and thereby constantly spreading and deepening its influence, and augmenting the happiness and value of life to all people, everywhere.[9]

HB knows that life under Khomeini was harsh, full of repression and loss. Many of his friends died during the eight-year war with Iraq. Others, including members of his family, were imprisoned or executed. Nevertheless, Hossein B. distinguishes between Khomeini as a person and Khomeini as an avatar. Khomeini stood for the transformation of the communal Shiite middle ground into a political order. This was an idea HB could both commit to and applaud.

He sees a similar middle ground spirit in Roosevelt's speech and in Lincoln's words. The Islamic Republic has been so intent on condemning every American idea and action, that his daughter's generation believes the United States is antithetical to Iran. Only one way of life can prevail, the young people say, and many of them think it will be the American one. HB thinks this existential conflict may be unreal.

For him, George W. Bush represented an abandonment of the middle ground in favor of a single, radical truth. Other presidents in U.S. history shared Bush's conservative opinions. Still, such presidents refrained from engaging with the world and preferred to focus their vision on the American people. HB believes that the Barack Obama is carrying out a spirited attempt to transform U.S. policy and restore it to its middle ground origins.

When HB considers the intellectual and political origins of the United States, the relationship to the middle ground is clear. The first U.S. polities were established by Englishmen of great conviction, fleeing political persecution in order to foster and promote their own big ideas. The founding documents of the United States, however, flesh out a polity of the middle ground, refraining from the sweeping rhetoric of the 1791 French Declaration on the Rights of Man.[10] The American declaration sees life as a dynamic process, defining

---

[9] See: http://www.theodore-roosevelt.com/images/research/speeches/maninthearena.pdf
[10] Online at http://www.hrcr.org/docs/frenchdec.html.

the basic rights as "life, liberty and the pursuit of happiness." There is no single road upon which one must walk in the American document.

Hossein B. has always taken an interest in American culture. His impression is that the middle ground plays an essential part in the law and politics of the country. This is demonstrated by the structure and application of criminal law in the United States. One of the hallmarks of state power is the ability to formulate and enforce social norms through criminal law.

American criminal law is split between federal and state authorities. Although egregious violations are often actionable under both federal and local statutes, there are disputes which are not necessarily resolved in favor of the federal authorities. HB has watched these disputes unfold many times on one of his favorite television shows, "Law and Order."

The federal constitution provides another example for the prevalence of middle ground logic within U.S. law. This cornerstone of America's legal order is applied through interpretation. Different from the codices of Europe, the constitution is not only a set of concrete instructions regulating specific circumstances; it is a document laying out both principle and instruction, composed and amended over a lengthy period of time.

HB has heard about the heated battles waged in the U.S. Supreme Court between schools of constitutional interpretation. Originalists claim the constitution should be read and applied in ways that would closely fit the intentions of its framers. Other, more liberal interpreters suggest that the constitution can remain valid only if it juxtaposes the original wording and current needs and contexts. Still, all ascribe to interpretation rather than literal execution.

HB listened to President Obama's Cairo speech of June 4 2009.[11] An Iranian blogger translated the speech into Persian. Hossein B. thought that Obama's words reflected an understanding that reality should not be reduced to a clash between absolute truths. The president spoke of critical risks underlying twenty-first-century life. He spoke of the Israeli-Palestinian conflict, as well as the general hostility between religious and secular visions. Obama focused on the importance of values, morals, and beliefs in the international arena. He recognized their existence by referring to them as a source for inspiration and commitment, rather than as a source for unequivocal obligation.

HB believes President Obama is firm in his conviction to reaffirm the middle ground as the American high ground. This represents a radical shift from the Bush doctrine. The United States under Bush committed itself to the worldwide promotion of neoconservative values, from superimposed democratization to the expansion of global markets. The Bush Administration was profoundly committed to realizing its vision. The U.S. global War on Terror caused officials to ignore regulations and protocol regarding the customary balance between national security and individual liberties which had characterized U.S. behavior

---

[11] For a full text of the speech, see http://www.huffingtonpost.com/2009/06/04/obama-speech-in-cairo-vid_n_211215.html.

in the past. Bush's policies sought dominance and rejected equilibrium, clearly indicating on most fronts who the United States considered "bad" and whom it considered "good." Obama appears determined to reread America's big ideas in light of the middle ground.

When Obama accepted his Nobel peace prize (December, 2009) in Oslo, HB understood his words as meant for Iranian ears:

I know that engagement with repressive regimes lacks the satisfying purity of indignation. But I also know that sanctions without outreach – and condemnation without discussion – can carry forward a crippling status quo. No repressive regime can move down a new path unless it has the choice of an open door.[12]

Hossein B. likes the message, but it is the tone he finds especially familiar and inviting. He has been disappointed by those who were supposed to share his convictions and faith. He is surprised by the kinship he feels when he hears Obama speak. Obama's middle ground is negotiated and honest, virtuous and dynamic. It pursues a higher truth but not just at any cost. HB knows that the United States and President Obama are not perfect. He feels that this is the point. No one is. We have to make do with what we have.

For HB, Obama's words meet the ultimate test of middle ground sincerity. Many leaders throughout the world are inspired, in their handling of reality, by the desire to realize a grand, unyielding vision. In contrast, Obama accepts reality even at its grimmest, while acknowledging its potential for change and expressing his commitment to reality's betterment. HB thinks Obama wants to change the world while remaining firmly within it.

The middle ground itself is a challenge, thinks HB. Life within it is a struggle which does not reward the meek. He remembers reading that one of Barack Obama's books was named *The Audacity of Hope*. HB has no doubt that Khomeini would have concurred. Despite their great differences, both leaders thought of hope as the audacious core of middle ground politics.

Khomeini hoped for divine deliverance beyond his knowledge and influence. Acknowledging this unbridgeable gap between his life and God's truth, Khomeini's hope returned simultaneously to both the here-and-now and its improvement. Obama hopes for a more just world, for nuclear disarmament and comprehensive social rights. Realizing that he cannot impose this, his hope is also projected onto his reality, shaping it gradually in the image of his ideal. Khomeini and Obama embark on very different journeys. Still, both journeys flow from and with their existing realities, and not against them.

HB was a part of the political sea change in Iran, heralded by the revolution of 1979. He has sensed a new wind blowing from the United States since the election of President Obama. Hossein B. finds these changes powerful because they are grounded in old, nearly timeless forces. Faith, community, a sense of

---

[12] For a full text of the speech, see http://realclearpolitics.blogs.time.com/2009/12/10/text-of-obamas-nobel-address.

vision – these all precede most political orders and are likely to outlive them. This vantage point, shared by Iran and the United States, has been obscured by the mutual understanding that both nations represent extreme perceptions of human values and international order. HB remains hopeful that in the coming years, U.S. and Iranian leaders will not repeat the blunders of the twentieth century, the age of extremes.

In HB's opinion, European ideals – or better yet, the absolute devotion to such ideals – are at the root of this extremism. The notion that an all-encompassing idea can be the source of both legitimacy and practice for a political order is, thinks HB, frivolous at best. The time of the "isms" has passed. Societies that have a longstanding middle ground heritage, like Iran and the United States, should commit to leading the global community toward the era of the middle ground. Other nations – in Latin America, Asia, the Indian subcontinent – are following suit. They require inspiration and guidance on the way toward fulfilling their potential. The United States and Iran, HB believes, must step up.

HB recalls Khomeini's famous words in the letter announcing his decision to sign the ceasefire with Iraq in 1988:

O' God! You are aware that we do not collude even for a moment with America, the Soviet Union and other global powers, and that we consider collusion with superpowers and other powers as turning our back on Islamic principles.[13]

Khomeini detested the notion of one nation seeking a position of dominance over others. He did not oppose political machinations, but felt that the unassailable title of "power" or "superpower" was morally wrong. True virtue does not lie at the extremes occupied by "powers," but in the middle ground. HB believed this was one of the most liberating aspects of Khomeini's words. Iranians no longer had to define themselves according to superimposed values, or debilitating dichotomies. Iran could be strong, powerful even, without becoming a "power." HB himself did not have to ascribe wholeheartedly to "liberalism" or to "traditionalism." He could be both or neither at the same time.

HB has since thought that Khomeini's words were the harbingers of change for the world. Ideas such as non-alignment and slogans such as "Neither East or West" had become popular in the world of the 1960s. Still, they had been seen as a compromise. Non-aligned nations were the freaks, those who could not find their place within the dichotomized global order of East and West. Khomeini was the first to claim that life in the middle ground was morally superior to existence at the extremes.

HB remains convinced that those states that still see the world as split down the middle are on their way out. Can anyone seriously claim that Iran is backward when one realizes it is a world Internet leader? Is anyone reading the

13 Online at http://www.cfr.org/publication/11745/letter_from_ayatollah_khomeini_regarding_weapons_during_the_iraniraq_war.html.

countless blogs put up by seminary students in Qom? HB knows only too well
how repressive the Islamic regime can be. Still, do the regime's repressive qualities deny the diversity to be found in Iranian society and culture?

HB has no doubt that this is all true elsewhere as well. The era of all-out vic-
tories and total defeats is nearly over. The dominance of states over other entities is on the decline. Non-state organizations, like Lebanese Hizballah, are as
powerful as their host states. Multinational corporations and social networks
are establishing lines of communication which make state-based global culture
less relevant. Iran is uniquely poised to make the most of this change. So are
several rising forces across the globe.

The Present Portrait of the Future

In the global arena, what high-ground conventional wisdom sees as a threat
is now transformed by middle ground politics into an incontrovertible truth,
a necessary reality. This reality brings together elements conventionally perceived as diametrically opposed. Profound ideas and daily life engage in the
middle ground. Escaping perfection, these visions and realities are imbued with
nearly limitless potential for evolution and adaptation. The emerging middle
ground order embraces neither full acceptance nor total rejection. Surviving
in a less-than-perfect world requires diversity and tenacity. "In dreams begins
responsibility."[14]

Leaderships occupying the middle ground can hardly be reduced to overriding principles or conditions obliging all its members and constituents. Middle
ground reality is characterized by mutually acknowledged difference and diversity. The ascendance of the middle ground order directly challenges the blunt
distinctions characteristic of today's world. The worldview epitomized by such
works as "The Clash of Civilizations"[15] and "The End of History"[16] is significantly undermined by the middle ground order. One can no longer reach one's
destination before embarking on the voyage:

If it be / now, 'tis not to come; if it be not to come, it will be / now; if it be not now, yet
it will come. The / readiness is all. (Hamlet, V ii, 234–237)

Turkey, India, and Brazil are three rising powers that reflect the emerging
potential of middle ground politics alongside the Islamic Republic of Iran. The
leaderships of all three are motivated by powerful communal heritages, along
with a commitment to changing their social and political reality. In all three,
diverse identities exist within a single national vision. The inherent tension

---

[14] William Butler Yeats, online at http://www.sacred-texts.com/neu/yeats/lpy/lpyo8o.htm.
[15] See Samuel P. Huntington, *The Clash of Civilizations and the Remaking of World Order*
(Touchstone, 1996).
[16] See Francis Fukuyama, *The End of History and the Last Man* (Free Press, 2006).

and coexistence between the national whole and its component parts underlies their shared notion of the middle ground.

In Turkey, the political leadership headed by Prime Minister Erdoğan has been challenging the foundations of the Kemalist Republic by advocating a place for Islam at the core of the secular state. This initiative relies on a growing popular will among Turks of different persuasions. The government has reformed the Turkish constitution by removing certain powers from the army and the judiciary and endowing them on elected representatives. For Erdoğan's leadership, democracy and religion are not mutually exclusive. Islamic heritage does not contradict integration into the European Union. These agendas are all legitimate without any single one dominating others. Within the Turkish middle ground, the coexistence of these seemingly contradictory paths is considered normal.

In India, ethnic and religious diversity is one of the greatest in the world. Estimates differ, but more than a 1,000 languages are spoken by Indians. Bengalis, Punjabis, Shiites, Sunnis, and Hindus, among many others, interact on a daily basis throughout the subcontinent. Indian leadership regulates and balances widely divergent needs and priorities, while remaining true to a unifying social and political vision. Attempting to sustain the world's largest democracy, Indian leaders cannot afford to embrace absolute truths. Indian policy, both domestic and foreign, is a tapestry in progress. The Indian ship of state remains afloat through commitment to social improvement. Its progress is dependent on acknowledgement of its diverse traditions. For Indians, the temptation of extremes does not defeat the necessary reality of the middle ground.

In Brazil, the middle ground provides possibilities for the expansion of economic parity and solidarity. The election of President Luiz Inacio Lula da Silva in 2002 ushered in a new era. Lula expanded assistance programs to Brazil's poor, mainly through professional training and the strengthening of local communities. Lula also undertook massive economic reforms to meet international standards. At the same time, he adopted independent opinions on diverse international issues, including nuclear negotiations with Iran. By doing so, Lula managed to create a unique voice for Brazil, enhancing a shared sense of identity and promoting increased economic solidarity. Brazil's stand on domestic and international issues has rejected superimposed dichotomies. Lula's heir, Dilma Rousseff, has been committed to his engaging position even when she has differed from his specific policies.

Despite their differences in focus – religion, ethnicity, and economics – Turkey, India, and Brazil provide a glimpse at the emerging, middle ground order. Opposites engage at the depths of such order and surface differently, more diffuse and permeable. Improbable connections form within this order, based on an incorporation of values, interests, and contexts.

The new middle ground order does not blindly accept conventional norms, nor does it absolutely reject the existing global order. Instead, it maintains a position of resistance. The middle ground position of this order produces a resistance of engagement and encounter toward what it perceives as the extremes of Western dominance. This resistance is not born from a desire to achieve hegemonic status instead of the West. Middle ground resistance provides a firm basis for friction and regulation.

The new Shiite leadership we have considered has been a prominent forerunner of the middle ground political order. This Shiite leadership is often perceived as extremist and uncompromising. Contrary to this view, we understand Shiite leadership to be driven by a desire to change the world while remaining firmly within it. The faith driving Shiite leadership lies in its ability to balance Divine truth and human contextually. It is this balance, which created a non-dogmatic religiosity, which has made Shiite leadership an unexpected pioneer of middle ground politics.

The challenge presented by the emerging middle ground to the conventional wisdom of the high-ground international order is as immediate as it is far-reaching. Today's world tends more toward exists in flux rather than stasis. It is defined by boundaries that are ambiguous and shifting rather than distinct and static. One cannot escape the conclusion that today's inconceivable will becomes tomorrow's inevitable. At first it will seem harsh and dissonant; later still, full of inspiration; and eventually, inescapable.

Epilogue

Shiite Leadership and the Emergence of the Middle Ground Regime

Middle ground Shiite leaderships are elusive. While it is in their middle ground nature to reject clear-cut definitions or typologies, they maintain durable, contact, and dynamic interaction with their high-ground ends and ultimate visions. These ends are a part of the middle ground and not its opposite. They enable the creation of the middle ground and sustain its dynamic with their rigor and conviction. The middle ground is thus the place where high-ground ends fuse and detach continuously.

Scholars and observers are often tempted to ignore the middle ground qualities of Iran and Hizballah's Shiite leadership and embrace the extremes at the ends. Perhaps the extremes lend themselves comfortably to analysis and deconstruction. The high grounds can be scaled by the professional eye, favoring detachment over immersion, conceptual clarity over concrete chaos. For students of International Relations and Area Studies, the "life" of the middle ground, its quality of unbridled motion, its reticence to confidently declare "for" or "against," is a critical challenge in the study of the Shiite political leaderships.

Bringing the middle ground to the foreground in the Shiite case reflects the rise of other middle ground leaderships in the Middle East and all over the world. Such leaderships emerge in context, between high grounds, ends and extremes that embody deeply held beliefs, convictions, and ideas. Middle ground leaderships engage in friction generated by cooperation, competitive relations, and confrontational interactions at both intra- and interstate levels. Middle ground leaderships are inspired by diversities rather than similarities and are motivated by diversity rather than similarity or unity.

One might consider these middle ground leaderships to be harbingers of a new political order, a middle ground regime. The new Muslim leaderships installed by the Arab Spring tend to be middle ground leaderships, placed as they are between extremist Salafists and ardent Westernizers or the faithful of the *ancien regime*. Turkey, India, Brazil, and even China; these may be recognized as a middle ground leaderships. Each independently embodies an ongoing interaction between local sensibilities and global necessities. Their leaderships take on such perceived contradictions without blurring the distinctions between both ends. The ensuing friction drives policies which are multifaceted and dynamic while remaining grounded in a sense of community and tradition.

The manifold presence of middle ground leaderships is reshaping the political and the economic global sphere, rattling old allegiances and promoting new alliances through incessant friction. At the domestic level, middle ground leaderships are enabling interaction between elements conventionally understood to be mutually exclusive – democratic, religious, non-state movements – and other forces, the interactions of which were usually thought too perilous for sustainable political leaderships.

Survival in the global arena was often dependent on affiliation with high-ground principles and a grand vision. This state of affairs left little room for local logic and context. This is no longer the situation. The politics of high-ground ends and extremes are deteriorating. The lenses used for observing the global politics of grand visions, once considered acute and penetrating, are growing blurry.

At the turn of the twenty-first century, survival in the global arena is hardly conducive to high-ground politics. Vested political and economic interests are defined within a relational, multilateral perspective. This perspective is friction-based and dynamic. Simply put, it would be impractical for a leadership to focus exclusively on predefined, clear-cut goals. Policy decisions based on the desire to undermine a rival's goals and intentions are equally impractical. The middle ground regime, as a global phenomenon, rejects such dichotomies just as it shies away from the certainties of triumph and defeat. Looking through the eyes of a would-be rival, middle ground leaders see themselves in an unexpected light. This unexpected view of oneself is as crucial to the middle ground worldview as are the latter's high-ground ends.

It may be useful to think about middle ground leaderships and the nature of the middle ground regime in the context of a stone thrown into a pond. Once the stone hits the water, ripples spread from the point of contact and water rises to fill the void created by the sinking stone. Imagine several stones being thrown simultaneously into a still pond, and you will have a notion of the middle ground regime. Each stone produces its own ripples, its own voids. Still, ripples intersect and shape each other. The same water fills different voids.

The middle ground regime introduces a general dynamic into the still global pond, shaking things up simply through its motion. Simultaneously, its component middle ground leaderships go about the business of filling voids and creating ripples in their own distinct ways. The lives of middle ground leaderships begin with the stones already having been thrown. Middle ground leaderships operate in the midst of both ripples and voids, negotiating between diverse dynamics and focal points. Its own ripples intersect with neighboring ones while remaining irrevocably linked to their stone of origin. The ripple fields of the various stones are distinct, yet cannot avoid connections.

Referring to the middle ground regime as a worldwide phenomenon does not mean that we should downplay the differences between middle ground leaderships. We mentioned three middle ground modes of behavior: conformist, revolutionary, and traditional. There are many related-yet-distinct modes to be explored, each unique to specific circumstance of politics, culture, and economics. Still, the common element is the gaze from the middle ground. It is an insider's gaze, observing the world from within a story already in the process of being told. Still, the middle ground gaze does not become assimilated to a single context or set of parameters. It is free-ranging within its given context, acknowledging its distinctions from other middle grounds while simultaneously seeking to engage them in friction.

The middle ground gaze may have many expressions. These can be found in a broad variety of leaderships within the global environment, from Iran to the United States, from Turkey to India, from Brazil to the leaderships born of the Arab Spring. In all of these cases, leaders attempting to make sense of themselves and their world do so with a middle ground gaze. Each leadership is keen on defining its own context, identifying and acknowledging its own high-ground ends. Still, such leaderships conceive and act mostly through dynamic partnerships, fulfilling diverse roles in diverse situations, at times simultaneously

The forces of the middle ground defy dichotomous distinctions. Middle ground leaderships do not reject ends and extremes. They incorporate them into the middle ground, thriving off the friction created by the clash of absolute truths, grand designs and ultimate visions. Recep Tayyip Erdoğan, the Turkish Prime Minister, provides a poignant example. He does not shy away from grand statements. He easily claims both Ottoman grandeur and European modernity as his birthright, acting in both modes or in either at different times and contexts.

The Palestinian Hamas provides an additional demonstration of the rising middle ground regime. Its mode of choice is resistance, similar to Lebanese Hizballah. Hamas acts as a sovereign state, as part of the Palestinian national struggle, and as a staunch foe of Israel. Still, it communicates regularly with Israel and routinely takes on the Fatah movement, its rival/partner in the Palestinian struggle. Its leadership does not seek to ameliorate the tensions between these elements. This tension, this friction, is what drives Hamas forward, allowing it to elude attempts to view it as one-dimensional, or as inextricably bound to singular, never-changing ideas and practices.

Non-state middle ground leaderships contribute to the rise of the middle ground regime around the world. The global arena was once open exclusively to sovereign states. This state of affairs is changing. Non-state entities are capable players in a game dominated by an insider's gaze. Other than a few radical exceptions, such as al-Qaeda, non-state entities see themselves intrinsically in relation to other factors – the state, the West, or other countries in the region. They do not stand alone. Survival is in the middle ground, the politics of friction; these are second nature to such organizations. Thus, one may speak of a middle ground regime without implying that all middle ground leaderships are categorically similar.

The challenge of maintaining the gaze from the middle ground lies with those who would observe it. If there is a methodological lesson to be learned from our meanderings, it may be that pursuing the middle ground involves adopting a middle ground gaze, with the limitations and boundaries of scholarly prudence. In the words of the writer Ursula K. Le Guin:

A yielding, an obedience, a willingness to accept these notes as the right notes, this pattern as the true pattern, is the essential gesture of performance, translation and understanding. The gesture need not be permanent, a lasting posture of the mind and heart; yet it is not false. It is more than the suspension of disbelief needed to watch a play, yet less than a conversion. It is a position, a posture in the dance (*The Telling*).

Glossary

Akhbari	Text-based Shiite school of thought that rejected the *taqlid*-based, personal authority of the *maraji*, the sources of emulation, in favor of a philosophical, ontological quest for deliverance and salvation.
Ashura	The tenth day of the month of Muharram. It is the main holiday of the Shiite calendar, commemorating the death of Imam Hussein in battle on the plains of Karbalah, in today's southern Iraq, in AD 680. During *Ashura*, the death of Hussein is commemorated in a passion play.
Fatwa	Religious ruling, a product of *ijtihad*.
Fuqaha'	Shiite legal scholars qualify as knowledgeable in *Fiqh* (Shiite jurisprudence). According to Khomeini, the most qualified to lead the Shiite community in the absence of an Imam.
Hadith	The sayings of the prophet Muhammad about what he said or did and about what he did *not* say or do. Shiites collect such traditions from the twelve Imams and their households as well.
Ijtihad	The practice of providing legal decisions based on religious knowledge. It is another name for the prerogative of the Shiite legal scholars, the *Fuqaha'*.
Imamah	The principle of Shiite leadership declaring that true leadership of the Shiite community lies with an infallible Imam, a descendant of the line of Ali, the first Imam. In the absence of such an Imam, or until the return of the Twelfth Imam as messiah, the nature of Shiite leadership remains unclear.
Ma'sumin	Infallible. Usually applied with reference to the twelve infallible Shiite Imams.

Majlis	The common name for Iran's parliament. Technically, the elected chamber of the Iranian parliament as opposed to the appointed chamber, the Guardian Council.
Marja-ye a'ala-ye taqlid	The supreme source of emulation.
Marja-ye taqlid	Source of emulation.
Muqawama	Resistance. A term encompassing a collective agenda and state of mind, directed most often against foreign military and cultural presence within the Islamic world. Most particularly, an approach and attitude to be adopted against Israel's presence and very existence.
Norouz	The Iranian New Year, celebrated on March 21, the vernal equinox, and a remnant of Iran's pre-Islamic past.
Rahbar	The Supreme Leader of the Islamic Republic of Iran.
Sharia	The Islamic law based on God's sovereign commandments and prohibitions.
Shura	Consultation. A basic practice demanded from Muslim rulers called to consult with elders and sages. In the case of Lebanese Hizballah, it is the supreme council of the organization.
Taqiyah	The Shiite doctrine allowing the faithful to maintain a low public profile when faced with threats to individual or communal existence.
Taqlid	Emulation. The Shiite doctrine which requires a lay believer, anyone who is not religiously qualified to practice *ijtihad*, to find a source of emulation. This requires a trained religious scholar to follow the source's rulings in all matters pertaining to worship and religious life.
Usuli	Source-based, original. A Shiite school of thought advocating personal authority of the scholars, *taqlid*, and the popularization of Shi'ism. The school emphasized the importance of both the public and private dimensions of religion. It remains the dominant strain of Twelver Shiite thought and practice.
Velayat-e faqih	The name of a book containing Khomeini's 1970–1 lectures in Iraq on the subject of Islamic government. Later on, the moniker for Iran's "Islamic ideology," describing an unprecedented assumption of political power by Shiite religious scholars.

Communal Space	A space that is local and grounded in the shared experience of its inhabitants. It includes residential arrangements, kinship systems, circuits of praxis, and networks of cultural-economic affiliations. This dimension also denotes social divisions between particularistic groups across residential, ethnic, and religious lines. Usually, it expresses an interest narrower than the state's territorial boundary.
Conformist Behavioral Mode	This strategic mode, related to the present, is affiliated with institutional space, usually that of the state. Guided by the aspiration to reduce the disadvantages of the existing order, the grand idea of the conformist mode is the preservation of the current state of affairs, avoiding significant change as much as possible, while making the present constantly more habitable.
Friction	The practical axis of the Shiite middle ground. Different voices and interests coexist; oppositions confront as well as cooperate with each other. Decisions are based on an ongoing process of regulations rather than clear-cut resolutions.
Frontier Space	A geopolitical as well as an imagined place, growing out of a mythical past, shared beliefs, common destiny, and a grand political design. It is the collective action of proponents of sectarian religious "unity of all believers," or supporters of ethnic, supra-state nationalism. Frontier's aspirations go beyond the territorial boundaries demarcated by the international order of the nation-states. This discrepancy is often expressed in an all-inclusive expansion of the political boundaries.
Interpretation	The main practice of the Shiite community in the absence of the Imam. With infallible authority suspended, no truth or order claims to be more than an interpretation. Interpretation is the core rationale of the Islamic Republic of Iran, just as it is the dominant dynamic allowing Lebanese Hizballah to remain unscathed.

Institutional Space

The spatial realm of the state, which provides the basic structure for this type of space. Its recognizable aspects are the executive organs of government. The sovereignty of this space is defined by national borders and nation-states' claims for legitimacy rather than community-based argument.

Revolutionary Behavioral Mode

The mode of action associated with the frontier outreach beyond the territorial boundaries of the current existing political order. This behavioral mode represents proactive conduct, rejecting and negating present reality, and placing its agents always "not here," "not now". It refers to the desired state of affairs or to the grand design of reality itself.

Traditional Behavioral Mode

A strategic mode affiliated with communal space. Behavior in the traditional mode has a flexible, network-oriented perception of reality. Commonly held traditions or beliefs, across residential ethnic and religious lines, all of which serve to provide context for traditional behavior.

Void

A hole or a vacuum at the heart of Shiite faith that begins with the absence of the Twelfth Imam, the Mahdi. The void, never fully whole, stands in direct contrast to the subjective, rational wholeness of the modern individual from which Western politics and philosophy emerge. It is the void of an ultimate religious authority that led to the emergence of interpretation and friction as a strategic compensation tool for dealing with daily reality.

Bibliography

Abrahamian, Ervand. *Iran between Two Revolutions.* Princeton University Press, 1982.

Khomeinism: Essays on the Islamic Republic. University of California Press, 1993.

A History of Modern Iran. Cambridge University Press, 2008.

Afary, Janet. *The Iranian Constitutional Revolution, 1906–1911: Grassroots Democracy, Social Democracy & the Origins of Feminism.* Columbia University Press, 1996.

Ajami, Fouad. *The Vanished Imam: Musa al Sadr and the Shia of Lebanon.* Cornell University Press, 1987.

Akhavi, Shahrough, Religion and Politics in Contemporary Iran. State University of New York Press, 1980.

Algar, Hamid (trans. and ed.). *Islam and Revolution.* Mizan Press, 1981.

Amir-Moezzi, Mohammad Ali. *The Divine Guide in Early Shi'ism – The Sources of Esotericism in Islam.* State University of New York Press, 1994.

Anderson, Benedict. *Imagined Communities.* Verso, 1991.

Arjomand, Said Amir. *The Shadow of God and the Hidden Imam.* Chicago University Press, 1987.

The Turban for the Crown: The Islamic Revolution in Iran. Oxford University Press, 1988.

After Khomeini: Iran under His Successors. Oxford University Press, 2009.

Auden, W.H. "The Sea and the Mirror" in *Collected Poems.* Modern Library, 2007.

Axworthy, Michael. *The Sword of Persia: Nader Shah, From Tribal Warrior to Conquering Tyrant.* IB Tauris, 2009.

Babayan, Katheryn. *Mystics, Monarchs and Messiahs: Cultural Landscapes of Early Modern Iran.* Harvard Center for Middle Eastern Studies, 2003.

Batatu, Hanna. *The Old Social Classes & The Revolutionary Movement in Iraq.* Saqi Books, 2004.

Bourne, Richard. *Lula of Brazil: The Story so Far.* University of California Press, 2009.

Brumberg, Daniel. *Reinventing Khomeini: The Struggle for Reform in Iran.* University of Chicago Press, 2001.

Caputo, John. *Philosophy and Theology.* Abingdon Press, 2006.

Clarke, Lynda. "The Shi'i Construction of Taqlid," *Journal of Islamic Studies* 2001 12(1): 40–64.

Cole, Juan. *Sacred Space and Holy War: The Politics, Culture and History of Shi'ite Islam.* IB Tauris, 2005.

Imami Jurisprudence and the Role of the Ulama, in: Nikkie Keddie (ed.). *Shi'ism: From Quietism to Revolution.* Yale University Press, 1986.

Dabashi, Hamid. *Theology of Discontent.* New York University Press, 1993.

Shi'ism – A Religion of Protest. Belknap Press, Harvard University Press, 2011.

Davari, Mahmood. *The Political Thought of Ayatollah Murtaza Mutahhari: An Iranian Theoretician of the Islamic State.* Routledge, 2005.

Ehteshami, Anoushiravan and Zweiri, Mahjoob (eds.). *Iran's Foreign Policy: From Khatami to Ahmadinejad.* Ithaca Press, 2011.

Fischer, Michael. *Iran: From Religious Dispute to Revolution.* University of Wisconsin Press, 2003.

Fischer, Michael and Abedi, Mehdi. *Debating Muslims: Cultural Dialogues in Postmodernity and Tradition.* University of Wisconsin Press, 2002.

Foucault, Michel. *Of Other Spaces.* Accessible online at: http://foucault.info/documents/heteroTopia/foucault.heteroTopia.en.html

Fukuyama, Francis. *The End of History and the Last Man.* Free Press, 2006.

Gadamer, Hans Georg. *Truth and Method.* Continuum, 2004.

Geertz, Clifford. *Interpretation of Cultures.* Basic Books, 1973.

Ghani, Cyrus. *Iran and the Rise of Reza Shah: From Qajar collapse to Pahlavi Power.* IB Tauris, 2001.

Gleave, Robert. *Iran under the Safavids.* Cambridge University Press, 2007.

Scripturalist Islam: The History and Doctrines of the Akhbari Shi'i School. Brill, 2007.

Religion and Society in Qajar Iran. Routledge, 2009.

Guha, Ramachandra. *India after Gandhi: The History of the World's Largest Democracy.* Harper Perennial, 2008.

Halberthal, Moshe and Margalit, Avishai. *Idolatry.* Harvard University Press, 1998.

Halper, Stefan and Halper, Jonathan. *The Silence of the Rational Center: Why American Foreign Policy Is Failing.* Basic Books, 2007.

Halper, Vanessa. *Islam and Modernism: The Iranian Revolution of 1906.* Syracuse University Press, 1989.

Hamzeh Nizar, Ahmad. *In the Path of Hizballah.* Syracuse University Press, 2004.

Hashemi, Ali. *Family Planning Program Effects in Rural Iran.* Virginia Polytechnic Institute and State University, Department of Economics, 2009.

Hathaway, Jane and Barbir, Karl. *The Arab Lands under Ottoman Rule: 1516–1800.* Longman, 2008.

Helm, Heinz. *Shi'ism.* Columbia University Press, 2004.

Hirschl, Ran. *Constitutional Theocracy.* Harvard University Press, 2010.

Huntington, Samuel P. *The Clash of Civilizations and the Remaking of World Order.* Touchstone, 1996.

Keddie, Nikki R. *Religion and Rebellion in Iran: The Iranian Tobacco Protest of 1891–1892.* Frank Cass, 1966.

Scholars, Saints and Sufis: Muslim Religious Institutions since 1500. University of California Press, 1978.

Kleist, Heinrich von. *On the Gradual Production of Thoughts Whilst Speaking* (ed. and trans. by David Constantine). Hackett Publishing, 2004.

Kuru, T. Ahmad and Stepan, Alfred (eds.). *Democracy, Islam and Secularism in Turkey.* Columbia University Press, 2012.

Lefebvre, Henri. *The Production of Space.* Wiley-Blackwell, 1992.

Martin, Vanessa. *Islam and Modernism: The Iranian Revolution of 1906.* Syracuse University Press, 1989.

Menashri, David. *Education and the Making of Modern Iran.* Cornell University Press, 1992.

Ayatollah Khomeini and the Velayat-e Faqih in: *Militancy and Political Violence in Shi'ism* (Assaf Moghadam, ed.). Routledge, 2011.

Mishal, Shaul. *The PLO under Arafat.* Yale University Press, 1986.

Moin, Baqer. *Khomeini: Life of the Ayatollah.* IB Tauris, 2009.

Momen, Moojan. *An Introduction to Shi'i Islam: The History and Doctrines of Twelver Shi'ism.* Yale University Press, 1987.

Moussawi, Ibrahim. *Shi'ism and the Democratisation Process in Iran: With an Emphasis on Wilayat al-Faqih.* Saqi Books, 2012.

Musa al-Nawbakhti, al-Hasan ibn. *Shi'a Sects (Kitab Firaq al-Shi'a).* Islamic College for Advanced Studies Press, 2007.

Nakash, Yitzhak. *The Shi'is of Iraq.* Princeton University Press, 2003.

Nakhleh, Emile. *Bahrain: Political Development in a Modernizing Society.* Lexington, 2011.

Newman, Andrew J. *Safavid Iran: Rebirth of a Persian Empire.* IB Tauris, 2008.

Noe, Nicholas (ed.). *Voice of Hezbollah: The Statements of Sayyed Hassan Nasrallah.* Verso, 2007.

Packer, James I. *Fundamentalism and the Word of God.* Eerdmans, 1958.

Panjwani, Imranali (ed.). *The Shi'a of Samarra: The Heritage and Politics of a Community in Iraq.* IB Tauris, 2012.

Patrikarakos, David. *Nuclear Iran: The Birth of an Atomic State.* IB Tauris, 2012.

Polk, William. *Understanding Iraq: The Whole Sweep of Iraqi History, from Genghis Khan's Mongols to Ottoman Turks to the British Mandate to the American Occupation.* Harper Perennial, 2006.

Powell, Walter and Dimaggio, Paul (eds.). *The New Institutionalism in Organizational Analysis.* University of Chicago Press, 1991.

Qassem, Naim. *Hizbullah: The Story from Within.* Saqi Books, 2005.

Rahnema, Ali. *An Islamic Utopian: A Political Biography of Ali Shariati.* IB Tauris, 2000.

Superstition as Ideology in Iranian Politics: From Majlesi to Ahmadinejad. Cambridge University Press, 2011.

Richard Norton, Augustus. *Hezbollah – A Short History.* Princeton University Press, 2009.

Ricoeur, Paul. *The Conflict of Interpretations: Essays in Hermeneutics.* Northwestern University Press, 2007.

From Text to Action: Essays in Hermeneutics II. Northwestern University Press, 2007.

Sachedina, Abdulaziz. *Islamic Messianism.* State University of New York Press, 1981.

The Just Ruler in Shiite Islam: The Comprehensive Authority of the Jurist in Imami Jurisprudence. Oxford University Press, 1988.

Salibi, Kamal. *A House of Many Mansions: The History of Lebanon Reconsidered.* University of California Press, 1990.

Savory, Roger. *Iran under the Safavids*. Cambridge University Press, 2007.

Schirazi, Asghar. *Islamic Development Policy: The Agrarian Question in Iran*. Lynne Rienner, 1993.

The Constitution of Iran, Politics and State in the Islamic Republic. IB Tauris, 1998.

Scott, James. *Domination and the Art of Resistance: Hidden Transcripts*. Yale University Press, 1990.

Shabestari, Mohammad Mojtahed. *iman va-azadi* (Faith and Freedom). Entesharat Tarh-e No, 1379.

Shah Pahalvi, Mohammad Reza. *Answer to History*. Stein & Day, 1982.

Singerman, Diane. *Avenues of Participation: Family, Politics, and Networks in Urban Quarters of Cairo*. Princeton University Press, 1993.

Sobelman, Daniel (Hebrew). *New Rules of the Game: Israel and Hizbollah after the Withdrawal from Lebanon*. Jaffee Center for Strategic Studies, Tel Aviv University, Memorandum 65, 2003.

Taheri, Amir. *The Spirit of Allah: Khomeini and the Islamic Revolution*. Hutchinson, 1987.

Thrift, Nigel. *Non-Representational Theory: Space, Politics, Affect*. Routledge, 2007.

Tuan, Yi-Fu. *Space and Place: The Perspective of Experience*. University of Minnesota Press, 2001.

Turner, Colin. *Islam without Allah? The Rise of Religious Externalism in Safavid Iran*. Curzon Press, 2001.

Turner, Colin, and Luft, Paul (eds.). *Shi'ism*. Routledge, 2007.

Wilber, Donald. *Riza Shah Pahlavi: The Resurrection and Reconstruction of Iran*. Exposition Press, 1975.

Winkler, David F. *Amirs, Admirals and Desert Sailors: Bahrain, the US Navy and the Arabian Gulf*. Naval Institute Press, 2007.

Yarshater, Ehsan (ed.). *The history of al-Tabari*. Volume 19, SUNY Press, 1991.

Electronic Resources

Blogs:
http://www.juancole.com/2012/06/behind-the-usisraeli-cyberattacks-on-iran.html
http://www.thenation.com/blogs/notion/443634
http://emperors-clothes.com/archive/hez.htm
Articles:
Abbasi-Shavazi, Mohammad Jalal. "Recent Changes and the Future of Fertility in Iran." *United Nations Population Division*, 2002: 425–39:
http://www.un.org/esa/population/publications/completingfertility/2RevisedABBASIpaper.PDF

Abu-Nasr, Donna. "Hezbollah Inspires Pride and Disgust." *The Boston Globe*, July 19, 2006: http://www.boston.com/news/world/middleeast/articles/2006/07/19/hezbollah_inspires_pride_and_disgust/

Addis, Casey L. "Iran's 2009 Presidential Elections." *Congressional Research Service*, June 22, 2009: http://fpc.state.gov/documents/organization/125709.pdf

Assl, Nima Khorrami. "Hezbollah: A State above the State." *Foreign Policy*, February 3, 2011: http://www.foreignpolicyjournal.com/2011/02/03/hezbollah-a-state-above-the-state/

Bailey, Norman A. "Iran's Venezuelan Gateway." *Foreign Affairs*, February 2, 2012: http://foreignaffairs.house.gov/112/HHRG-112-FA-WState-NBailey-20120202.pdf

Bassiouni, Mahmoud Cherif et al., "Report of the Bahrain Independent Commission of Inquiry." December 10, 2011: http://files.bici.org.bh/BICIreportEN.pdf

BBC News. "Bahrain doctors on trial over anti-government protests." *Middle East*, June 19, 2011: http://www.bbc.co.uk/news/world-middle-east-13966073

BBC Charts Iran's Complex Political System: http://news.bbc.co.uk/2/shared/spl/hi/middle_east/03/iran_power/html/expediency_council.stm

Beirut A. P. "Lebanon Vote Lets Hezbollah Keep Weapons." *The New York Times*, December 10, 2009: http://www.nytimes.com/2009/12/11/world/middleeast/11lebanon.html?_r=1&ref=hezbollah

Bevan, Tom. "Text of Obama's Nobel Address." *The Real Clear Politics Blog*, December 10, 2009: http://realclearpolitics.blogs.time.com/2009/12/10/text-of-obamas-nobel-address

Borger, Julian. "Text of the Iran-Brazil-Turkey deal." *The Guardian*, May 17, 2012: http://www.guardian.co.uk/world/julian-borger-global-security-blog/2010/may/17/iran-brazil-turkey-nuclear

CNN Wire Staff. "Timeline of Iran's controversial nuclear program." March 6, 2012: http://articles.cnn.com/2012–03–06/middleeast/world_meast_iran-timeline_1_nuclear-program-iran-signs-iran-s-natanz?_s=PM:MIDDLEEAST

Cook, Jonathan. "Israel's "Dahiya Doctrine" Comes to Gaza." *The Electronic Intifada*, January 20, 2009: http://electronicintifada.net/content/israels-dahiya-doctrine-comes-gaza/8006

The Constitution of the Islamic Republic of Iran: http://www.iranonline.com/iran/iran-info/Government/constitution.html

Declaration of the Rights of Man and of the Citizen, Human and Constitutional Rights Resource: http://www.hrcr.org/docs/frenchdec.html

Ditz, Jason. "Iran Clerical Rift Widens as Rafsanjani Relatives Arrested." *Antiwar.com*, June 21, 2009: http://news.antiwar.com/2009/06/21/clerical-rift-widens-as-rafsanjani-relatives-arrested/

Duss, Matt. "Mousavi and Iran's Nuclear Politics." *Think Progress*, November 4, 2009: http://thinkprogress.org/security/2009/11/04/175724/mousavi-and-irans-nuclear-politics/?mobile=nc

Eisenstadt, Michael and Khalaji, Mehdi. "Nuclear Fatwa: Religion and Politics in Iran's Proliferation Strategy." *The Washington Institute*, September 2011: http://www.washingtoninstitute.org/policy-analysis/view/nuclear-fatwa-religion-and-politics-in-irans-proliferation-strategy

Escobar, Pepe. "Iran Won't Crack." *Asia Times*, July 7, 2012: http://www.atimes.com/atimes/Middle_East/NG07Ak03.html

Esfandiari, Golnaz. "Iran: President Says Light Surrounded Him During UN Speech." *Radio Free Europe*, December 16, 2012: http://www.rferl.org/content/article/1063353.html

Exum, Andrew. "Hizballah at War: A Military Assessment." *The Washington Institute Policy Focus 63*, December 2006: http://www.washingtoninstitute.org/policy-analysis/view/hizballah-at-war-a-military-assessment

Fathi, Nazila. "In a Death Seen Around the World, a Symbol of Iranian Protests." *The New York Times*, June 22, 2009: http://www.nytimes.com/2009/06/23/world/middleeast/23neda.html

Fulton, Will, Voxman, Andrew, and Lichtenbaum, Annika. "Iran-Lebanese Hezbollah Relationship Tracker 2012." *Iran Tracker*, April 10, 2012: http://www.irantracker. org/military-activities/iran-lebanese-hezbollah-relationship-tracker-2012

Guardian Council, Iran, June 15, 2009: http://topics.nytimes.com/topics/reference/ timestopics/organizations/g/guardian_council_iran/index.html

Hakimian, Hassan. *How Sanctions Affect Iran's Economy*. London Middle East Institute, Le Point International, June 1, 2012: http://www.lepointinternational.com/it/ economia-e-finanza/medio-oriente/867-how-sanctions-affect-irans-economy.html

Hein, Avi. *Israel-Hizbollah Prisoner Exchange*. Jewish Virtual Library, January 20, 2004: http://www.jewishvirtuallibrary.org/jsource/Society_&_Culture/prisonerswap 012904.html

Henzel, Christopher. "US Embassy Cables: Bahrain's Relations with Iran." *The Guardian*, February 15, 2011: http://www.guardian.co.uk/world/us-embassy- cables-documents/164906

"Hezbollah Chief Rejects Call by UN to Disarm." *Al-Jazeera*, January 15, 2012: http:// www.aljazeera.com/news/middleeast/2012/01/20121154542742500.html

"Hezbollah Chief Says Group Gets Support, Not Orders, from Iran." *Al-Arabiya*, February 8, 2012: http://english.alarabiya.net/articles/2012/02/08/193327.html

hoda@iran. "Sayyed Nasrallah Stressed Iran's Supports of Hezbollah." *The Iran Project*, February 8, 2012: http://theiranproject.com/blog/2012/02/08/sayyed-nasrallah- stressed-irans-supports-of-hezbollah/

Hokayem, Emile. "Iran and Lebanon." *The Iran Primer*, October 11, 2010: http:// iranprimer.usip.org/resource/iran-and-lebanon

Imam Khomeini, *Islamic Government: Governance of the Jurist*. The Institute for Compilation and Publication of Imam Khomeini's Works, International Affairs Department: http://www.al-islam.org/islamicgovernment/

Imam Khomeini's Islamic Revolution Web site: http://www.inminds.co.uk/khomeini. html

Imam Khomeini's Letter to Mikhail Gorbachev: http://www.ghadeer.org/english/imam/ letter%20Imam/callto/callto2.html

Iran – Constitution Changes: http://www.servat.unibe.ch/icl/ir00000_.html

Iran, Political Sanctions Timeline: http://www.mapreport.com/citysubtopics/iran-p-0. html

Iran Profile, Nuclear Threat Initiative. July 2012: http://www.nti.org/e_research/profiles/ Iran/Nuclear/chronology.html.

"Iran Protesters Defy Rally Ban." *BBC News*, June 15, 2009: http://news.bbc.co.uk/2/ hi/middle_east/8099952.stm

Kahl, Colin. "Supremely Irrelevant: Iran Tried to Take Advantage of the Arab Spring. It Failed, Miserably". *Foreign Policy*, January 25, 2012: http://www.foreignpolicy. com/articles/2012/01/24/supremely_irrelevant

Katz, Yaakov. "The Dahiya Doctrine: Fighting dirty or a knock-out punch?" *The Jerusalem Post*, January 21, 2010: http://www.jpost.com/Features/FrontLines/ Article.aspx?id=167167

  "Barak Reveals Conditions for Iran-West Talks." *The Jerusalem Post*, April 4, 2012: http://www.jpost.com/IranianThreat/News/Article.aspx?id=264839

Khalaji, Mehdi. "Khamenei's Military Coup in Iran." *The Washington Post*, June 15, 2009: http://www.washingtonpost.com/wp-dyn/content/article/2009/06/14/ AR2009061401758.html

Khomeini, Ruhollah Musavi. Letter from Ayatollah Khomeini regarding weapons during the Iran-Iraq war, 1988: http://www.cfr.org/publication/11745/letter_from_ayatollah_khomeini_regarding_weapons_during_the_iraniraq_war.html

Klein Halevi, Yossi. "The Iranian–Israeli War: When will Israel and Iran Go to War? They Already Have." *The New Republic*, March 11, 2008: http://www.tnr.com/article/politics/the-iranian%E2%80%93israeli-war

The Lebanon National Pact (al Mithaq al Watani): http://countrystudies.us/lebanon/77.htm

Lucas, Scott. "Iran and WikiLeaks 2010: Esfandiar Rahim-Mashai 'A Key Advisor for the Increasingly Isolated President.'" *EA Iran*, April 22, 2011: http://www.enduringamerica.com/home/2011/4/22/iran-and-wikileaks-2010-esfandiar-rahim-mashai-a-key-advisor.html

Mansharof & Rapoport. "Iran Wants Bahrain 'Back.'" *The Lid*, August 3, 2007: http://yidwithlid.blogspot.co.il/2007/08/iran-wants-bahrain-back.html

The "March 14" Movement Web site: http://www.14march.org/

McGregor, Andrew. "Hezbollah's Tactics and Capabilities in Southern Lebanon." *The Jameson Foundation*, August 1, 2006: http://www.jamestown.org/single/?no_cache=1&tx_ttnews[tt_news]=860

Milani, Abbas. "Is Ahmadinejad Islamic Enough for Iran?" *Foreign Policy*, April 29, 2011: http://www.foreignpolicy.com/articles/2011/04/29/is_ahmadinejad_islamic_enough_for_iran?page=0,1

Mitnick, Josh. "Was Israel behind Iran Nuclear Scientist's Assassination?" *The Christian Science Monitor*, January 12, 2012: http://www.csmonitor.com/World/Middle-East/2012/0112/Was-Israel-behind-Iran-nuclear-scientist-s-assassination

Molavi, Afshin. "Invoking the Arab Spring, Iran Rewrites its Own History." *The National*, April 6, 2011: http://www.thenational.ae/thenationalconversation/comment/invoking-the-arab-spring-iran-rewrites-its-own-history

Morozov, Evgeny. "Iran Elections: A Twitter Revolution?" *The Washington Post*, June 17, 2007: http://www.washingtonpost.com/wp-dyn/content/discussion/2009/06/17/DI2009061702232.html

Mousavi's "5 Stages to Resolution" Statement: http://enduringamerica.com/2010/01/02/iran-document-mousavis-5-stages-to-resolution-statement-1-january/

Nasrallah, Hassan. "Victory Speech." *The Arabist*, translated by Issandr El Amrani, August 14, 2006: http://arabist.net/archives/2006/08/16/nasrallahs-speech-full-text/

Op-ed, "Behind the Protests, Social Upheaval in Iran." *The New York Times*, June 23, 2009: http://roomfordebate.blogs.nytimes.com/2009/06/23/behind-the-protests-social-upheaval-in-iran/

Parsi, Trita. "Who's Fighting Who in Iran's Struggle?" *Time World*, June 16 2009: http://www.time.com/time/world/article/0,8599,1904989-2,00.html

Payvand News, May 10, 2003: http://www.payvand.com/news/03/may/1048.html

Persepolis Celebration: http://www.angelfire.com/empire/imperialiran/persepolis1.html

Roosevelt, Theodore. "Man In The Arena" speech: http://www.theodore-roosevelt.com/images/research/speeches/maninthearena.pdf

Roudi-Fahimi, Farzaneh. "Iran's Family Planning Program: Responding to a Nation's Needs." *Population Reference Bureau*, June 2002: http://www.prb.org/pdf/iransfamplanprog_eng.pdf

Rumi, Jalal al-Din. *Tales from Masnavi* (translated by A.J. Arberry): http://www.kha-mush.com/tales_from_masnavi.htm#The%20Elephant

Saad-Ghorayeb, Amal. "The Israel-Hizbollah Prisoner-Deal." *Open Democracy*, July 14, 2008: http://www.opendemocracy.net/article/the-israel-hizbollah-prisoner-deal

"The Israel-Hizballah Prisoner Deal." *The Electronic Intifada*, July 16, 2008: http://electronicintifada.net/content/israel-hizballah-prisoner-deal/7619

"The Hizbollah Project: Last War, Next War." *Open Democracy*, August 13, 2009: http://www.opendemocracy.net/article/the-hizbollah-project-last-war-next-war

Sanger, David E. "U.S. CyberAttacks Iran Nuke Plant." *Islam Newsroom*, June 14, 2012: http://islamnewsroom.com/news-we-need/1877-obama-cyberattacks-iran-nuke-plant

"Obama Order Sped Up Wave of Cyberattacks Against Iran." *The New York Times*, June 1, 2012: http://www.nytimes.com/2012/06/01/world/middleeast/obama-or-dered-wave-of-cyberattacks-against-iran.html?pagewanted=all

Sayed Hassan Nasrallah Conference Speech, YouTube Video, May 8, 2008: http://www.youtube.com/watch?v=6hRwn3kJ_xE

Sayyah, Syma. "Tehran's Great Green Silence March." *Payvand Iran News*, June 16, 2009: http://www.payvand.com/news/09/jun/1163.html

Sayyed Nasrallah in live address: Cooperation with Army is Top priority, January 4, 2008: http://www.english.moqawama.org/essaydetailsf.php?eid=722&fid=11

The Shia Post, Sheikh Issa Qasim Slams Bahrain's Brutal Crackdown Against Protesters: http://en.shiapost.com/?p=2441

SKY News. "Iran's Supreme Leader: 'No Nuclear Weapons.'" February 22, 2012: http://news.sky.com/story/928077/irans-supreme-leader-no-nuclear-weapons

Slackman, Michael. "In Iran, Struggle beyond the Streets." *The New York Times*, July 7, 2009: http://www.nytimes.com/2009/07/08/world/middleeast/08clerics.html

Special Tribunal for Lebanon Web site: http://www.stl-tsl.org/

State of the Green Movement Web site: http://www.foreignpolicyi.org/event/iran/greenmovement

Sunday Times: Mossad Agents behind Iran Scientist Assassination. *Haaretz*, January 16, 2012: http://www.haaretz.com/news/diplomacy-defense/sunday-times-mossad-agents-behind-iran-scientist-assassination-1.407593

"Timeline: Iranian Election and Aftermath." *Reuters*, June 18, 2009: http://www.reuters.com/article/worldNews/idUSTRE55H3TE20090618

Totten, Michael. "Hezbollah Riots in Lebanon." *Middle East Journal Blog*, January 22, 2007: http://www.michaeltotten.com/archives/001369.html

The Union of Islamic World Students, Sayyed Hasan Nasrallah Hails New Lebanese Government, 26 Jan 2011: http://www.rohama.org/en/news/3977/sayyed-hasan-nasrallah-hails-new-lebanese-government

"U.S. President Obama Speech in Cairo University of Egypt." June 4, 2009: http://www.huffingtonpost.com/2009/06/04/obama-speech-in-cairo-vid_n_211215.html

Vick, Karl and Klein, Aaron J. "Who Assassinated an Iranian Nuclear Scientist? Israel Isn't Telling." *Time World*, January 13, 2012: http://www.time.com/time/world/article/0,8599,2104372,00.html

Voice of Democratic Iran Web site: http://www.khandaniha.eu

Wehrey, Frederic. "The Rise of the Pasdaran Assessing the Domestic Roles of Iran's Islamic Revolutionary Guards Corps." *RAND Corporation*, 2009: http://www.rand.org/pubs/monographs/MG821.html

Wisdom Bestows Well-Being, Persian Proverb: http://www.biblegateway.com/passage/?
search=Proverbs+3&version=NIV

Worth, Robert. "Iran's Power Struggle Goes Beyond Personalities to Future of
Presidency Itself." *The New York Times*, October 26, 2011: http://www.nytimes.
com/2011/10/27/world/middleeast/in-iran-rivalry-khamenei-takes-on-presidency-
itself.html

  "Effort to Rebrand Arab Spring Backfires in Iran." *The New York Times*, February
2, 2012: http://www.nytimes.com/2012/02/03/world/middleeast/effort-to-rebrand-
arab-spring-backfires-in-iran.html?pagewanted=all

Yeats, W.B. *Responsibilities*, 1914: http://www.sacred-texts.com/neu/yeats/lpy/lpy080.
htm

Zisser, Eyal. "The Return of Hizbullah." *Middle East Quarterly*, Fall 2002, Vol. IX:
Number 4: http://www.meforum.org/499/the-return-of-hizbullah

Index